Shy of the Squirrel's Foot

Contents

List of Illustrations vii
Preface ix

Introduction 1

CHAPTER ONE
Jammin' the Greek Scene (Jargon 13c) 16

CHAPTER TWO
Letters to Christopher (Jargon 47) 38

CHAPTER THREE
Notches along the Bible Belt (Jargon 98) 62

CHAPTER FOUR
The Lyrix of Col. Hampton B. Coles (Ret.) 82

CHAPTER FIVE
Bibliographical Checklists of the Jargon Society's Books including Prospective Titles and Authors 105

Epilogue 135
Corn Close
ANNE MIDGETTE

Afterword 138
Channeling Bibliography
NICOLE RAZIYA FONG

Notes 143
Index 171

© 2024 Andrew Martrich
All rights reserved
Set in Merope Basic by Westchester Publishing Services
Manufactured in the United States of America

Library of Congress Cataloging-in-Publication Data
Names: Martrich, Andy, author.
Title: Shy of the squirrel's foot : a peripheral history of the Jargon
   Society as told through its missing books / Andy Martrich.
Description: Chapel Hill : The University of North Carolina Press, 2024. |
   Includes bibliographical references and index.
Identifiers: LCCN 2024029894 | ISBN 9781469682501 (cloth) |
   ISBN 9781469682518 (paperback) | ISBN 9781469682525 (epub) |
   ISBN 9781469682532 (pdf)
Subjects: LCSH: Jargon Society—History. | Jargon Society—Bibliography. |
   Williams, Jonathan, 1929–2008. | American poetry—Publishing. |
   Publishers and publishing—North Carolina—History. | BISAC: LITERARY
   CRITICISM / Poetry | BIOGRAPHY & AUTOBIOGRAPHY / Editors,
   Journalists, Publishers
Classification: LCC Z473.J19 M37 2024 | DDC 070.509756/982—dc23/eng/20240723
LC record available at https://lccn.loc.gov/2024029894

Cover art: Jonathan Williams photographing Ray Kass in 1977. Copyright Sally Mann, courtesy of Gagosian Gallery. Photograph courtesy of the Poetry Collection of the University Libraries, University of Buffalo, State University of New York.

Shy of the Squirrel's Foot
*A Peripheral History of the
Jargon Society as Told through
Its Missing Books*

Andy Martrich

The University of North Carolina Press CHAPEL HILL

Illustrations

Holly Beye in Woodstock, New York 6

Jonathan Williams on the set of *The Beautiful People* 8

Jonathan Williams at Black Mountain College 18

Charles Olson at Black Mountain College 21

Williams's portrait of Merle Hoyleman 1 43

Williams's portrait of Merle Hoyleman 2 43

"Red Hots," a poem by Richard C. 66

Ad for a cowboy-themed church service 77

One of Richard C.'s spreads from his "Christian Athletes" folder 80

Tom Patterson with Jonathan Williams at St. Andrews College 83

The Jargon Society at James Harold Jennings's *Art World* 87

Billy McPherson and Bruce Hampton on the cover of
Outside Looking Out 96

Preface

In the first century A.D., the Roman epigrammatist Martial questioned the purpose of gathering his poems into a book, even considering it paradoxical: "We have arrived at the bosses, but you, reader, want to go further . . . as though you had not finished what was already finished on page one."[1] The epigrammatic form—which treats a given epigram as a brief, stand-alone poem—ensures that the book containing them can be started or finished on any page. His observation is a criticism not just of presumptive reading habits, but also of what it means to collect at the expense of the material collected. If Martial's epigrams are to be treated as "the same poem over and over again," as the statement above suggests, then their convergence—and their compiler's misunderstanding—may imply the dissolution of their closed form and invite a more narrative temporality; as Martial challenges, "quid prodest brevitas, die mihi, si liber est? (What is the use of brevity, tell me, if it constitutes a book?)."[2] His rhetorical query implies certain teleological principles and limitations for both the book and epigram, which, according to Martial, are incompatible. But while an authority who has assembled a collection may disguise its self-reflexive disjunction as things gathered in a group, collections are rarely—if ever—so fixed, and not all collectors are merely aloof.

Shy of the Squirrel's Foot takes as its foundation a kind of collection—that is, an enumerative list of books—with consideration for what lurks behind that collection's proverbial curtains. At the behest of its components, a bibliographical structure can be viewed empirically, enabling a closer look at the parts, or, more accurately, the ideas of those parts, what they reflect about themselves, and their aggregation; however, as Craig Dworkin writes in *The Perverse Library*, "The move from accrual to taxonomy sets in motion an endless chain-reaction of tantalizing remove—a perpetually retreating horizon—as categories proliferate just beyond the reach of the collection that would seek to compass them." A bibliography, which is composed of systematic descriptions of ostensible materials, is "haunted" not only by what its components signify (e.g., other materials and groupings not contained by the collection) but also by catalogic processes which, as Dworkin points out, result in a "negative ontology." By default, any library insinuates "a phantom shelf in the sense that one might speak of a phantom limb," which "accounts for the vague feeling conjured by even the most capacious collections that something is missing." Dworkin takes this to its logical stalemate, concluding that "libraries are defined not by what they have on their shelves, but by what they exclude from them," and compiling bibliographies of his personal collection alongside absent and imagined books, essentially turning his library into an infinite matryoshka doll.[3] Perhaps worse than what Martial feared, a collection of his poems wouldn't only neglect poetic form but would also appear to proliferate phantom epigrams ad infinitum.

This book focuses on the collected books of the Jargon Society, the writer's press Jonathan Williams founded and ran from 1951 until his passing in 2008. I started writing about Williams and Jargon with an underlying premise in mind, gleaned from Thomas Meyer's 1982 introduction to Williams's first collection of essays, *The Magpie's Bagpipe*: "A publishing memoir of the Jargon Society, and its titles, to describe its founding, direction, and influence as a writer's press . . . is long overdue."[4] It still is. In the spring of 2021, with the support of my friend and former executive director of Jargon, Tom Patterson, I decided to try my hand at it.[5] Early on in my research I was distracted by what perhaps signals a publisher's equivalent to the library's phantom shelf: a section from the minutes of the Jargon Society board meeting held on March 5, 1987, called "Lacunae," which lists some of Jargon's own absent and imagined books. Apparently, the materials presented in its catalogs, prospectuses, and bibliographical checklists aren't always "books" as advertised.

Of course, missing books are nothing new and span a variety of fates, such as those lost or destroyed, as documented in Fernando Báez's *A Universal History of the Destruction of Books*; those fragmented and rendered incomplete, including surviving works by Alkman, Archilochos, and Sappho; and, most relevant to this project, possible or prospective books, as explored in Ben Segal and Erinrose Mager's *The Official Catalog of the Library of Potential Literature* and Veronica Scott Espinosa's directory *The Missing Books*, respectively. It's not uncommon for a press—particularly a small one dedicated primarily to poetry—to plan for books that don't make it to publication. There isn't much support, money, or a reading public, the latter of which Guy Davenport refers to as a "charming fiction."[6] Jargon lost money on nearly every book it published, and it lacked the infrastructure to handle consumer demand, as evidenced by its one financial success— Ernest Matthew Mickler's *White Trash Cooking* (Jargon 101)—having to be sold to another publisher.[7] But it's the financial hardships coupled with

Williams's impressive network that makes Jargon's trail of "Lacunae" projects unique.

While *Shy of the Squirrel's Foot* explores the missing books of the Jargon Society, it's important to note that navigating its materials can be tricky. James S. Jaffe, compiler of *Jonathan Williams: A Bibliographical Checklist of His Writings, 1950-1988*, alleges that it would be impossible to assemble a comprehensive list of everything Williams wrote and published.[8] Obviously, this becomes even more difficult when trying to include everything that Williams *wanted* to publish. Another complication arises when one realizes that Williams was his own archive. Richard Owens—who, along with Jeffery Beam, edited the seminal encomium *Jonathan Williams: The Lord of Orchards*—writes, "Williams himself was the living institution through which one might approach these incomplete and spatially dispersed materials."[9] Yet, as Dworkin suggests in *The Perverse Library* and its documentation of the absent and imagined, a reference bibliography represents a collection, but only as a form of intellectual control. There are no physical objects per se, but Jargon's enumerative series—however partial—might be viewed as a window to "the *processes* of things" (emphasis in the original).[10] Williams writes this in reference to the photography of Bill Brandt, but it's a phrase that we may borrow in sketching a peripheral history; through an exploration of Jargon's fractured, unfinished, and lost projects, a novel silhouette of Williams and the Jargon Society takes shape.

OF COURSE, A SILHOUETTE IS dependent on a light source, and in this matter, I'm indebted to more than a few individuals for their luminescence. First and foremost, Thomas Meyer—whose correspondence and friendship over the last few years I have cherished—is central to this project, as well as Tom Patterson (as mentioned above), who initially encouraged me to take my fandom for the Jargon Society to a different level. Meyer and Patterson provided numerous resources, additional content, and editorial advice throughout the duration; simply put, this book wouldn't exist without them. To Lola Galla, who read and provided commentary on numerous drafts and listened to me talk incessantly about this project from its inception, my gratitude is beyond words. Anne Midgette not only gave me the honor of contributing to this book by way of her brilliant epilogue but personally spent hours poring through her stepfather Donald B. Anderson's archives, selecting, scanning, and advising on materials that proved to be singular resources.[11] I've had the pleasure of collaborating with Nicole Raziya Fong on several projects, including this book; their response to the text, which

Preface xi

appears as an afterword, and correspondence had me going back to chapters with fresh eyes and fleshing out ideas according to their sage observations. I'm so grateful for the support of my dear friends J. Gordon Faylor—whose edits to drafts of the introduction and chapters 1, 2, and 4, were integral in turning a fledgling manuscript into this book—and Marc Maffei, who proffered advice during the revision process that enabled me to finalize several chapters. Many of the concepts and musings found in these pages were discussed with Michael Martrich, who provided guidance, suggested additional readings and sources, and edited the first draft of chapter 3. Other interlocutors whose correspondence, advice, and/or writings are central to this book include Jeffery Beam, Thorns Craven, Simon Cutts, Jonathan Gorman, Jonathan Greene, Ross Hair, Eddie Hopely, James S. Jaffe, Mark Francis Johnson, Clara B. Jones, Whitney Jones, Ray Kass, Sally Mann, Niland Mortimer, Craig J. Saper, Kyle Schlesinger, Alice Sebrell, Mark Sloan, Danny Snelson, Ted Stimpfle, and Ian Young. I would also like to thank Lucas Church and Thomas Bedenbaugh at The University of North Carolina Press for their generous support, and my two anonymous peer reviewers, whose enthusiasm for the project and recommendations for revision greatly improved the manuscript.

Chapter 1, which explores Jonathan Williams's missing book "Jammin' the Greek Scene," was initially inspired by Ross Hair's essay "'Hemi-demi-semi barbaric yawps': Jonathan Williams and Black Mountain," which appears in the *Journal of Black Mountain College Studies*, volume 3. An adaptation of chapter 1 was published in volume 14 of the same journal, and I thank the editors Ant M Lobo-Ladd, Thomas E. Frank, Carissa Pfeiffer, and Kira Houston for their suggestions and comments, which played a role in developing the finalized version that appears in this book. Chapters 2 and 3, which address Merle Hoyleman's *Letters to Christopher* and Richard C.'s "Notches along the Bible Belt," respectively, were essentially written in conversation. Chapter 2 would be entirely different if not for the collaboration of two of Hoyleman's friends: Ken Chute, who arguably knows more about Hoyleman than anyone alive, and Mike Vargo, who filmed and directed a profile on Hoyleman and provided care to her during her twilight years. During the writing of chapter 2, I was in frequent touch with Chute, who happily shared his knowledge and extensive research and fielded my many questions. Chute and Vargo also read and provided edits to the chapter; I'm ever grateful for their wisdom and encouragement. I'd like to thank Lisa A. Miles, whose book *This Fantastic Struggle: The Life and Art of Esther Phillips*—which Chute recommends as "essential to understanding Merle"—is cited throughout the chapter.[12] I also want to express my appreciation to Hoyleman's grand-nephew Rhese S. Hoylman III.[13]

Chapter 3 was written in close communication with the North Carolina–based curator and art writer, and close friend of Richard C., Huston Paschal. Paschal shared in-depth knowledge of her experiences working with the artist, and in many cases, she served as an intermediary for helping Richard C. answer some of my more elaborate, prying inquiries. Paschal also did a lot of legwork, conducting her own research, sharing contacts, and shipping me lots of catalogs and books. I'm so very thankful for her generosity and keen interest. Of course, I'm humbled by Richard C.'s support for this project and extremely grateful to him, especially for sending me his files related to "Notches along the Bible Belt." Regarding chapter 4—which takes as its subject "The Lyrix of Hampton B. Coles (Ret.)," an unpublished collection of lyrics by Col. Bruce Hampton—I want to express my appreciation to Hampton's biographer Jerry Grillo, whose book *The Music and Mythocracy of Col. Bruce Hampton* is a central resource. Also, Patterson, who was Hampton's close friend, provided essential inputs and edits. Chapter 5 consists of bibliographical checklists for Jargon's published, unpublished, and prospective books, and it benefited from readings and additions by Beam, Cutts, Greene, Jaffe, Jones, Meyer, Midgette, Paschal, Patterson, and Caroline Vaughan. I'd also like to again thank Carissa Pfeiffer, who assembled the checklist that appears on the Black Mountain College Museum + Arts Center's website, which I use as a foundational reference.

Much of this book was written during a time when travel and access to archives was restricted, and so I was dependent (more so than usual) on the work of archivists, librarians, and researchers, principal among them Alison Fraser and James Maynard of the Poetry Collection at SUNY Buffalo, and Ross Cooper and Greta E. Browning of the Belk Library at Appalachian State University. Fraser and Cooper, in particular, are perhaps the pinnacle of archival reference services: super quick, knowledgeable, and enthusiastic; as a fellow archivist, I'm inspired by their dedication and passion for the field. Others who aided in this project include Keith Adams, Scott Ross Adams, Marcus Aurelius, Melissa Watterworth Batt, Apala Bhowmick, Danny Bigdips, Michael Black, Lil' Stevie Bon-Bon, Rory Brown, Tom Cahill, Liz Campion, Parker Cipolle, Paul Christensen, Dolores Colón, Roger Conover, Carole Crews, Doug DeLoach, Eric Dillalogue, Patrick Eyres, Cara Gilgenbach, Flournoy Holmes, Neal Hutcheson, R. Michael Johnson, Joanna

Keane Lopez, Mind Lucent, Susan Maldovan, Roger Manley, Elizabeth Matheson, Charles McNeill, Edric Mesmer, Abigail Michaud, Joel Minor, Kari Salisbury, Natalia Sciarini, Kathy Shoemaker, Benjamin Snyder, Nicky Steeltoes, Julie J. Thomson, Tom Ward, and Michael Weiss.

Shy of the Squirrel's Foot is dedicated to the memory of the artist William Anthony (September 25, 1934–December 24, 2022).

Shy of the
Squirrel's Foot

Introduction

> good time
> to plant corn
>
> when the hickory buds
> are as big
> as a squirrel's foot
>
> —JONATHAN WILLIAMS, "May"

The Jargon Society is perhaps best known as the publisher of singular and profoundly influential books by Robert Creeley, Larry Eigner, Lorine Niedecker, and Louis Zukofsky. It's typically associated with Black Mountain College, which Jonathan Williams attended on and off from 1951 until its closure in 1957 and which was where Jargon evolved from a fledgling experiment into the publisher of *The Maximus Poems*, the magnum opus of Charles Olson, Williams's mentor, and much else thereafter. Jargon helped launch the careers of eminent writers (e.g., Denise Levertov, Michael McClure, Paul C. Metcalf, and Joel Oppenheimer); spotlighted neglected artists and brought them into print (e.g., Bob Brown, Mina Loy, and Alfred Starr Hamilton); coined the term "visionary folk art" and was a champion of its practitioners (e.g., Georgia Blizzard, St. EOM, Dilmus Hall, Annie Hooper, and Mary T. Smith); and represented an apex for gay and queer publishing (e.g., books by Jeffery Beam, James Broughton, Robert Duncan, Ronald Johnson, and Thomas Meyer). Jargon is much more than a press, and direct affiliation with any one achievement, book, institution, or writer (other than Williams himself) is transitory at best, and misleading at worst. Here, "processes of things" are properties of Williams's imagination, enacted dynamically across a network cultivated in constant movement and awareness. Thomas Meyer, who was Williams's partner for forty years and arguably knew him better than anyone, writes, "The world is a mare's nest of interlocking details . . . so dense and so extensive that it is unlikely that any hierarchy, any ranking of things can finally survive the glorious welter of particularities. Hence it is the function of attention to isolate for a moment the single, luminous detail. Hence the lists, the compendia, the dispatches which constitute Jonathan Williams's natural form, poetic and prosaic."[1] Following suit, *Shy of the Squirrel's Foot* considers Jargon as an ongoing work of attention, fostered on diverse and often overlooked strains of artistic practices in North America and the United Kingdom throughout the latter half of the twentieth century and beyond.

Of course, something that Jargon isn't known for is what it *didn't* publish, and therefore its missing books—that is, projects that Williams wanted to issue but wasn't able to—may seem a strange entry point to a history, peripheral or otherwise. These projects, however, are exemplary of the "processes of things" at the core of Jargon's operations over its fifty-seven-year tenure, perhaps even more so than its published content. James S. Jaffe noted shortly after Williams's passing on March 16, 2008, "There are more than a few libraries around the country waiting for books that Jonathan announced a long time ago but was never able to publish."[2] Technically, they still are waiting. These missing books radiate dynamic potential within the collection in a tangible way, given the expectation, unreasonable or not, that they may one day arrive. As Wyatt Gwyon—the painter, art forger, and protagonist of William Gaddis's *The Recognitions*—aptly points out, "There's something about . . . an unfinished piece of work . . . where perfection is still possible . . . because it's there, it's there all the time."[3] This observation speaks to this study, which takes a bibliographical approach to exploring Jargon as a dynamic repository.

In *Archive Fever: A Freudian Impression*, Jacques Derrida proposes that the archive is "always dislocating itself" due to its unstable temporality.[4] As a shifting framework of past and future possibilities that can never be realized, the archive is fundamentally self-destructive. Consequently, the archivist is a kind of enthusiast in the throes of a manic episode (i.e., archive fever), obsessing over the preservation and restoration of an infinite regress. The bibliographer suffers a similar delirium, well expressed by the pursuit of an "ideal copy," which Fredson Bowers defines as "the most perfect state of the book as the printer or publisher finally intended to issue it."[5] As Philip Gaskell explains, an ideal copy is precisely what the bibliographer sets out to capture: "The bibliographer examines as many copies as possible in order to construct a notional ideal copy of the edition he is studying. A description of this ideal copy would note all the blank leaves intended to be part of its gatherings, and all excisions, insertions, and cancellantia which belonged to the most perfect copy of the work."[6] Of course, this equates a kind of speculation, since no two copies of a physical book can be the same. Yet, following Gwyon's remark, a missing book—which circumvents its issuing—simultaneously articulates its own potential and sustains an ostensible perfection. Thus, in treating Jargon as a work in progress, its prospective and possible projects provide a direct representation of its active and energetic creative processes. Perhaps, then, one may more accurately approach its bibliographical repository in the context of M. C. Richards's conception of centering, which draws parallels to the inclusiveness of a potter's technique, working outward from a foundational point toward the unknown; along the way, a kind of sculpture or vessel may be formed.

In approaching Jargon's complexities as a repository of both published and unpublished materials, it should be stressed that any inquiry into its processes is inevitably corollary to the peculiarly magical attention of Jonathan Williams; to peripatetic encounters of a calculated and improvisational kind; to exploration of social and cultural margins; and, oddly enough, to serial subscriptions. To address the latter first: the effect of subscriptions to a collection may seem trivial, but it's essential to understanding where most of Jargon's missing books come from, and, more generally, it remains unsung in the history of American letters. As Millicent Bell writes, "That publishing poetry 'pays' is assumed by *no* publisher, of course; that small, exquisitely-produced books should even succeed in keeping the creditors at bay is obviously most unlikely. Yet Williams . . . has somehow kept the Jargons coming. Subscription has helped in the case of many of the books and still continues to be his reliance."[7] Williams implemented subscriptions with the intention of financing in advance the publication of books as he planned them, although it didn't exactly work that way. In "Issue #6 of an Occasional Jargon Newsletter," dated January 2, 1962, Williams writes, "Jargon is stuck, has been stuck, I have said so many times. The subscribers I need (libraries and individuals) with sufficient confidence to invest for a ten-year period for $100.00, they are hanging back." This is just one of hundreds, if not thousands, of references pointing to Jargon's constant financial difficulties. Regardless of whether the subscription model was Williams's intention from the beginning, it informed Jargon's structure very early on, not only as a means of "paying the printer" but also to arrange for an enumerative series.[8] Numbers were assigned to most projects as they were planned, and in some cases they were reassigned to new projects, or reassigned to later publications. Perhaps the most striking example of the latter is Louis Zukofsky's teacher's guidebook *A Test of Poetry*, which was originally slated to be published in 1958 as Jargon 26. Instead, it became Jargon 12 (replacing the first volume in a series of translations by Kenneth Rexroth that was never released by Jargon) and was published in conjunction with Corinth Books in 1964.[9]

Thus, Jargon's catalog has a jumbled chronology, a non-ordinal ordinality caused by difficulties and precarities of planning future books, broadsides, and other materials. Joel Oppenheimer's *Just Friends / Friends and Lovers* (Jargon 57) took nearly twenty years to publish, while others simply never materialized, usually falling victim to financial instability.

In the late '50s and '60s, Williams was the recipient of small grants from several foundations, which helped to keep Jargon afloat, but were typically only enough for a few publications (if that). In 1968, Jargon officially became the Jargon Society, which as Ross Hair explains in *Avant-Folk: Small Press Poetry Networks from 1950 to the Present*, "arose out of practical financial needs," but was also a result of "the breakdown of Williams's relationship with Olson."[10] The rift with his mentor grew as Williams continued to distance himself from the Black Mountain coterie and to publish writers of whom Olson disapproved (e.g., Kenneth Patchen, Mina Loy, and Buckminster Fuller). Regardless, the change opened further funding possibilities and led to Jargon taking on a non-profit status. As Meyer relates in our correspondence, "Jargon had just received a grant from the newly formed National Endowment for the Arts to publish three new titles. In order to accept that support the press had to incorporate as a not-for-profit foundation. The involvement of the Feds here made getting that tax status secure. . . . Although for Jonathan it was more a matter of backing into the situation, Jargon Press or Jargon Books or plain old Jargon was now the Jargon Society, Inc." But this only temporarily relieved some of the budgetary burden, and Williams's relationship with foundations was anything but jovial. From the mid-'60s onward, Williams relied on several wealthy benefactors for Jargon's (and often personal) funds, principal among them Donald B. Anderson and R. Phillip Hanes.[11] That said, the publication of books still depended on Williams's constant fundraising efforts, largely conducted via his "begging bowl" letters, or—as photographer and former Jargon treasurer Dobree Adams calls them—"whine-o-grams."[12] Described by Thomas Lask, poetry editor at the *New York Times*, as "ripsnorting, curmudgeony missuves [sic]," the letters contain some of Williams's most sardonic prose, often peppered with threats to end Jargon unless a certain amount of money was donated.[13]

As one might expect, these letters occasionally caused problems. Andrew Rippeon's *Letters to Jargon: The Correspondence between Larry Eigner & Jonathan Williams* documents the difficulty of raising funds for Eigner's *On My Eyes*, which was published as Jargon 36 in 1960. In several begging bowl letters, Williams publicizes the amount of money he owed; for example, in one from 1959 titled "Further Tired Fried Homilies," he writes, "I have found that poetic enthusiasm does not pay printers, to whom I still owe $3000 from previous propagations of the intimate poem. If I could find one American who felt that $1000 spent on a volume of Larry Eigner was more important than 16% of a Cadillac, I'd go to press immediately."[14] Although the letter was a sincere attempt to raise funds for the book, the fact that Williams owed this amount of money to the printers caused much tension in Eigner's household. Eigner had been soliciting his family for donations on Jargon's behalf, and at the sight of this debt, his mother threatened to cut off correspondence with Williams. Others were more skeptical of Williams's efforts, including Lask, who writes that "prosperity would be the ruin" of Williams: "You know very well that if somebody guaranteed Jargon its deficits for the next ten years, provided you with six months of readings, kept your books in print in three editions . . . and funded your favorite charities . . . you would just go to pieces."[15] Lask and Williams were friends, and his comments are likely facetious, but they articulate something of a valid point: Jargon's structure is contingent on conflict of a peculiar sort. Whitney Jones sheds light on this in correspondence: "When [Williams's] archives were organized . . . they found unopened envelopes with uncashed checks inside. . . . Jonathan frequently thought whatever someone gave was not enough."[16] This quixotic relationship to money is perhaps representative of a deeper, internal struggle, or at least stubbornness, confirming Diana C. Stoll's observation that "only hardheaded individuals run small presses for fifty-year stretches."[17]

Perhaps exemplary of this disposition is an anecdote from Holly Beye's memoir *120 Charles Street, The Village: Journals and Writings from 1949-1950*, which details her time living in New York with her then-husband David Ruff, with whom Williams studied at Atelier 17 under Stanley William Hayter.[18] Williams spent a lot of time at Beye and Ruff's apartment, which sustained severe damage after a fire engulfed their building in the winter of 1950. In a journal entry from May 25, 1950, Beye writes,

> David cooked a luscious dinner. Chuck steak, onion soup and mushrooms. Jonathan, who was determined to hear Toscanini, sat by the radio and held on tight to the aerial. (NBC, QXR, and CBS were knocked off the radio by the fire and we can only hear them by gripping the aerial). David, anxious to get back to the Atelier, kept urging Jonathan to eat, finally cut his steak for him and even fed it to him piece by piece while Jonathan, torn between indignation and the desire to hear the program, gripped the aerial hard and tried to push him away.[19]

Introduction 5

Holly Beye in Woodstock, New York. Williams, Beye, and her then-husband David Ruff were frequent traveling companions, often visiting Kenneth and Miriam Patchen at their cabin in Old Lyme, Connecticut. In 1951, they spent time with Henry Miller at Big Sur and with Kenneth Rexroth in San Francisco; the latter meeting led to the first Jargon publication. Photo by Jonathan Williams, courtesy of the Poetry Collection of the University Libraries, University of Buffalo, State University of New York.

As Beye mentions in other entries, this was a rare dinner for the three impoverished artists in those days. If the image of Williams in this awkward position isn't the consummate prophecy of Jargon, it's at least testament to his perseverance. Much later, Williams would say, "I've been doing this and losing money for fifty years and I'm still eating regular," even if someone else was providing the meals.[20] In the spring of 1950, Jargon was only becoming a possibility. He and Ruff were already making poetry plates at the Atelier and, in need of money for food and rent, selling the prints around the city, or at least trying to. Over ale and porter at the White Horse Tavern, their frequent haunt, they would discuss books and publishing ambitions. Williams had already served as amanuensis to Kenneth Patchen, typing up *Fables and Other Little Tales* as it was dictated to him;[21] the collection would become the sixth Jargon publication three years later. Williams had intended to publish *Fables* as early as the fall of 1950, making it among the very first planned, although it wasn't yet Jargon, a name he would take from his friend the painter Paul Ellsworth later that year.[22] According to Beye, it could have been called "Bubkis [sic]" or "Gorilla."[23]

Before discovering Patchen's books, Williams had a "H. P. Lovecraft frenzy" in his adolescence, and included authors like Frank Baum, Beatrix Potter, and J. R. R. Tolkien among the most cherished and influential authors of his childhood.[24] It may be argued that in these early encounters with books, one glimpses a kind of protolithic Jargon. Williams frequently cites the Oz series, Potter's tales, and *The Hobbit* (among others) as imported simulations; for instance, in Monty Diamond's 1975 documentary *Jonathan Williams: By Eye and by Ear*, Williams says, "I'm interested in the notion of creating the books of childhood, the magic books over again." [25] For him, these books were sacred objects that commanded care and attention. The lack of these qualities, very much evident in the hawkishly obtuse US culture, became a catalyst for later activism. Patchen said that the role of the artist is to "protest against evil," and Williams's staunch opposition to Western inattention, anti-intellectualism, and negligence may be viewed in this light.[26] The critic Hugh Kenner famously refers to Jargon as the "custodian of snowflakes," which Williams acknowledges as indicating that "Poetic culture in this country is evanescent and deliquescent as snowflakes are. If they aren't caught and turned into books almost everything around us can disappear without a trace. . . . It's something that has to be fought just as much as you would fight for conservation or ecological balances."[27] Indeed, Williams felt that poetry would eventually be studied as a branch of ecology.[28] Jargon functioned as a type of conservancy focused on the work of neglected artists and writers (e.g., Alfred Starr Hamilton, Mina Loy, and Lorine Niedecker) as opposed to writers who would've garnered larger audiences (e.g., Allen Ginsberg and William S. Burroughs, whose *Howl* and *Naked Lunch*, respectively, Williams had rejected).[29]

Williams's variety of responsive conservation was a complement of an active lifestyle and incessant travel. Tom Patterson alleges that Williams "probably logged more cross-country driving miles than Neal Cassady."[30] In the mid-1950s, Williams began traversing the country in his Volkswagen Bug, selling books, giving readings and lectures, searching out artists on their own turf. An avid hiker, he backpacked throughout North America and Europe,

Williams on the set of William Saroyan's *The Beautiful People* circa 1947. Photo by Highlands Playhouse, courtesy of the Poetry Collection of the University Libraries, University of Buffalo, State University of New York.

in such places as the Black Forest, Swiss Alps, the Lake District, and his beloved Appalachian Trail, which he and his then-partner the poet Ronald Johnson trekked along, from Georgia to New York, in 1961. This type of constant movement is an important distinction that Williams makes in connection with his own practice: "I don't sit around waiting for these people to sort of materialize. I go out and find them. I guess it has to do a lot with the life I lead, a lot of which is led on foot. I like to walk and I find that I do find things if I do go out and hike. And I find poems about as easily as I find people."[31] Williams found the poets and, like the visionary poet John Clare before him, "the poems in the fields and wrote them down," to such an extent that Hugh Kenner crowned him "the truffle hound of American poetry."[32] In addition, Williams wrote letters almost obsessively, a practice he considered necessary to the maintenance of his network. Anne Midgette writes of her stays at Corn Close, the seventeenth-century Cumbrian cottage that her family shared with Williams and Meyer: "Anyone staying overnight . . . woke to the sound of Jonathan's electric typewriter . . . thwacking out essays and poems and letter after letter against a background of whatever music caught Jonathan's fancy that day. . . . The correspondence was the central, continuous leitmotif."[33] The network, which was essentially Williams's overlaying process for active discovery and care, again reflects his rejection of the literary establishment. Jonathan Greene writes that Williams "'networked' before the word existed . . . across disciplines and in altruistic fashion."[34]

Williams's peripatetic output may be construed as impromptu, given his travels and correspondence, particularly during Jargon's inception. Indeed, Jargon's first publication, *Garbage Litters the Iron Face of the Sun's Child*, a collaboration between Williams and David Ruff, was printed somewhat spur-of-the-moment at Ruff's Print Workshop in San Francisco in June of 1951.[35] The next month found Williams at Black Mountain College, where he published Joel Oppenheimer's *The Dancer* as Jargon 2, which Oppenheimer printed on the small Kluge in-house press at the college. As Williams notes, "Oppenheimer had the facility, had the training, to make these things possible," as had Ruff before him.[36] In 1952, Williams's application for conscientious objector status was denied, and he was drafted and stationed with the Army Medical Corps in Stuttgart, Germany. Nonetheless, this fortuitously put him within short distance of several printing houses, including that of Dr. Walter Cantz, "one of the best printers" in the country.[37] Having received a $1,500 inheritance from his friend Charles Neal, he was able to publish *Four Stoppages / A Configuration* (Jargon 5) and the first Jargon books: Patchen's *Fables and Other Little Tales* (Jargon 6), Olson's

The Maximus Poems / 1–10 (Jargon 7), and Robert Creeley's *The Immoral Proposition* (Jargon 8).[38] Whether or not these books would've been published if Williams hadn't been drafted and hadn't received the inheritance, they certainly would've looked different, as the books printed by Dr. Cantz are some of Jargon's finest and most sought-after publications to this day, among them *The Maximus Poems / 1–10* and Louis Zukofsky's *Some Time* (Jargon 15). Jargon's spontaneity and unpredictability may also be glimpsed many years later. Williams had initially considered rejecting *White Trash Cooking*; it was Thomas Meyer who recommended publishing what became Jargon's greatest commercial success.[39]

Whether projects were plotted, improvised, or serendipitous, Williams's fluidity and Jargon's bricolage affectations came to embody a wide-ranging and unique set of aesthetics. Of course, the contents are independent in nearly every way. As Kyle Schlesinger writes, "One of the most satisfying things about seeing a bunch of Jargon Society books together is the differences between them. No rules, no template, no formulas, no reruns; each book is built around its content. In Williams's words, if there is any commonality between Jargon's authors, it is that they are 'homemade,' 'nonacademic,' 'non-urban' writers working on their own terms."[40] Additionally, Ross Hair points out that in the context of community, "the knowledge of not being alone is crucial to the broader dynamics of Jargon's society," which reflects the caliber of Williams's conservational networking, particularly among those considered to be outside the mainstream.[41] After all, Jargon is a society inclusive to not only writers and artists cultivated under the imprint, but also to the books themselves, entwined together in an enumerative series; the number 1 assigned to *Garbage Litters the Iron Face of the Sun's Child* and the number 117 assigned to *The Tom Patterson Years: Cultural Adventures of a Fledgling Scribe* constitute the bookends of the collection, and what's found in between establishes this numerical record as one of the most important small press operations of the twentieth century.

While there's no comprehensive bibliography of Jargon Society materials, there are several bibliographical checklists. In 1963, Millicent Bell published one of the first not assembled by Williams himself, which includes the first forty-five Jargon books, its broadsides, and several other titles involving Williams. J. M. Edelstein, who served as the librarian of the National Gallery of Art and was the bibliographer of Wallace Stevens, put together what is typically credited as the foundational resource related to the enumerative bibliography: *A Jargon Society Checklist 1951–1979*.[42] Printed for Williams's fiftieth birthday, it contains the first ninety-two books with gaps at numbers 59, 60,

63, and 64. Edelstein apparently wanted to assemble an official bibliography and was even referred to by Williams as Jargon's bibliographer, but nothing was ever completed beyond the checklist. *Jargon at Forty: 1951-1991*, published twelve years later by the Poetry Collection at SUNY Buffalo, includes additions by then-associate curator Michael Basinski, expanding the list of books to 109, with gaps at 98, 102, 104, 105, and 108, and it remains the only resource to contain separate lists for Jargon postcards and billboards. Richard Owens and Jeffery Beam bring the list to 114 in "A Checklist of Jargon Society," featured in *Jonathan Williams: The Lord of Orchards*. And finally, the Black Mountain College Museum + Arts Center posted a list of 115 books (missing Jargon 116 and 117, as of this writing) to their website. But there's no resource that lists the many pamphlets, newsletters, and ephemera that Williams published throughout his life, reaffirming Jaffe's contention that a complete bibliography is probably not possible.[43] Of course, assembling a comprehensive list of all the materials that Williams planned on publishing is even more challenging.

Williams may have been the "custodian of snowflakes," but some were more difficult to catch than others. Exemplary are the projects officially considered part of Jargon's book series—that is, they continue to hold a numerical spot in the bibliography, despite never being published—which are discussed in the following pages. Chapter 1 focuses on "Jammin' the Greek Scene," which was slated as Jargon 13c, and was to be the third volume of Williams's *Poems: 1953-1956* (Jargon 13). Six proof copies were printed in Karlsruhe in 1959, and while it was never officially released, many of its poems were published in journals, anthologies, and some of Williams's later works. Its story reflects Jargon's first period, from its inception through to the late '50s and early '60s. Williams went to Black Mountain College in July 1951 to study photography, which was certainly one of the most important decisions in his life. It was at the college that he established lifelong friendships with many of his fellow students—including Lyle Bongé, Fielding Dawson, Francine du Plessix Gray, and Joel Oppenheimer—and studied with teachers who would profoundly impact his art, including Harry Callahan, Lou Harrison, Aaron Siskind, Stefan Wolpe, and, principal among them, Charles Olson, who contributed an introductory note to "Jammin' the Greek Scene." Although Williams was writing poems prior to attending Black Mountain, Olson was responsible for Williams's commitment to poetics, and Jargon, as a fledgling press, erupts out of this influence. During its first few years, Jargon mostly published writers affiliated with Black Mountain and/or Olson's circle—those known today as the Black Mountain poets.[44] Yet, by

Introduction 11

the time the college closed in 1957, Williams already had one foot out the door and was consciously inching away from Olson's domineering presence. The following year, Williams met the poet Ronald Johnson in Washington, D.C., which led to his first long-term relationship.[45] "Jammin'" is Williams's first openly gay work, and while this may have had something to do with why it was never published (as discussed in chapter 1), it simultaneously signals his initial forays into the sexual content featured in many of his later poems and his breaking from Olson's influence, which weren't exactly mutually exclusive.

Chapter 2 represents a post–Black Mountain phase where Williams was focused on publishing those he referred to as mavericks and eccentrics—Guy Davenport, Buckminster Fuller, Alfred Starr Hamilton, Mina Loy, Ralph Eugene Meatyard, and the poet Merle Hoyleman, whose magnum opus *Letters to Christopher* was scheduled to be published as Jargon 47. *Letters to Christopher* is a lucid, autobiographical work of prose poetry, which features the routine experiences of the protagonist Phoebe being turned into mythology via correspondence with her lover Christopher. Its poems had several champions, including the poet and publisher James Laughlin—who published selections in the 1937 edition of *New Directions in Prose & Poetry*—and Rae Beamish, who planned on including some of the letters alongside Hoyleman's first and only officially released poetry book, *Asp of the Age*.[46] Williams had slated *Letters to Christopher* for publication in 1960, but it was initially held up due to the usual financial constraints, and then by Hoyleman's refusal to sign the contract that she insisted Williams provide to her. This decision reflects a deeper issue related to certain health problems Hoyleman struggled with throughout her life. From her upbringing in Ponca City, Oklahoma, to her adult years in Pittsburgh, Hoyleman suffered from severe physical and mental illness, the latter of which led to several institutionalizations and extreme reclusiveness up until her death in 1984. Prior to the 2000s, very little was known about Hoyleman's life.[47] Her singular and mysterious works *Asp of the Age* and *Letters to Christopher* prompted speculations that her poems were the result of paranormal communications. However, while some form of channeling may have played a part in Hoyleman's writing process, the claim that she received her poems from spirits is challenged by her friends. While Williams was never able to release *Letters to Christopher*, Hoyleman self-published a very limited edition of twenty-five copies in 1970, and chapter 2 takes a look at the contents of this version.[48]

"Notches along the Bible Belt" (Jargon 98), which is explored in chapter 3, was supposed to be a collection of photos and clippings of odd evangelical ephemera discovered by Richard C. (a.k.a. Richard Craven, a.k.a. Richard Canard), a North Carolina–based artist and curator, and a central figure in Ray Johnson's New York Correspondence School. Its story is part of Jargon operations during a particularly dynamic period starting in the late '60s when it became a non-profit and Williams met the love of his life, Thomas Meyer.[49] It was also during this time that Williams started to supplement Jargon's bibliography, predominantly composed of poetry works, with photography books and other visually oriented projects like "Notches along the Bible Belt."

While Richard C.'s oeuvre is quite diverse, he's primarily known for his correspondence art and found poems. After he added Williams to his mailing list in the mid-1960s, the two became friends and mutual admirers. Williams was such a fan of Richard C.'s work that he began to brainstorm a Jargon publication, eventually landing on the premise for "Notches along the Bible Belt," based on a strain of religious spoofing running through Richard C.'s practice. Williams pitched the idea at some point in the mid- to late '70s,[50] but Richard C.'s modest assumption that his work didn't warrant a book, coupled with concerns over copyright, had him dragging his feet. By the time he started seriously working on the project (nearly a decade later), Williams's enthusiasm had waned, in part due to the difficulties that surfaced with the publication of *White Trash Cooking* in 1986.[51] Although materials were gathered over the years, the manuscript was never completed, and any attempts to complete the project fizzled out.

Many of Jargon's prospective books that were forecasted and then nixed from planning were taken on by other presses, including Jess Collins's translations of Christian Morgenstern's *Gallowsongs* (Black Sparrow Press), Kenneth Patchen's *But Even So* (New Directions), and Kenneth Rexroth's *One Hundred Poems from the French* (Pym-Randall); but some have yet to find a publisher, such as the subject of chapter 4, "The Lyrix of Col. Hampton B. Coles (Ret.)," a selection of lyrics by the performance artist and bandleader Bruce Hampton, complemented with drawings by the visionary folk artist James Harold Jennings. That the book was taken on by Jargon for a time was the result of Tom Patterson's friendship with Williams and his management of the Southern Visionary Folk Art Preservation Project, a three-year endeavor to bring awareness to artists and environments in the US South. While the project didn't include Hampton's work, Patterson considers Hampton's performance and lyrics as being cut from similar visionary cloth. In 1982, Patterson included the lyrics to four of Hampton's songs in the Red Hand Book series, which he edited and released via the Pynyon Press imprint. Patterson also had plans to publish a full-length collection, but they were stunted two years later when he moved to Winston-Salem to work for Jargon.

After Patterson introduced Williams to Hampton, Williams became a big fan of Hampton's then-band The Late Bronze Age, which is somewhat surprising given Williams's harsh opinion of music that was neither jazz nor classical. Patterson pitched "Lyrix," and Williams apparently liked it enough to slate it for publication as Jargon 102. Yet, only a few years later, its number was stripped.[52] Although there were several factors involved in canceling the project—not least of all Patterson's departure from Jargon in 1987—Williams was initially reluctant to publish it once he saw the way the lyrics looked on the page.

Chapter 5 consists of two bibliographical checklists. The first is for Jargon's book series, expanded to incorporate entries and notes on all prospective projects that received a number. Highlights include its only slated LP, "Olson / 'By Ear,'" a recording of Olson reading from *The Maximus Poems* and *In Cold Hell, in Thicket*, among other poems; selected works that Williams edited for Bob Brown, Robert Duncan, Ian Hamilton Finlay, Mason Jordan Mason, and Joel Oppenheimer; and several photography books, including collections by Kay DuVernet, Art Sinsabaugh, and Caroline Vaughan. Alternate titles—that is, books that were given the same number as another work and apparently forgotten—also appear. The second checklist consists of as many forecasted projects without a number that I could find cited in correspondence, newsletters, catalogs, and prospectuses. Breaking away from the enumerative book series allows for the discovery of surprising projects that Williams wanted to do but that never made it far enough in the planning stages to be slated for publication.

Some of these projects came out with other publishers, such as Mahalia Jackson's *Movin' on Up* (Hawthorn, 1966), Charles Mingus's *Beneath the Underdog* (Alfred A. Knopf, 1971), and Celia and Louis Zukofsky's translations of Catullus (Cape Goliard Press in Association with Grossman, 1969); others remain unpublished, including Edward Dahlberg's "Oracular Essays," Baby Dodd's "Book of Drumming," and LaVerne George's "The Notebooks of Arthur Dove"; and some projects never evolved beyond an idea or an invitation to submit, like the unknown titles by Ann McGarrell, Stuart Mills, R. B. Kitaj, and Hilda Morley. It's important to note that this second checklist is nowhere near comprehensive; it's my hope that other Jargonauts will expand on it.

Each of these chapters intends to show how Jargon's missing books function autonomously within its broader collection, with each work projecting its own unique and vibrant world, demonstrating the fragile dynamism and difficulties facing small presses.

Many presses face their own bibliographical gaps, whether in unrequited wishes for particular manuscripts, imaginary books never to be conceived, or projects that fail after years of work. Missing books, when considered by academia at all, are often treated as a by-product of a press's activities.

James S. Jaffe's comment about libraries waiting for Jargon publications exudes material potential, implying the expectation of services promised. And, who knows, these spectral books may very well arrive in physical form some day. Their having never been published will always necessitate this potential, suggesting that they *will* be published. They're not lost—just waiting to be plucked out of limbo.

This anticipation will dwindle with time. People forget, pass away; an institution undergoes structural change, allowing the records of the lost records to become lost themselves. The non-existence or stunting of these projects' physical manifestations grants them a unique spatial nature, haunting both inside and outside the collection as a kind of possibility.

The continuation of the Jargon imprint under the auspices of the Black Mountain College Museum + Arts Center, which took over Jargon's inventory and rights in 2012, suggests that many of these projects could finally take shape. It should be noted that several Jargon books were conceived and/or published after Williams's passing, including Jeffery Beam's compilation of Williams's quotes *A Hornet's Nest* (Jargon 108) and Reuben Cox's *Corn Close: A Cottage in Dentdale* (Jargon 116).[53] In the meantime, perhaps this little book is the next best thing, as an assembly of the stories, fragments, and correspondences that comprise incipient buds shy of the squirrel's foot—not quite the right time for planting.

CHAPTER ONE

Jammin' the Greek Scene (Jargon 13c)

Jonathan Williams's three-volume set *Poems: 1953-1956* (Jargon 13) comes out of a formative and very productive period for Williams as a publisher and writer. From 1953 to 1956, Jargon published its first books, eleven publications in total, which included some of its most beautiful and coveted productions, such as Charles Olson's *The Maximus Poems / 1-10* (Jargon 7) and Louis Zukofsky's *Some Time* (Jargon 15). It was also during this time that Williams was exploring and shedding influences to refine his poetry, particularly at Black Mountain College under Olson's often imperious tutelage. "Jammin' the Greek Scene"—which was scheduled as Jargon 13c, the third and final volume of *Poems: 1953-1956*—is exemplary of Williams's poetic development. Oddly enough, given Olson's biases as discussed in this chapter, it's also Williams's only book to feature an introduction from him. Yet, although there are six scattered proof copies, "Jammin' the Greek Scene" has remained unpublished for over sixty-five years. This chapter takes an in-depth look at its story, spanning Williams's forays into poetry and gay literature, his complicated relationship with Olson, and his maturation as a publisher and writer, all of which have something to do with why "Jammin'" was never released in its entirety.

    Before Williams became Olson's student, his primary mentor had been Kenneth Patchen, whose work he discovered while visiting Ben Abramson's Argus Book Shop during a field trip to New York City in his late teens. Williams occasionally refers to his first poems as "Patchenesque," and consequently they met with Olson's disapproval on his arrival at Black Mountain.[1] As Williams tells Martin Duberman in *Black Mountain: An Exploration in Community*, "I couldn't write poems worth a damn. I wrote a sort of horrible cummings/Patchen pastiche—really hopeless, full of fog and gold singing snakes! When I met Olson he was antagonistic toward me because he didn't admire Patchen or cummings. . . . He ripped the stuff to pieces. . . . It was a good thing to do so, but as a result, it took us about two months before we got friendly at all."[2] Olson's animosity toward Patchen was generally a criticism of his anarchist/pacifist politics. Having worked in government for several years, Olson was invested in certain notions of political power, which he didn't exactly relinquish even after abandoning his political career in 1945. Despite Williams's lifelong affection for Olson, he refers to him as a "monster" during his interview with Robert Dana in the mid-1980s, indicating Olson's temperament as Black Mountain's rector and patriarch, with students and faculty either fallen in line or browbeaten.[3] Michael Rumaker affirms this in his memoir *Black Mountain Days*, revealing how Olson openly played favorites, and how, at Olson's behest, he and others heckled an unnamed "pacifist playwright" who "sneaked off into the night after his flop of a reading, and was never seen again."[4]

Those left out of Olson's inner circle, particularly women students, weren't subjected to the same treatment his "boys" received.[5] Francine du Plessix Gray, who studied at Black Mountain and was a close friend of Williams, was resistant to Olson's misogynist tendencies and "thought he was a total crock."[6] But any antagonism that Williams felt eventually shifted to admiration, and he described Olson to Dana as "full of the blarney. But very impressive, extremely impressive, and amazingly energetic. You felt you'd never quite experienced anybody like this before. . . . He was forty-one, in full vigor, writing The Maximus Poems like mad and cranking them out. Full of himself, as he always was . . . full of it, but great. . . . After the laid-back, bored Ivy League professors I'd had at Princeton, he seemed like a new world. . . . Give you more time than you wanted. . . . No let up."[7] Olson's total availability, energy, and unconventional teaching was exactly what Williams was looking for after dropping out of Princeton and the Institute of Design.[8] As he writes in a letter to the London *Times* on Olson's death in 1970, "Who else living gave courses called 'Ovid's Metamorphoses & Mayan Glyphs' or, simply, 'The Present?'"[9] Who else, as Williams mentions in several interviews and writings, could hold a class for twenty-four hours straight?[10]

Olson introduced Williams to a line of descent stemming from the work of Ezra Pound and William Carlos Williams, whose poetics substantially influenced Olson's own writing, as expressed in his seminal essay "Projective Verse." Many of the ideas found there would not only have an impact on Williams's writing but also complement his proclivity for homing in on the nuances of speech. As Olson writes, "Listening for the syllables must be so constant and so scrupulous, the exaction must be so complete, that the assurance of the ear is purchased at the highest—40 hours a day—price."[11] Williams didn't realize it at the time, but discovering the epigrams of Catullus and Martial—the latter of whom Williams name-drops as his mentor for "Jammin'"—reawakened an interest in found speech and material that started in childhood. Much of the language he spotted or heard around his family's summer home in Scaly Mountain, North Carolina, eventually made

Williams at Black Mountain College. Courtesy of Jonathan Williams Photographs, Yale Collection of American Literature, Beinecke Rare Book and Manuscript Library.

its way into epigrammatic poems, as in "The September Satisfaction of Uncle Iv Owens": "I got / a rat-proof / crib!"[12] A proclivity for the homespun and "elaboration on simple words" led to an appreciation and use of a specific kind of epigram, which Williams was experimenting with while working on "Jammin'."[13] Although the epigram's Hellenistic progeny took on various styles and subjects, Williams's reference to Martial implies the mode associated with his name—one that was witty, sarcastic, and "required frank speech."[14] The latter refers to Martial's use of obscenity, as expressed by his "contention that epigrams cannot 'please without cock.'"[15] However, the emphasis on frankness also reflects the unrefined, earthy language that Williams was introduced to in the mountains of North Carolina. In his introduction to Williams's *Niches Inches: New & Selected Poems, 1957–1981*, Eric Mottram writes, "[Williams's] urge, increasingly, is to condense to the state of epigram (his longer poems are often branches of epigrams), clerihew, pun chains, palimpsests in parvo, brief acts of what Joyce termed verbivocovisual on the word. His ear for people's speech . . . enables him to record impulses to idiosyncrasy he finds around him into poems of discovery rather than acceptance."[16] A good example of the epitaph for Uncle Nick Grindstaff, which Williams found engraved on a remote stone monument while hiking the Appalachian Trail, and later adapted as a poem:

LIVED ALONE
SUFFERED ALONE
DIED ALONE[17]

This is epigrammatic in the traditional Hellenistic sense, as a commemorative inscription. But what intrigued Williams about this epitaph was the way that language could be presented in such a succinct and compelling manner and, in this specific case, how the local shopkeeper who wrote it "could get those words to work like that."[18]

Olson believed that a poem's intensity was intrinsic, waiting to be discovered and "transferred from where the poet got it . . . by way of the poem itself to, all the way over to, the reader," propelled from the mouth as a kind of music. Expanding on Pound's notion of composing via the "musical phrase," Olson sought to free the poem's energy from the rigidity of the metronome toward an individual sense of rhythm carved by the poet's breath; thereby, poetic form could never be "more than an extension of content," a dictum that Olson and Robert Creeley developed in correspondence.[19] As Amiri Baraka relays in *The New American Poetry*, "There must not be any preconceived notion or design for what a poem ought to be. 'Who knows what a poem ought to sound like? Until it's thar' says Charles Olson."[20] Olson's poet was essentially an intuitive medium, likewise reflected in Williams's own practice, as one immersed in the search for poems that already exist but require an active channeling (via attention) to reach. But Olson intensified this idea via his understanding of projective procedure as a sort of time traveling or conjuring, resulting in the return to or summoning of an archaic order that existed prior to the development of Greek philosophy, the latter of which he held responsible for humanity's estrangement from nature. His poetics appear to have been built out of the failure of Western thought, which was particularly evident after World War II and well expressed by prominent thinkers (e.g., Ludwig Wittgenstein) calling for an end to philosophy itself.

However, Olson called instead for a redemptive, process-oriented poetry, which would reunite the poet with the "totality of nature."[21] In his essay "At the Boundary of the Mighty World: Charles Olson and Hesiod," Gary Grieve Carlson explains that Olson used Hesiod as a portal to "a total placement of man and things among all possibilities of creation, rather than that one alone, of modern history and politics." He goes on to quote Olson from his 1965 manifesto "Proprioception": "A work which would free much of the encumbrance upon man as himself a universe . . . would start with Hesiod, taking him as a base-line and saying anything after him as 'lost' something and that all which he does show and include is a beginning of dimension of man's place in the cosmos as it had been imagined before Homer. . . . What I am gesturing in, is a 'literature' (of which Hesiod seems to be a conclusion) which is now for the first time again available."[22] Apparently, Olson's poetics react against the subsequent line of Western literature (i.e., pretty much everything written after Hesiod) and wind up as an activation of a pre-Hellenic consciousness.

Not surprisingly, such dogmatic poetics and coaching left Williams feeling burned out and struggling to "get out from under Leviathan J. Olson."[23] As his poems began to change to something that wouldn't be torn to shreds by the teacher in front of the class, his friends and mentors (e.g., Edward Dahlberg, Louis Zukofsky, and Kenneth Rexroth) cried foul, going as far as to accuse Olson of bullying.[24] As Duberman writes, "Among the divergences was Olson's occasional tendency to treat Williams like a servant" and "to patronize his talents as a poet."[25] The poet Susan Howe testifies to the distinction between influence and outright apprenticeship when noting Olson's impression on her own early writings, saying that "[Olson] showed me what to do. Had he been my teacher in real life, I know he would have stopped my voice."[26] Fortunately, Williams concluded that Olson's influence had to be slipped for his own good. Ross Hair writes that Williams "found his own voice . . . by assimilating Olson's dominant voice with other valuable models and influences," perhaps most notably, Dame Edith Sitwell, whose writing provides a stark contrast to the ultra-masculine campus life, which Robert Duncan expresses when remarking that at Black Mountain it was "easier to announce that you are a homosexual than to say you read Edith Sitwell."[27]

Aside from introducing Williams to a second line of descent composed of the French Symbolists, Sitwell's poetics reflect a visionary quality, emphasizing the "many aspects of words. What color they are. If they leave shadows. How much they weigh," echoing a kind of magical curiosity similar to that found in Williams's cherished books of childhood, such as Beatrix

One of Williams's portraits of Olson at Black Mountain. Prone to cold intolerance, Olson typically had a shawl on hand, even in the summer. Courtesy of Jonathan Williams Photographs, Yale Collection of American Literature, Beinecke Rare Book and Manuscript Library.

Potter's tales and J. R. R. Tolkien's *The Hobbit*. Sitwell was also concerned with getting words into their right place, and against the use of extraneous or unnecessary language in poetry.[28] She writes that "images which are meaningless and unrelated to the material and shape of the poem—is bad poetry."[29] Thus, she simultaneously appealed to Williams's playfulness and imagination within brevity and constraint, as glimpsed in her treatment of musical patterns as arbiters of form and content. As Sitwell writes in *Taken Care of: An Autobiography*, "From the thin, glittering, occasionally shadowed, airy, ever-varying texture of that miracle of poetry, the instinct was instilled into me that not only structure, but also texture, are parents of rhythm in poetry."[30] Although Sitwell's poetics are markedly different from Olson's, she too believed in the channeling capabilities of poetic rhythm, which functioned as a translator "between dream and reality" and an aural equivalent to visual light.[31] But where Olson was more open to intuitive variations of the breath, Sitwell was more lyrical in her use of musical composition, reflecting what would become the qualities of cadence and timing emblematic in Williams's own poetry. In his introduction to *Jonathan Williams: A Bibliographical Checklist, 1950–1988*, Guy Davenport credits Williams's use of "the musical phrase with tricky rests and harmonic surprises" as that which "sets his poems apart."[32] Sitwell's writing showed Williams an alternative to projective verse by using structured musical textures alongside what Duncan refers to as a wish "to include the inventions of the imagination, spoofs, fancies, allegory, fable, all."[33]

"Jammin' the Greek Scene" is a unique embodiment of a mélange of ostensibly conflicting influences, such as Sitwell's lyrical structures and Olson's improvisatory breath; open and closed forms (e.g., projective and epigrammatic techniques); and found materials and raw speech rendered into aphoristic melody. Williams was excited enough about it in 1956 to plan for an edition of 300 copies to be published alongside the first two volumes of *Poems: 1953–1956: Amen/Huzza/Selah* (Jargon 13a), and *Elegies and Celebrations* (Jargon 13b), which came out in October 1960 and summer 1962, respectively. "Jammin'," on the other hand, was published only in "scraps and pieces," with "The Switch Blade (Or, John's other wife," for example, appearing in *The New American Poetry*:[34]

> men share perceptions (and
> their best friends' wives, in lieu of
>
> a perverse tangling of arseholes
>
> —so if you don't dig that sound get down together
> on the wrestling mat mit your
> Blutsbrüderschaft,
>
> > Mr Caesar, Mr Seizure, Mr Man
>
> (every man's woman and every
> woman's man, said Suetonius[35]

The anthology situated Williams as a member of the Black Mountain poets—with Olson at the groups' center—a label that would follow Williams throughout his career despite his rejection of it. "The Switch Blade" is the most published poem from the "Jammin'" set, appearing in multiple journals and books, including Williams's bilingual selection of poems in English and Italian, *Affilati attrezzi per i giardini di Catullo*, which erroneously lists "Jammin'" on the copyright page as having been published in 1966, the last date attributed to its release. Two years later, nearly half of the manuscript was featured in a section titled "From: Jammin' the Greek Scene" in *An Ear in Bartram's Tree: Selected Poems, 1957-1967*.[36] By 1969, plans to distribute the full volume had petered out with any ambitions Williams had for *Poems: 1953-1956* as a whole, and it's likely that the number given to "Jammin'" was never reassigned due to its alphabetical sub-position in the collection as 13c. In a Jargon newsletter dated June 4, 1969, Williams writes, "There were 50 copies [of *Amen/Huzza/Selah*] on special laid paper which were to be boxed later with Jargon 13(b) and Jargon 13(c) in a case designed by René Laubiès with a photo of JW by Creeley. Jargon 13(c), JAMMIN' THE GREEK SCENE, was, however, never released and the laid-paper copies of (a) and (b) have been scattered."[37]

Although it was never published in its entirety, proof copies were produced in 1959 by Verlagsdruckerei Gebr. Tron in Karlsruhe, Germany—the same printer used for the companion volumes, as well as several earlier Jargon editions including Patchen's *Fables and Other Little Tales* and Creeley's *The Immoral Proposition*.[38] James S. Jaffe records the proof as follows: "JAMMIN' THE GREEK SCENE, Poems by JW, Note by Charles Olson. Karlsruhe, Germany, 1956 [sic]. 5⅜ × 7¹³⁄₁₆ inches; 18 leaves. Orange paper wrappers, printed dust jacket on proofing paper with statement by JW dated Summer, 1959 on front flap. Jargon 13 (c). Approximately 4 proof copies were produced for a projected edition of 300 copies, but the book, with a cover designed by Fielding Dawson, was never published."[39] In later correspondence, Jaffe increased the estimated number of proof copies to six, with the locations of only two known: Jaffe's collection at Yale, and the Jargon Society collection at SUNY Buffalo. Visually, the proof is somewhat misleading, as it's similar in design and format to the first two volumes of the series and is marked on the colophon as having been published in "Summer 1956." It's technically Williams's first perfect bound book—an achievement that may otherwise be attributed to *The Empire Finals at Verona: Poems 1956-1957* (Jargon 30)—as his prior publications were single-sheet objects. The dust jackets of all three volumes contain brief statements from Williams, providing lists of influences and mentors (Catullus, Kenneth Rexroth, Olson, and Martial); authors he was reading at the time (Catullus, Li Po, Yosa Buson, Andrew Marvell, Ovid, Robert Graves, and Jane Harrison); and contextual anecdotes (e.g., "When a hip square asked me on the CBC in Montreal, 'Man, are you Beat?' I replied quickly, coolly and mindlessly: 'Sir, I'm a Southerner.' Ask a stupid question, you get, etc.") alongside some lovely typos (e.g., "to draw a bead [sic] on the old androgynous gods"). Although the books are meant to be a unified work encompassing his early poems in what Williams describes as "late-Roman up-tempo style," each one embodies Williams's poetic explorations of the 1950s, distinguished by unique prefaces from three of his mentors (Zukofsky, Duncan, and Olson for volumes a, b, and c, respectively).[40] Williams also assigns specific intentions to each book: (a) "to delight" (calling to mind Zukofsky's idea that the purpose of poetry is to "record and elate"); (b) to "decry and exalt" (i.e., his rendering of the first words of Catullus 85: "Odi et amo"); and (c) to spoof the gods of Greek mythology at the expense of "pious mythographers." These distinctions ultimately led to the proof's separation from the Jargon archive at SUNY Buffalo, where it was instead cataloged as a published book. One of the few indications of its proof status is a faulty credit on its dust jacket, stating that the "covers and title-page drawing are by Fielding Dawson," which Williams had apparently received in the winter of 1956 but didn't include in the proof.[41]

Exactly why "Jammin'" wasn't released is somewhat elusive. Williams had been very close to publishing it and was taking money in advance (via subscriptions) for all three volumes as early as 1956. "Jammin'" was listed as "forthcoming" in Jargon's newsletters and prospectuses up until 1966, after which it typically appears with a note indicating its non-release. In an email from Thomas Meyer to Jeffery Beam in 2008, he writes that why "Jammin'" wasn't published "is still an unanswered question," and he goes on to suggest that Williams's enthusiasm for it may have dwindled after the publication of the first two volumes.[42] Meyer is onto something here, and there's even evidence that Williams had cooled on the entire series as early as 1957; in a Jargon newsletter dated the same year, Williams writes, "Since the Guggenheim Committee apparently liked the ms. of some of [*Poems: 1953-1955*] enough to grant me a Fellowship, I will try to get them finally published, as early in 1958 as possible. The problem of old work, and how to stay interested in it."[43] Around this time, Williams was working on *The Empire Finals at Verona*, which follows a similar theme to "Jammin'" while taking it to another level in terms of production and Fielding Dawson's collaborative role as artist and co-designer.[44] In 1962 the Auerhahn Press published *In England's Green & (A Garland and a Clyster)*, which Williams considered to be his first book in his own voice, implying that his previous books had been weighed down by certain influences. Clearly, he felt the need to move on from his early work. That said, in a lecture delivered for the Hanes Foundation in 1989, Williams points out that the proof contains a vital clue by way of Olson's introduction: "'Why didn't ["Jammin' the Greek Scene"] get published?' . . . 'Money, most likely.' But also something Olson put his finger on: 'I'm sure we got askance from utter shyness. They made us shy, the whole thing fronted so. We winced. And we's wincin' back. I mean, we's shy. Bro Jonathan, he shy.'"[45] Olson overtly states that Williams is too timid to publish "Jammin'," a strange accusation to come from the book's intro. Why would Olson write this? One may only speculate, but there's evidence that it had to do with the role of obscenity in "Jammin'."

At first glance, the title may not appear to be suggestive of anything "obscene"; rather, it indicates that Williams is running Greek mythology through an instrument, with immediate reference to his use of the musical phrase, and this is partly correct. As Ronald Johnson writes, "If we take lyric in its first sense as song from a lyre, then we understand that in Williams's poetry, from the early book *Jammin' The Greek Scene* [sic] . . . in which he turns up rather like Edith Sitwell playing Ovid on the saxophone in a New Orleans dive . . . his words present themselves, one after the other, as equivalents of notes of music plucked still ringing from the air. He stands as one always in dialogue with Orpheus himself."[46] Williams confirms the central role of sound in *An Ear in Bartram's Tree*, where he writes that the idiom "jammin'" is taken "from Charles Brown, Bud Powell, Blakey and Miles," an important point that he leaves out of his statement in the proof. Since *An Ear in Bartram's Tree* marks the first time these poems were published together under the "Jammin'" moniker, the initial impression of the word is related to slang and affiliated with jazz, of which Williams was an obsessive listener. He also held friendships with many influential musicians, including Charles Mingus, who was on the advisory board of the Nantahala Foundation, essentially an early incarnation of the Jargon Society.[47] In the proof, Williams elaborates on "Jammin'"'s connection to music with an anecdote, apparently gleaned from Olson, which he attaches to the meaning of obscenity: "The results suggest the time Aeschylus put megaphones in the hands of some of his thespian-type Errinys, so six came on, screaming like fifty. People gave birth, etc., on the spot."[48] The correlation between sex and sound is a main theme here. The words "jam" and "jazz" have sexual connotations, such as the former's somewhat conflicting meanings of a cis heterosexual male (i.e., an acronym for "just a man") and "a spontaneous party often ending in a spirited orgy."[49] "Jazz" has etymological ties to the word "jasm," meaning "energy, spirit," which came to be affiliated with music that was initially called "jas" or "jass," which is slang for sex.[50] The composer and musician Eubie Blake notes that the change in spelling was a thinly veiled attempt at masking its sexual connotations as the music began to reach larger audiences on the cusp of the Jazz Age.[51] Williams's comparison of an amplified Aeschylus performance to the bebop of the mid-1950s is hypersexualized and, according to him, obscene; he writes in his statement to the proof that "such sounds were ob scena; therefore, for off-stage purposes."

Following suit, many of the "Jammin'" poems seem to consist of "language being spoken off stage," invoking another definition of "jazz": "Unnecessary, misleading, or excessive talk."[52] "Jammin'" reflects the vernacular more than its companion volumes, with much of the tone, texture, and form emblematic of musicians' speech, broken up as if overheard, discussing what's about to be played rather than actually performing, or just idly chatting away. For example, in "The Priapupation of Queen Pasiphaë," Williams writes:

> say, lay
>   off the doll biz, Daedalus,
> construct me
>   a stately mansion, dad, a conveyance
> for my
>   quote most monstrous lust unquote!
> got just the rig, doll, try this
>   cow on—
> for size . . .[53]

By fracturing the story of Pasiphaë's curse into one shooting the shit backstage, Williams inserts the possibility for an interlocutor to respond, who in this case calls the storyteller's bluff in the poem's final lines:

> white bulls, sacred to poseidon,
> don't fool
>   that easy, that's
> for sure (which is sort of
> the first cock & bull story
> for sure

If one accepts the multiple authorship view of the Homeric question—that is, that Homer consists of many writers over several generations—the fragmenting of myth into conversational chatter reflects the oral tradition of early-period Homer. Williams confirms Johnson's notion of the bardic role in "Jammin'" by rendering portions of the epics into their inceptive textless form (before re-transcribing them). This may also be viewed as a projective operation via Olson's belief in an archaic, pre-Hellenic literature apparently resurfacing during the '40s and '50s. However, Williams's evident use of childish humor and spoofing—a technique that Robert Duncan treats as a rebuff of Olson's projective verse[54]—and his emphasis on the sexually obscene may have been a gibe at Olson.

While "The Priapupation of Queen Pasiphaë" refers to the Minoan myth, in some cases the ascribed myth is either not apparent or non-existent, with not much happening aside from the evident sexual/musical act. For instance, in the two-word poem "The Jam of Sage Euhemerus": "Whoopee, Priape!" The image of whoopee (Jazz Age slang for sex) with the fertility god Priapus doubles as an exclamation uttered during the "jam," whether that be musical or sexual. In what is easily the shortest poem in "Jammin'," the ensuing blankness of the empty page may lead to the speculation that Williams is accentuating everything that happens offstage, even silence and awkwardness after bad sex or improvisation. A similar effect occurs in the preceding poem, "Idyll," with the consecutive space implying certain sounds associated with a sexual/musical act:

> a soft heart and a hard
> cod
>
> song is down
> in the mouth,
>
> heating

Simultaneously, the "song" is "heating" or forming in the mouth—alluding to projective verse and Olson's proclamation that "the song is heat!"—and going "down in the mouth," implying oral sex.[55] Mythology, if cited at all, is used as a vehicle for sexual innuendo, and there isn't much stock in the details, other than its corollary to a "scene" where it might be concurrently played with musically and deviously. Both "The Jam of Sage Euhemerus" and "Idyll" indicate that the "jam" may also be considered as a nonce poetic form—essentially a half-lyrical, half-projective epigrammatic jest—starting with the cover. The title "Jammin' the Greek Scene"—simultaneously reflecting the jam as a purposeful occlusion, a musical performance, and what might happen before or after the show, whether that be chitchat, practicing, or engaging in some kind of sexual act or orgiastic scene—constitutes its own Martialian epigram with shifting meanings. Its poems not only echo what's happening offstage but also pull the curtain back to reveal the deeds, putting them front and center as the main performance with the aim to "shock and amuse," in the vein of Martialian obscenity.[56]

Considering the nature of the subject matter, coupled with Williams's direct reference over thirty years later to Olson's introduction as an inhibition to publishing "Jammin'," it's obvious that Olson's accusations of "shyness" and "wincin' back" have merit. As Jeffery Beam proposes, "Later on Jonathan was clearly less shy about publishing sexual content, but perhaps that early in his career, not?" He believes this may have had something to do with the project's unconcealed gay references, starting with the title—that is, "Greek" as a shortened form of "Greek love." Beam notes that Williams's comment "about being 'fronted' and 'shy' speaks volumes about the time," given the very real dangers for gay and queer people. Consequently, there was no expectation for coming out either. As Beam explains, "Suddenly we just had boyfriends and then partners and any girlfriends just vanished away."[57] That said, Williams was also suspicious of any categorization, believing that anyone—regardless of being gay or straight—could be had. In his essay "'Hemi-demi-semi barbaric yawps': Jonathan Williams and Black Mountain," Ross Hair discusses the role of "sexual ambiguity" in Williams's "wider mistrust of, and resistance to, abstracting labels," and quotes him from his and Meyer's joint interview with John Browning for *Gay Sunshine*: "The words male and female must have been invented by the same crowd that talks about Truth and Beauty—abstractions that can be made to pay off commercially and politically when spoken out of the moola-side of the mouth."[58] Similarly, as Kenneth Irby points out, Williams was wary of the difficulties of writing about sex, in requiring "many techniques to keep it from being platitudinous, too easy, too indulgent."[59] But his reluctance to publish gay content in the mid-'50s had less to do with skepticism than with the fact that he was still a student of poetry under the tutelage of certain patriarchs including Patchen, Kenneth Rexroth, and, of course, Olson. Robert Duncan was Williams's first openly gay mentor, and he provided a way out from Olson via his poetics—which were even more "open" than Olson's open-form projective verse—and those of others such as Edith Sitwell; this was crucial to Williams finding his own voice, as reflected in 1962's *In England's Green &* (*A Garland and a Clyster*).

If the queer and sexually explicit poems of "Jammin'" were a sticking point for Williams in and around 1956, they certainly weren't by the end of the decade, signaled by the publication in 1959 of *The Empire Finals at Verona*, which, as already mentioned, is similar in theme and content. Of course,

"Jammin'" was still slated for publication at the time, and this is where Meyer's point about Williams's lack of enthusiasm for publishing his early work comes in—along with Jargon's limited finances, it played a major role in permanently sidelining "Jammin'" in the mid-'60s. That said, Olson's introduction caused initial hesitation, and one can't help but note the unfairness of this when considering Williams's vulnerabilities as a young gay man still gaining confidence as a poet. As Maria Damon writes of Williams's friend Jack Spicer, "The incriminating sentence becomes . . . a central problematic in gay poetry."[60] While Olson may have been unaware of this, some of the things he said to his students may suggest that he wasn't merely aloof but perhaps held certain prejudices.[61] Williams's reluctance to publish "Jammin'" presents the necessity for an important distinction—was it Williams's timidity or Olson's comment about it that was the bigger barricade? Williams seems to relay the former in his 1989 lecture for the Hanes Foundation; nevertheless, Beam also suggests that Olson likely disapproved of some of the "Jammin'" poems despite his introduction.[62] Although Beam didn't say this, his contention implies that Olson's comment about Williams's reticence may have been a tacit (albeit, successful) attempt to prevent the book's release.

In his poem "Maximus to Gloucester: Letter 27 [withheld]," Olson proclaims, "No Greek will be able / to discriminate my body,"[63] and while this line carries weight as a reference to his critique of Western metaphysics, it also reflects certain notions regarding his sexuality. Williams and Olson's falling out is often attributed to differing opinions regarding publishing and the Black Mountain community more broadly. Although it's true that they disagreed on these issues, Hair suggests that a kind of sexual tension may have been a factor as well: "Olson may have proclaimed that 'the song is heat!' and proposed a proprioceptive, 'corporeal poetics' very much centered on physiognomy, but in his own lifetime, Williams implies, Olson was 'a cold man pretending to be hot.' . . . Olson was one of the many heterosexual male 'counter-cultural' poets of the 1950s who remained ambivalent about, or resistant to, what [Rachel Blau] DuPlessis describes as 'the sexual frankness and body consciousness of gay male poets.'"[64] Hair explores this idea across several poems, including "Funerary Ode to Charles Olson"—where Williams casts Olson as Orpheus—and "Jammin'"'s "Always the Deathless Mu-sick," noting that its title not only is a reference to Olson's "Maximus to Gloucester: Letter 2" but also proclaims that "Orf's awfully gay / despite Eurydice."[65] Williams's use of Olson as an Orphic proxy ends up revealing a shortcoming in Olson's poetics, hinting that Olson may not have taken "openness" as seriously as the "40 hours a day . . . price" he himself required.[66] This can also be observed in how Williams challenges heteronormative biases by using projective technique to transmit gay and queer anecdotes, as in "The Honey Lamb":

> the boysick, by gadzooks thunderstruck, Rex Zeus, sex expert, erects
> a couple temples
>   and cruises the Trojan coast
>
> eagle-eyed, spies,
> swoops, swishes
> into town;
>
> ponders whether tis nobler . . . or
> to bullshit, leeringly,
> brown, or go down
> on, on
>   that catamite cat,
>   Kid Ganymedes,
>   mead mover
> erst-while eagle-scout
> bed mate

In the tenth book of Ovid's *Metamorphoses*, Orpheus sings about Jupiter's transformation into an eagle for the abduction of prince Ganymedes—a mythological symbol of gay desire—to become both his lover and cupbearer to the gods. Williams overtakes the Orphic role via his own rendition of the bard's tale in the projective style of Olson coupled with the Uranian mode, spoofing through both obscenity and slang, and ultimately presenting Olson as a kind of sexually half-assed Orphic Zeus.

"Jammin'," then, isn't about Greek mythology per se, but rather a kind of exposure; and if its primary objective is "to draw a bead [sic] on the old androgynous gods, to make them come clean from the torpor of pious mythographers," as Williams writes in his statement, then this may also imply exposure corralled by a sort of caricaturist methodology. Williams tells the reader that "the facts . . . are courtesy of Golding's Ovid, studies by Jane Harrison and Robert Graves' edition of the Greek Myths."[67] He wasn't the only one at Black Mountain College engaged by these texts. Graves's writings on the subject, notably *The Greek Myths* and *The White Goddess: A Historical Grammar of Poetic Myth*, are cited as having direct influence on *The Maximus Poems* (particularly the latter two books) and Robert Creeley's *A Form of Women* (Jargon 33).[68] But there's nothing in "Jammin'" to suggest that Williams actually read these books. He very well may have, but it's just as easy to assume that he flipped through "the facts" and pulled out various references, as a spoofing of the act. "Jammin'" certainly toys with the idea of what a poem can be, which calls to mind Amiri Baraka quoting Olson in *The New American Poetry*, "Who knows what a poem ought to sound like? Until it's thar'."[69] Some of Williams's poems, such as "The Jam of Sage Euhemerus," seem to have been purposefully stopped short of Olson's "thar."

Williams and his Martialian "frank speech" also test the notion of what can be codified as poetic language, including appropriated menacing. In the second poem of the proof, "Catullus: Carmen XVI," Williams starts off with a warning:

> I'll pedicate and irrumate
> you, Mr Pathic and Miss Catamite!
>
> You two who dig me 'immodest',
> just because of some voluptuous-type sounds.

The title clearly cites "Carmen XVI," a Catullus poem considered so offensive that a full English-translation didn't appear in print until the twentieth century, nearly 2,000 years after its writing. Its first line is particularly shocking, threatening two of Catullus's critics with "Paedicabo et irrumabo" (sodomizing and face-fucking).[70] The beginning of Williams's poem is an adaptation of the original, and it goes on to proclaim:

> We Sacred Poets come on chaste—
>   yet our verse
> is as wide as
> the world

Williams associates "frank speech" with an all-encompassing poetic language, and what might be thought of as the obverse of the obscene or the vulgar—cleanliness. As he writes in his statement, "Only way to have clean, vatic-variety ears is to let all sorts serpents lick them, swore Hercules."[71] Although Olson accuses Williams of shyness, he also writes that Williams's use of parody and "vulgarism" wind up as a kind of honest representation of mythology, especially when contrasted with mythology depicted by "pious mythographers." In his introduction, Olson writes, "Everything got treated as scalar for the 2500 years immediately preceding. And indeed the Gods. . . . What Brother Jonathan does in hyar is to keep up the velocity at the same time that the things are let be. Ganymedes, or Echo, or that one Io, get back, by vulgarism, their patent vector powers. In his lightness the spoof."[72] Olson acknowledges the unique role of "vulgarism," and by default, the obscene, as an accurate premise by which to depict the gods, even to the extent that such a portrayal may end up reinstating their authentic "powers." It's with an eye to such flattery that Olson's introduction is often referred to as an accolade by, for example, Ronald Johnson and Eric Mottram. Paul Christensen echoes this sentiment in *Charles Olson: Call Him Ishmael*: "[Jonathan Williams's] humor is in control in the beautifully witty poems of *Jammin' the Greek Scene*, where the imposing conceptions of Greek mythology are translated into American slang. Olson wrote a foreword to these poems, praising the frank, honest, and amusing use Williams had made of his subject and arguing that Williams's attitude was one that Americans had to acquire after so long a reverence for Europe."[73] Christensen's sketch isn't inaccurate, but it ignores the possibility that Olson's introduction may have been tongue-in-cheek at the very least. While Williams was indeed a part of Olson's circle, Duberman reveals that "Olson was more interested in [Ed] Dorn, John Wieners, and later LeRoi Jones and Ed Sanders than in Williams."[74] Olson's introduction to "Jammin'," which could easily be construed as a generous compliment, also includes reference to Williams's "lightness" and use of "the spoof." As already mentioned, the latter is cited (by Duncan) in opposition to projective verse, and the appearance of it in Olson's note, coupled with accusations of cold feet, raises some red flags. Perhaps this is an early example of a criticism that Williams faced throughout his career, as a poet of light verse; but a closer reading of "Jammin'" exposes the depth of Williams's early epigrams, ostensibly set up to poke fun at conservative renderings of Greek mythology, while just below the surface spoofing Olson alongside his poetics.

If we take the proof as the definitive setup for "Jammin'" (as opposed to the selection published in *An Ear in Bartram's Tree*), we first encounter the four-line epigraphic poem "Paen to Black Mountain":

    thar'll be
        Paideuma in the sky,
            in the sweet,
                by and by

Initially, this little poem may seem out of character with the objectives laid out in Williams's statement; but when considered in the shadow of Olson's introduction, which it directly follows, it introduces an approach for engaging with the proceeding poems. Williams conjures Olson's voice by adopting his use of the dialectical variant for words ending in *-ere* (in this case, "thar'll"), a technique employed throughout "Jammin'." But the most striking word of this little poem is "paideuma," an intricate expression coined by the German ethnologist Leo Frobenius, who defines it as "the soul of a given culture in history."[75] While it may be mistaken as a synonym of the word "zeitgeist," "paideuma" differs in its unique prosopopoeial implications, with culture treated as an actual entity with spiritual qualities, and in the role that education plays in the development of its "soul."[76] This complements the paen as a song of praise; although historically tied to the worship of Apollo, the use of "paideuma" here indicates praise to a cultural/educational organism, evidently Black Mountain College, as revealed in the title.[77] The notion that the poem may be a whimsical celebration of Black Mountain at its closing in 1957 is reinforced by its use of the nineteenth-century Christian hymn "In the Sweet By-and-By." Consequently, it takes its final two lines—"in the sweet / by and by"—from the hymn's chorus, therefore summoning the lyrics that follow—"We shall meet on that beautiful shore"—as a ghost line constituting the poem's actual ending, perhaps evoking the closing image of Black Mountain's Lake Eden campus. But of course, as with the majority of poems in "Jammin'," "Paen to Black Mountain" is a double entendre; the shift in meaning occurs when read in mind with the hymn's numerous parodies, the most famous being Joe Hill's 1911 song "The Preacher and the Slave," which is the origin of the skeptical phrase "pie in the sky": "You'll get pie in the sky when you die (that's a lie!)."[78] The pun "Paideuma in the sky," sung in a mock Olson voice, suggests a fantasy or wishful thinking rolled back on Black Mountain and its patriarch as another sort of caricatured mythology. Parody of one mythology is set up to lampoon another—in this case, Williams's own mythology, with Olson as his Orphic Zeus, and Black Mountain as a crumbling Parthenon. As Williams writes, "Princeton was one club, and Black Mountain was another. I made distance from each as quickly as possible."[79] If we take "Paen to Black Mountain" as a Martialian epigram, then it's both "a means of commemorating and preserving" and "an elegant waste of time not intended to outlast its occasion."[80] With Black Mountain and Olson chronicled as transitory parody, they're made easier to get away from. What better way for Williams to signify this break than with a final

Jammin' the Greek Scene   33

prank—getting Olson to write an introduction to a book that was to feature such frivolous limericks as

> A dizzy old goddess named Demeter
> Got pomegranate seeds in her catheter;
> She lit a Pall-Mall,
> Slapped Kora in Hell,
> And yelled for her son-in-law, Lucifer.

It can be argued that Williams went even farther by getting Olson to essentially give his okay to a text that's at odds with his politics. "Paen to Black Mountain" marks the inclusion of Christian mythologies via its use of "In the Sweet By-and-By," which likewise introduces context for the particular sort of piety of those "pious mythographers"—that is, reverence for the American religion, which distorts all preceding mythologies, Greek or otherwise, in its own capitalist fun-house mirror. This suggests that Williams intended to jam the American mythos by way of its moral treatment of mythologies (and much else), thereby exposing aspects of its bigotry. In one of the final poems in the "Jammin'" sequence, "The Beast-Scene," Williams writes:

> "you can tell
> what sort a man is by his
> Creature
> that comes oftenest
> to the front"

whar?
Fraternity
where?

The poem starts out by quoting Mr. Raven from George MacDonald's 1895 novel *Lilith*, a book replete with Christian mysticism. Mr. Raven's preceding lines are as follows: "Every one, as you ought to know, has a beast-self—and a bird-self, and a stupid fish-self, ay, and a creeping serpent-self too—which it takes a deal of crushing to kill! In truth he has also a tree-self and a crystal-self, and I don't know how many selves more—all to get into harmony."[81] The title suggests that the "Creature that comes oftenest to the front" is the "beast-self," revealing the title as a pun with anti-war connotations.[82] The poem continues to echo Mr. Raven, who after taking Vane, the novel's protagonist, to "the region of the seven dimensions," points out the deficiency of Vane's human-centric conceptions of place and position. Again,

Williams channels Olson's voice via the dialectical variant "whar?," only this time, it sounds a lot like "war," in association with "Fraternity," a nod to Olson's political conservatism in opposition to pacifism. As Rumaker relates in *Black Mountain Days*, Olson had decidedly broken from Black Mountain's "Quaker, passive-resistant past," noting that he taught his students that they should prepare "'for the marauders over the hill,' as well as the marauders in oneself."[83] The Olson / Mr. Raven figure orders Williams off to war in the poem's final line, "Join Up—or, Go to the Jungle!"—calling to mind Olson's cold shoulder when refusing to support Williams's conscientious objector status. After being threatened with substantial jail time, Williams was drafted into the army in 1952, but he maintained his pacifism while serving—refusing to pick up his weapon when initially assigned to a rifle company in Fort Knox, Kentucky, and eventually being sent to the medics.[84] "The Beast-Scene" recalls Williams's anti-war stance and suggests that the preceding poems be read in a similar light, as a peaceful protest against moralism and its various hypocrisies, including war and violence.

Did Olson miss these political undertones, the evident parodying of himself and projective verse, and the satirizing of his own heteronormative bigotry, when he gave the work his ostensible stamp of approval? It's possible. Perhaps Olson was too smart to be fooled in this way, although his tremendous ego, or addictions, could've prevented him from noticing certain implications. Could he have been perfectly aware of the extent of Williams's hijinks, and in turn played a counter-prank in the form of an introduction, that would have a role in preventing the book's publication? This adds an intriguing layer to the book's mystique, but it seems too calculated; on the other hand, it certainly wasn't beyond Olson's skills as a rival. Was he in on the joke and being a good sport? While the answers don't appear in the archives, I'm more inclined to believe the latter. While Olson may have treated Williams poorly at times, they were friends, and Williams was valuable to Olson, particularly as a publisher. Not only was Williams the first to take a risk on *The Maximus Poems*, but he was also publishing others affiliated with Olson's circle throughout the 1950s. As Williams tells Dana, "Olson had aspirations of me coming in and having the Jargon Society of *my* thing, and then becoming publisher to the college and printing a program of books he was interested in, i.e., *his* list."[85] While this appears to be a compromise, it could have been an attempt to gain more control over Williams and get him to move on from Jargon, a name that Olson didn't exactly care for.[86] Williams accepted the role as Black Mountain's publisher, but the college closed shortly thereafter. It's unlikely that Williams would've been able to maintain both operations, given the combination of Olson's expectations and Williams's sensitivity to Jargon's sustainability (i.e., threatening to end Jargon pretty much from its inception). Had Olson been left to look over Williams's shoulder, a project that he would've undoubtedly tried to axe is the subject of the next chapter, Merle Hoyleman's *Letters to Christopher*, a book that was never published by Jargon for very different reasons.

Whether "Jammin' the Greek Scene" was shelved due to a lack of finances, disinterest, a reluctance to publish "obscene" material, or all the above, it represents a turning point where Williams was coming into his own as a writer and publisher. It's also one of the strangest peripheral records of Black Mountain College's demise, as a literary representation of the iconic teacher and student bickering, simultaneously praising and slighting each other. The break with Olson didn't happen overnight. Although their relationship was complicated from the beginning, the 1962 publication of *Untitled Epic Poem on the History of Industrialization* (Jargon 44) by one of Olson's great antagonists, Buckminster Fuller, may have been a parting shot.[87] But "Jammin'" was already full of patricidal imagery, as in "The Case of the Castrated Space Cadet," where Williams assumes the role of Cronos, "grabs Dad by the nuts, / and cuts him"; in "Always the Death Less Mu-Sick," where his Olsonian "Orpheus / floats out to sea, he / bleed indefinitely";[88] and in "Stag or Drag (Come as you are," where he even references a murderer's message left at the crime scene, "Stop Me Before I Kill More"—Williams appears to have been more than ready to overtake daddy Olson. He notes that "Olson and I hardly met the last ten years of his life," which Williams regretted.[89] But the split was necessary not only for Williams's development as an artist and publisher but also for his mental health, and that of others; occasionally he'd "take people to his family's summer home in nearby Highlands to protect them from, or nurse them through, a crack up."[90] Perhaps, then, "Jammin'" was written out of necessity, which shines peculiar light on the language in Olson's introduction. Maybe Williams wasn't shy about publishing "obscene" content, but reluctant to share, however masked, the details of the strained relationship with his mentor.

Poems from "Jammin' the Greek Scene"
(in order of appearance in the proof):

"Paen to Black Mountain"
"Catullus: Carmen XVI"
"The Case of the Castrated Space Cadet" *

"Always the Death Less Mu-Sick" *
"The Curse"
[untitled limerick]
"The Priapupation of Queen Pasiphaë" *
"Idyll" *
"Grecque Musique D'Ameublement (Bar-Fixtures Dept."
"Stag or Drag (Come as you are" *
"The Jam of Sage Euhemerus"
"The Honey Lamb" *
"Love O Death O Careless Love"
"Hearts of Stone" *
"The Switch Blade (Or, John's other wife" *
"Ovid, Meet a Metamorphodite"
"That Old Original Phrygian Ball-Buster" *
"The Beast-Scene"
"Are you there? (A Placement Test"
"The Cold-Hearted Copulatrix"
"And so to Avalon (Fable Pasodoble Fable Pasodoble, with Moral"

* Appears in *An Ear in Bartram's Tree*

CHAPTER TWO

Letters to Christopher (Jargon 47)

While Jonathan Williams sometimes provides clues to why certain books such as "Jammin' the Greek Scene" were never released, in other cases he's more cryptic. The following blurb for Merle Hoyleman's magnum opus *Letters to Christopher* appears in *Uncle Gus Flaubert Rates the Jargon Society in One Hundred Laconic Présalé Sage Sentences*: "James Laughlin[1] and Jonathan Williams being among the few who grieved when the orphic ashes of Merle the Pearl floated down the Monongahela River headed for Outer Cosmic Infinity,[2] publication of this legendary arcanum remains unfixed."[3] Williams provides no hints as to why it remains "unfixed," yet it's a good word to keep in mind while exploring *Letters to Christopher*—a spiritual autobiography composed of over 200 "letters"—that is, concise, and often confessional, prose poems directed to the elusive Christopher. Because *Letters* is a mythological account of the poet's life, a reading of it benefits from some background details related to Hoyleman's extraordinarily difficult circumstances; therefore, this chapter presents a rare portrait of her and an overview of her writing, which sheds light on why Williams was never able to issue this singular work.

Letters to Christopher was technically published—a fact which, given the scope of this work, requires some elaboration. In 1970, Hoyleman printed it in a very limited edition of twenty-five copies for distribution by James Lowell's Asphodel Book Shop in Cleveland. The scarcity of this version aside, *Letters* remains a missing book, as Hoyleman never considered the self-published edition official, and of course, the Jargon edition is technically still waiting in the wings. Williams received and accepted the manuscript in the autumn of 1960, only to let it linger in Jargon's scheduling thenceforth.[4] What's curious about his implicit optimism (i.e., that he ostensibly planned to publish it for nearly fifty years) is that any real hope of releasing the book was essentially quashed in 1969 when Hoyleman refused to sign the contract that Williams sent her, even though it had been drafted in accordance with her wishes. That said, Williams's patience left Jargon as the only press in line to publish the completed manuscript after Hoyleman's death in 1984.[5]

Complicating the possibility for the posthumous publication of *Letters* is that Hoyleman has no open estate. She was very isolated during the last few years of her life, having cut off contact with everyone except for her social worker, Helen Bonn. Consequently, her personal possessions were nearly destroyed, including her massive collection of personal manuscripts, correspondence, and notes related to her many research projects—on teaching, local folklore, and Black history, for example—"scattered about an inch thick" across her apartment.[6] In a letter dated July 21, 1984, Williams expresses interest in stepping in: "I am trying to reach [Robert J.] Bertholf[7] and have him put in a bid for the papers, in storage—no heirs and no instructions, of course. Probably can be had for free. Either Buffalo or Yale would make sense, in terms of JARGON SOCIETY and New Directions."[8] There isn't any documentation to suggest how serious Williams was about placing the papers, but he was ultimately unsuccessful. Fortunately, they were rescued by two of Hoyleman's loyal associates, Ken Chute and Mike Vargo.[9] Along with Bonn, they cleaned out Hoyleman's apartment, which as Vargo notes "was a dodgy endeavor for . . . the phenomenal extent of cockroach activity. . . . And the legal questions of who had the right to do what with which of Merle's belongings."[10] Chute and Vargo paid for and managed the safekeeping of the papers at A-1 Self-Storage in North Oakland, Pittsburgh, for over thirty years.[11] In addition, Chute cleaned and organized the collection and conducted his own research, from which much of the following biographical information is taken.

Hoyleman was born on January 18, 1905, in Arkansas City, Kansas.[12] Her family settled in Ponca City, Oklahoma, where she spent most of her youth; however, they moved often, primarily with the intention of improving Hoyleman's physical health, with which she struggled her entire life. Although it isn't clear when she started writing, she composed poems and short stories in her adolescence and went on to study English-language writing at Northwestern State Teachers College and Central State Teachers College, both in Oklahoma. In her late twenties, she relocated to Pittsburgh, the city she would adopt as her home, to stay with her younger brother Wayne and receive medical care. It was during this period that she fell in with a group of artists, which included the writer Gladys Schmitt and the visual artist Esther Phillips. The latter became one of Hoyleman's closest friends, and even after Phillips left Pittsburgh at the end of 1936, she remained a crucial presence in Hoyleman's life, as explored in Lisa A. Miles's *This Fantastic Struggle: The Life and Art of Esther Phillips*. Phillips and Hoyleman lived minimal, bohemian lifestyles, wholly dedicated to their art regardless of the cost, which included nearly constant unemployment, severe poverty, hunger, and estrangement from family.[13] For a time, the two found much-needed support in each other and within their circle.

While Hoyleman may have discovered a community of artists and friends on arrival in Pittsburgh, the move also commenced a lifelong battle with her brother Wayne, and what she would later refer to as "systematic destructionist's attacks" on her.[14] Initially, the attacks began with Wayne halting financial support for her studies at the University of Oklahoma, which she attended on and off from 1931 to 1934 without taking a degree.[15] But the acts against Hoyleman grew more serious and, according to her, turned into attempts on her life. Possibly the most severe attack took place in the winter of 1951. Hoyleman was very ill from what was likely a reaction to various medications, including doses of radioactive isotope, which she'd been prescribed as experimental treatment for thyroid cancer.[16] Her older brother Rhese, who was still residing in Oklahoma, had been alerted to Hoyleman's serious health issues and came to Pittsburgh. When he showed up at Hoyleman's apartment, he found that his sister not only didn't recognize him but also demanded that he find an attorney who could prove his identity. Rhese ended up taking her to Shadyside Hospital, where, after a brief stay, she was declared insane. She was then transferred to a psychiatric hospital, Mayview State, and subjected to electric shock therapy and inhumane conditions that she documents in her writings and correspondence. In a detailed letter dated July 17, 1951, to the poet and literary critic George Marion O'Donnell—a frequent correspondent and a major proponent of her work—Hoyleman describes the situation in depth, as well as the conditions of the hospital, which she summed up thus: "I have never read a description of hell in any literature that equals this place; there is no record of such in the Bible. The stench of human bodies rotting with TB, cancer, epilepsy, venereal, kidney, asthma, nervous disorders, etc. is without parallel. Life and death are one."[17]

Like many other women at the time, Hoyleman was the victim of a notoriously subpar and sexist mental healthcare system. Miles elaborates on this point in *This Fantastic Struggle*, particularly in the context of Esther Phillips's institutionalization at Harlem Valley Hospital from 1942 to 1949. Although Phillips's experience wasn't as awful as Hoyleman's, Miles contends that the maltreatment of supposedly "insane" women at the hands of an ostensibly "sane" patriarchy wasn't only socially acceptable but also essentially a pastime. Hoyleman was unnecessarily—and probably illegally—committed, misdiagnosed, and subjected to abuse at Mayview State.[18] Even more disturbing is that Mayview State rescinded their claim that Hoyleman was insane and sent papers for her release that were left unanswered; as a result, Hoyleman had to endure another three months in the hospital.[19]

This abandonment is an important event for Hoyleman's practice. Rachel Blau DuPlessis's observation has particular relevance concerning Hoyleman's poetry: "For the woman writer, the family is the muse. If it turns nasty, and it can, it is the combined hydra-head of a monster/herself. For she need not have come to terms with the many heads inside her. . . . They will teem inside her; team up inside her."[20] Hoyleman's reference to the injustices suffered at the hands of her brother Wayne as "systematic destructionist's attacks" relays an additional component of what she considered to be a nearly fatal neglect; she found the disregard for her life to be calculated, and this developed into an extreme distrust of people.

Hoyleman suffered from mounting paranoia and a "nervous condition," which she believed was exacerbated by the electric shock therapy she had undergone.[21] She was convinced that "secret agents followed around the leading artists" and was herself "on alert for possible agents."[22] In a letter to O'Donnell dated April 15, 1953, Hoyleman details her perseverance in the wake of the "conspiracy against [her]": "I am too revolutionary to please an enemy. I cannot have a telephone & no one visits me unless they have known me five to ten yrs. I am forced to live in almost total reclusion. I am addressed on the streets of [Pittsburgh] in foreign languages & my photograph is snapped in public places, car drivers try to knock me down on main thoroughfares, my conversations are listened to in public telephone booths, men try to pick me up. . . . I give everybody a run for his money. I am large, fast moving & undaunted."[23] Of course, Hoyleman's suspicions weren't baseless, as various government agencies (e.g., the FBI) were actively keeping tabs on artists (including those from her circle) due to suspected affiliations with Marxist and communist organizations. Hoyleman was known as a resolute individual who wasn't just always on the defensive but could also handle herself. Miles relates her "shrewd discourse" via an anecdote told in Hoyleman's words: "Planned to go to town early and sit in Wm. Penn Lobby. I enjoy surveying the crowd there—such a 'hodge-podge' of humanity. Last time I was there some old buck wanted to take me to dinner. I gave him a run for his money too. (He didn't anticipate it either.) I dressed him down. He frankly admitted he couldn't stand me for daily diet—but I HAD A MIND AND KNEW HOW TO USE IT."[24]

Hoyleman sincerely believed that she was being stalked by her enemies, whom she referred to as "the Scum," and whom Chute stresses "would be impossible to over-rate" as a presence in her life: "The Scum traces back to Merle's work on the legends of the steelworkers and her understanding of steel.[25] The Scum . . . might form in the process of steel making, maybe on the top of the liquid metal. She viewed the Scum as the people, among others, who put her in Mayview in 1951."[26] Chute describes the Scum as not having "a mystic element," but rather being representative of Hoyleman's intense suspiciousness of people, which increased with age: "In later years she became more and more distrustful and chased away friends, Meals on Wheels, visiting nurse[s], the person who delivered groceries."[27] Nevertheless, there's speculation that the Scum went beyond unwitting suitors, malicious siblings, and government agents, and that Hoyleman was guided by and collaborating with paranormal entities, which Williams apparently witnessed while visiting Hoyleman in 1961.[28]

That Hoyleman was being harassed by apparitions seems to be corroborated in Megan Shay's article "Passion for Paint: The Life of Esther Phillips," which includes an anecdote told by Henry Bursztynowicz, a professor at Carnegie Tech (now Carnegie Mellon University): "[Bursztynowicz] recalls Hoyleman describing to him how 'they' would get on a bus, sit next to her, and goad her into confrontation. 'She would say, "I know who you are and what you want and you won't get away with it!" Then, with a certain amount of disgust and satisfaction, she would announce that "they" inevitably got off at the next stop.'"[29] Given that there was little information available on Hoyleman until fairly recently, secondhand accounts of her interactions with the Scum have a tremendous (if not terrifying) impact on how one might engage with her poetry. However, Hoyleman's close friends Chute and Vargo (the latter of whom was one of the few people she trusted even after ostracizing nearly everyone else in her life) never heard her refer to the Scum in this way. Hoyleman writes in detail about her life in her journals, outlines, and correspondence—much of which is accessible at the University of Pittsburgh—and while she frequently (perhaps even obsessively) refers to the Scum, she doesn't mention that it includes a phantasmic element, let alone that she was working with spirits. She was an incredibly proud person, and the suggestion that her writings were the result of a collaboration, uncanny or otherwise, would likely have offended her. Of course, Hoyleman was haunted by things of which one can only speculate, and it's not the goal of this chapter to demystify certain readings of Hoyleman's poems. In any case, it's important to note that Chute and Vargo contend that to believe that she received her poems via the Scum is to "fundamentally misunderstand Merle's poetry and Merle."[30]

Regardless of what Williams witnessed at Hoyleman's apartment in the early '60s, the two were friends, and they remained so despite the difficulties of their arrangement. They maintained a rich correspondence, and Williams

Williams's portraits of Merle Hoyleman, taken during his visit to the poet in 1961. These were snapped in front of the bowling alley across the street from Hoyleman's apartment in Pittsburgh. Courtesy of Archives and Special Collections, University of Pittsburgh Library System.

even cites the importance of their letters when shopping the Jargon papers to the Duke University archives in the 1970s: "Should the Duke University Press—or anyone else—be interested, entire books of correspondence might be constructed from the holdings by . . . Merle Hoyleman (posthumous fame if I ever publish *Letters to Christopher*)."[31] Hoyleman refers to Williams lovingly as her "favorite scoundrel,"[32] and he includes her among his treasured "mavericks,"[33] a term that the art historian Charlotte Streifer Rubinstein defines as a "deeply rebellious personality who created [her] own forms from [her] personal visions," and perhaps a designation that Hoyleman may have been comfortable with.[34] As Williams shifted away from publishing writers affiliated with Charles Olson's circle and Black Mountain College, he concentrated Jargon's efforts on "mavericks and eccentrics"— including Mina Loy, Alfred Starr Hamilton, Guy Davenport, Ralph Eugene Meatyard, and, of course, Hoyleman. Williams related to these writers and pushed Jargon toward preservation of those he saw outcasted by society, "to protect the Margins, because that's where I live."[35] But Williams had visited Hoyleman at her home in 1961 on account of the challenges she presented with respect to the release of *Letters*. Her suspicions extended to pretty much everyone she came across, and Williams was no exception. For example, Williams's first public reference to Hoyleman appears in a circular dedicated to raising money for the publication of Bob Brown's *1450–1950* (Jargon 29): "I, for one, want to help preserve the work of [Bob Brown] because I believe he was one of the life-lines of the American avant-garde—a man of incredible good humor and very considerable accomplishment. I can get very gloomy and say with Kenneth Rexroth: whatever happened to R.E.F. Larsson, or Wallace Gould, or Merle Hoyleman—or Bob Brown?"[36] Innocuous and certainly complimentary, this quote nevertheless caused a bit of a stir. In a letter to O'Donnell from April 26, 1960, Hoyleman expresses that she doesn't like Williams talking about her without her permission.

Williams was walking on eggshells around Hoyleman, but he was determined to publish *Letters* despite desperate straits. That said, the feeling of "difficulty" appears to have been mutual. In a letter to O'Donnell dated September 18, 1960, Hoyleman writes, "I have been in too many 'pickles & stews' to jump into anything. I am tired. Maybe you can handle Williams. It's evident I can't. He kept publishing others' works, & certainly good but not excitingly new."[37] On October 6, O'Donnell replies, "I think [Jargon] is the best possibility of publication that *Letters* has had in a long time. . . . As for your proposal that I should 'deal with' Jonathan Williams, I couldn't possibly do that. . . . I don't see that it is necessary for *anyone* to 'deal with'

J. W. He is in the publishing business only to see printed what he *can* see printed of the literature he likes. Far from making profit, he operates at a constant loss of his own money. . . . If he does the book, he'll give it as good a format as possible."[38]

Correspondence between Hoyleman and Williams indicates that the usual financial issues delayed publication of *Letters* in the early '60s, and that Hoyleman didn't appreciate her work being pushed aside while Williams spent money on other projects. But this shouldn't detract from Williams's efforts. He had started planning nearly as soon as he accepted the manuscript. In customary Jargon fashion, the book was to include visual work, initially "monoprint decorations" by Enid Foster, along with an introduction from O'Donnell.[39] Foster was eventually replaced by A. Doyle Moore as the book's artist, as noted in an article titled "Parson Weems & Vachel Lindsay Rent a Volkswagen and Go Looking for Lamedvovnik #37; Or, Travails in America Deserta," where Williams includes *Letters to Christopher* as one of his books slated in 1965:

> Miss Hoyleman, a remarkable writer of prose-poetry, lives in Pittsburgh, a virtual recluse and a virtual pauper. Her work was recognized for its singular radiance and wit, akin to the best of Emily Dickinson, by Lincoln Kirstein, James Laughlin, and George Marion O'Donnell back in the early 30s. She has been ignored since. I have little hope of securing the attention of many readers for her very singular work, but *Letters to Christopher* is a real achievement in its time and its place is secure. Doyle Moore, who operates the Finial Press in Urbana, Illinois, and who teaches in the University, has contributed very lovely botanical pressings to grace the text.[40]

A few years later, when Jargon was in the process of becoming a "society" and non-profit, Williams scheduled *Letters* alongside Lorine Niedecker's *Tenderness and Gristle: Collected Poems (1936-1966)* (Jargon 48) and Alfred Starr Hamilton's *Poems* (Jargon 49), to be funded via a $10,000 grant from the National Endowment for the Arts. At that point, *Letters* was held up due to Hoyleman's request for a contract. For the first eighteen years of its existence, Jargon's books were mostly based on agreements established verbally or in correspondence, making publishing contracts rare.[41] At Hoyleman's request, the contract for *Letters* was adapted from the one she had signed for her first and only officially published book, *Asp of the Age*; regardless, she refused to sign it, even with her advocates O'Donnell and his longtime partner Gordon Roysce Smith encouraging her to trust Williams and publish with Jargon.[42]

For instance, well after O'Donnell's passing in 1962, Smith writes to Hoyleman: "Mr. O'Donnell always said that the reason LETTERS had never been published was that you spent all your energies denouncing anyone who wanted to publish them as someone who was trying to do you out of something. . . . I do hope you can reconcile your doubts about Jargon. . . . But I know you won't. And LETTERS is no closer to being published today than it was forty years ago. . . . In the 25 years I've known about LETTERS . . . it has become an obsession with me to see them printed. It is ironic that their creator should be the chief obstacle in their way."[43]

Publishing full-length work was always a struggle for Hoyleman, but it wasn't always her fault. Despite Hoyleman and the efforts of her supporters—including Edward Donahoe, a fellow writer, dear friend, and probable lover from Ponca City—it took nearly three decades for *Asp of the Age* to see the light of day in 1967.[44] The finding aid to Hoyleman's papers, which is constructed largely from Ken Chute's research, notes that Donahoe "sent *Asp of the Age* to Lincoln Kirstein and *Letters to Christopher* to George Marion O'Donnell"; the former resulted in Hoyleman's first publication in the October–December 1931 issue of *Hound and Horn*, which Kirstein edited.[45] Chute includes Kirstein's acceptance note in his timeline: "Edward Donahoe sent me your poem 'Withering Fruition.'[46] I think it is really the most interesting piece of work in verse that has ever come to my hands. . . . I mean as far as intensity—graphic phrasing—a profound insight into the methods and limits of verse—why I don't think there are four other people in the country who can write as well. . . . Please send me everything you care to. . . . It's a very great pleasure to read such distinguished poetry."[47] Selections from *Asp* would appear in several journals over the years, but it also had several suitors who wanted to publish it in its entirety, principal among them Rae Beamish's Black Faun Press, an affiliate of the Decker Press. Beamish had accepted the manuscript in the winter of 1941 and planned to include among the three poems comprising *Asp* (i.e., "Asp of the Age," "Mind Province of the Tenth Month," and "A Latter Beast in the Noon") selections from *Letters to Christopher* and at least two prose pieces, "Unfinished Portrait" and "Body." At the behest of Hoyleman, Beamish asked O'Donnell to expand on his article "The Work of Merle Hoyleman," which appeared in *River: A Magazine of the Deep South* in 1937, to be used as an introduction.[48] The 1967 edition of *Asp* includes this intro, which is unchanged and therefore a bit confusing in its references to the 1941 book (which was never published) and *Letters to Christopher*, even though none of the letters appear in the 1967 version. Beamish had planned to put *Asp* into production in April 1941 but was initially held up by O'Donnell submitting his piece three months late, and then by Beamish requesting changes that O'Donnell refused to make.[49] Despite Hoyleman signing two contracts, the project folded when Beamish enlisted in the army during World War II.

Asp of the Age was eventually published in an edition of 326 copies by Ronald Caplan, printed at Wood Printing in Toronto, and distributed by James Lowell's Asphodel Book Shop in Cleveland.[50] As a physical object, it's quite striking. At 33 cm × 28 cm, it's longer and wider than a phone book, and its large cover featuring blood-orange leaf prints is offset by its green tape binding. All text on and in the book, including O'Donnell's introduction, are facsimiles of the poet's handwriting in green ink. Its unique design, coupled with content that Ruby Mars describes in her 2019 review as "a mucky documentation; a very measured trawl through a seemingly alien landscape in an attempt to experience recognition," present *Asp* as an artwork rather than a typical collection of poems.[51] Of course, the writing is equally unconventional. For the reader's pleasure, I include the entirety of "the white bull," part VI of *Asp*'s second poem, "Mind Province of the Tenth Month" as it appears in *New Directions in Prose & Poetry* (1937):[52]

> And a garment of elderberry ferment was spread
> In the running face of the white bull,
> The maddened enemy who came from the fortress of wrath
> To exchange the crystal eye of power to lip the breast of
>   cream
> From the she wolf that devoured the fire of cormorant grief
> Engendered by the leach-sucking bat
> Lest she give birth and triumph to the hood
> And lie in pregnantless beauty with the bull.
> His strength, as a leaping torch, came from the kingdom of
>   waters
> With the thickness of dark figs upon the snow sinews of his
>   throat
> And fissures of the rock dry sea closed behind him.
> But the false fig fruit when the trumpets of the vine blared,
> (And gourds, dry in perpetuation, beat and rasp the kingdom
>   of walls
> Where the auger of beauty drills like a cat through globule
>   mercury,
> Sets with body lotion sporing in the confusion of sex.

Sweet but lewd be the nets for the stranger portion of people
But none shall defend the face of habitation,
For the water of mind-birth shall dry men's souls
Into pin heads and cushion them in strange whorl.
Tell us if their worm-gossed blood is the ransom for beauty?
Dark flaws lose and fuse the image of flesh and warm hair.
Mother of compassion, plumes for still, unbroken vessels,
Who blows black the effluvium in spread of self retention
Where are the healing in tools for furrows and foam?
Bracelets are wet to the moon, and the seed of the east
Directs the batons of warm, dark wombs:
And murmur of sea-tyrant's cello bares the keeper of women
Where rumor mortars and buds upon prophetic yokes[53]
That touch and efface the fertile contagion of nothingness.
Barren intercession mongrels the white bull
In a crepitated passage over wasted bodies
To let glassened desire fall without purpose or quarrel,
And the sterilist of torches shall inform the blind of
 unfitness,
That, in the eyes of the end, a viper's egg shall break in dead
 men
Who pit the stars against a fatland, where none declare, nor
 weep, nor reprove
Now that the high coast of reason swells after the flesh's
 desert.
It is dark birth, mortared in the ill swabbed province of
 gourds.
Teach the buds of corruption to strike the scepter of
 prophecy,
To cry out, and make the age-hags rotting in the oliveyard[54]
Before the conspiracy of imagination conjures the golden
 ass' ear;
And, with bellows and brass, the rising noon fastens up the
 man-worm
That scorns the mouth of love and teeth of impotency
 wasting together;
And leanly climbs into the sky the strength of word
As daughters of the bat return to shameless men
Marking the garments of their scented beds.

Such is the mind province of the tenth month
Laughing away the swallowing of the ages.
And the white bull unspheres his fury into the mind's quiet,
Leaves unlettered passion steeping in the calves of women
    who wait
The period of unusual stars, the instruction of seven thrones.
What place has been raised up for the first fruit of all the
    fruit of the mind?
What controversy of dust has been made lean without blood?
Let the white bull ascend the pivotal stair of emerald
    remoteness,
And descent of body torches signal the pollution of fruitage.
The stripping of numbers from the garden fag curls as
    sulphur stench.
(O singing that is unsung in the days man forgot
Who shall destroy the roots of the dark fig tree?
What stalk has grown up beside the flesh, miscarried
    conception?
And the inhabitants of the other land shall seal the altar
With rejoicing with the milk of the white fig.)
Accumulation of the moment perishes as tall factors for
    fiends.
Excellent are the dead without slaying.
None but the white bull flogs the portion and noise of nations
And calls to the court of rocks that know the dust gavelled
    song.
Elastic dominions, burn the blood of the undisclosed earth
Where images feed like the dead upon understanding.
The soilure of the lamb blossoms where the east and west
    shackle together
And the scale-knife[55] splices the flights of time,
Smears between the teeth brew for the croak of snores,
Gloating cosmos, lean rods of the damp, and the unwound
    navel cord.
Shape consumptive puppets in error of fever's horn.
Where is the eye's kingdom with cowards braying in the
    color of insurrection?
The hot udder of contempt sponges the cockpit of forget-
    fulness,[56]

Mounts not, but maddening compulsion spouts,
And instant secretion becomes ulcered time.
Compound of monotone, discourse of oblivion directs the
    nose.
See time filches her breed and nests an unsexed egg;
O men born to rise in the birth of the tomb
Or exchange the eburnated beauty and hunger of tongue
For a moment's arrangement of matter
The velleity of the hooded bat devours the sap of the waste
In a mouthful where fat is perpetuated by a breath
Strangely sterilizing the wind. Let the northeast's tongue
Lick shiver of nails into our spines because none shall tell,
None shall bread the trust between the unbroken clods
Nor wisdom will out of civilization's belly speak of birth

In his introduction, O'Donnell discusses the mystical qualities of Hoyleman's poetry and considers both *Asp of the Age* and *Letters to Christopher* as "vision or 'wisdom' literature" with a foundation in "objective human experience." The latter is certainly less apparent in *Asp*, as evidenced by the startling juxtapositions and feverish imagery of "the white bull," which one may be tempted to read as a surrealist text. O'Donnell, however, explicitly warns against this: "Miss Hoyleman's mythology makes her seem surrealist because it ignores formal logic and scientific or naturalistic knowledge. But Miss Hoyleman simply abandons formal logic for poetic logic—the logic of the imagination—under which she organizes a vision of the world that is non-realistic (in the scientific sense) but coherent within its own terms."[57] "The white bull" demonstrates how Hoyleman refracts mythology (e.g., the Minoan myth) to render a personal reality that operates in contrast to "the more real than real world behind the real" associated with surrealism.[58] In addition, *Asp of the Age* appears to be calculated, as if aware of itself as a (possibly dangerous) spiritual doctrine, which Ruby Mars aptly points out: "The visual vocabulary of the pieces is vibrantly unrecognizable, but that doesn't mean it's unreal. There is something behind the difficulty and headiness that is very, very tangible. Sometimes it feels like the labyrinthine nature of the wordings and syntactical structures are protecting the reader from the full spiritual force of their implications."[59] That Hoyleman's "terms" may have developed as a kind of safety measure sheds ominous light on Charles Olson and Robert Creeley's axiom that "form is never more than an extension of content," and it's difficult to ignore that this has implications for the book's peculiar design.[60] That every single letter in and on the book is handwritten in green not only lends a compulsive quality to the text but also reveals how form spills over its medium. Although the book is beautiful, its size and layout make it somewhat difficult to read comfortably; as CAConrad notes, on being introduced to Hoyleman's work, "[Williams] handed me [*Asp of the Age*] with a magnifying glass."[61] If Mars's insight is extended to the object, then the book becomes a kind of meta-talisman, providing protection against itself.

Asp is dedicated to James Laughlin, who along with his mother Marjory was a financial supporter of Hoyleman for a time. Laughlin had discovered her writing by way of O'Donnell's piece in *River* ("The Work of Merle Hoyleman") and subsequently invited her to contribute to *New Directions in Prose & Poetry* (1937), where she appears alongside O'Donnell, Jean Cocteau, Lorine Niedecker, Gertrude Stein, e.e. cummings, and William Carlos Williams, among others.[62] The anthology features a selection from *Letters to Christopher* and parts IV and VI from "Mind Province of the Tenth Month."[63] This was Hoyleman's most important publication to date and it wouldn't be outdone until the publication of *Asp* thirty years later. It also fortified the reputation established by her earlier publications. For example, in a letter to Hoyleman dated January 24, 1940, Elizabeth Bishop writes, "Ever since I saw your wonderful poem, ASP OF THE AGE, in HOUND AND HORN a long time ago I have been interested in your work and so disappointed not to see more of it. . . . Then your things appear in NEW DIRECTIONS. . . . I think everyone feels that their work is going unnoticed and unloved and I wanted to tell you how you have made at least one very good admirer."[64] She wasn't the only admirer of Hoyleman's work; other fans include Caresse Crosby, Gael Turnbull, and John Gould Fletcher, who remarks of *Letters*: "Forgive me if in my exaltation, I go beyond what you wish. You have, in these letters, caught the rarest quality of all writing; something that abides when writing is finished; an overtone, an echo, to which the listening spirit can return again and again."[65]

In the late 1930s, Hoyleman seemed to have the necessary standing and literary contacts to publish whatever she wanted. It was also during this time that she was employed by the Works Progress Administration (WPA) to research and write on various subjects, including the "folklore and song" of steelworkers, and Black history in Pittsburgh from 1750 onward.[66] But her efforts to publish both *Asp* and *Letters* were for the most part unsuccessful. Many years later, she writes to Williams, "Upon the advice of an editor, fall

1959, I wrote approx. one hundred publishers. These that indicated any interest I sent the first published sequence from *Letters to Christopher*. . . . Thus far only two publishers asked to see large ms. I investigated both & learned that neither are reliable."[67] By the 1950s, decades of rejections and frustrating dealings with publishers led her to explore other possibilities for her poems, especially *Letters*, which she was very interested in turning into "a musical, a play, or motion picture scenario."[68] She searched for someone to transpose the manuscript and was actively networking with contacts in New York City and Los Angeles, including Oscar Hammerstein III, Margaret Webster, and staff at Disney. She was apparently even offered "a writing job in Hollywood" in 1955, which she declined, telling O'Donnell that she was "not strong enough to go."[69]

That said, Hoyleman did have a bit of luck in the medium of television in 1972, when Mike Vargo produced a segment on her for a "local general-interest show" called *Lifestyle* which aired on WQED-TV. Vargo elaborates on how it came about:

> One segment, in the latter part of '71 I believe, was about an outsider artist & jazz musician named Chuck Barr. Soon after it aired I got a phone call at home. Shrill, raspy, old-lady voice on the other end. She knew Chuck Barr, from when he had lived in her neighborhood. She said that her art was equally if not more deserving of attention. Merle rattled off credentials and names: literary magazines in which she had been published, a grant she once received, friends like Caresse Crosby, Lincoln Kirstein, Jonathan Williams. . . . So I set out to make what film-school instructors call a "neat old fart" film: a short about an old person who, unknown to most of the world, had lived a fascinating life and did amazing stuff.[70]

The segment, now lost, provided an overview of Hoyleman's life and writing and featured a local actress reading portions from Hoyleman's work, apparently despite Hoyleman's wishes, as she explains in a letter to Williams: "They wanted the young girl to read the first section of *Asp of the Age* (her voice too frail). . . . I said 'no' to their request. I told WQED-TV to ask for Richard Burton. . . . I still believe Richard Burton would read *Asp of the Age* for the children of America."[71] Nevertheless, she was ultimately proud of Vargo's profile, also telling Williams: "They continue to show the *Letters to Christopher* feature at WQED-TV. From Jan 10, 1972 to Oct 1972 it was on seven times. This, I know because different friends told me about seeing it.

52 CHAPTER TWO

May have been shown more times as the producer hasn't kept track of it. . . . It means more than a million persons now have heard the title of *Letters to Christopher*. It all seems quite pointless after forty years with this revolutionary ms pending!"[72] That she wrote this two years after the self-publication of *Letters* indicates that she still thought of the Jargon edition as forthcoming.

Hoyleman started writing *Letters to Christopher* in Pittsburgh during the spring of 1933, and she began shopping its poems soon thereafter.[73] A selection first appeared in 1934 in the literary journal *Space*. The title was adopted from this sequence, as the editor B. A. Botkin used "Letters to Christopher" in lieu of Hoyleman's original title *Phoebe-Christopher Letters*, named after Hoyleman's maternal great-great-grandparents Christopher Columbus Williams and Phoebe Pollard, which she chose because they were "the loveliest . . . in the family lineage."[74] O'Donnell observes of *Letters* that Phoebe is cast "as protagonist and the perceptible world as antagonist" in a "loose novel of character": "To portray Phoebe's maturing experience of the world, her conflicts with it, the moments of her spiritual defeats and victories, Miss Hoyleman writes for her . . . a series of letters to her beloved, Christopher. Each letter is a kind of impressionist interior-monologue in disguise."[75] O'Donnell's reading of *Letters* as a novel is intriguing, but the notion that Hoyleman is writing for Phoebe is a bit misleading. Hoyleman clearly *is* Phoebe, apparently in the throes of a spiritual autobiography, and any affiliation with Christopher Columbus Williams and Phoebe Pollard seems to end with their names.[76] Chute speculates that Christopher is based on Edward Donahoe, whom Hoyleman was very close to, and most likely romantically involved with.[77] But Hoyleman identifies Christopher only, rather cryptically, as "an ideal,"[78] which recalls Helen Vendler's concept of "invisible listeners": "The odd practice by which certain poets address their poems . . . to someone they . . . cannot set eyes on. . . . George Herbert speaks to God; Walt Whitman to the reader in futurity; John Ashbery to a painter of the past."[79] Throughout the text, there's "a single voice, alone, recording and analyzing and formulating and changing its mind," which occurs through the manifestation of the ideal as a silent, concealed correspondent.[80] Consequently, the letters addressed to Christopher surface as a nonce poetic form.

The "letters" that comprise *Letters to Christopher* are concise prose poems in first-person perspective. Their stanzas, if they can be called that, appear as small paragraphs—first line always indented—consisting of one to eight well-punctuated sentences, and sporadically interjected with other minimal poetic structures. For example:

> Tonight I am very tired. When I work too hard I ache and feel mean.
> A dirty house detracts from my peace—yet I cannot determine which is the mc uncomfortable.
>
> These brief lines are formless but you will, I hope, engage in the mood.
>
> | | |
> |---|---|
> | To touch, to kiss | To warm breath |
> | thy light, O spring | Upon thy whiteness, |
> | And turn thy pink | Leans no one blade |
> | Against the blue | To out-mimic |
> | Upholding a pageant | Thy fragrant miracle. |
> | Above winter's hood. | O spring, too much is mine. |
>
> Have you, did you mind the long darkness before?[81]

Perhaps the most defining trait of each poem, at least in terms of overall structure, is that it takes the date of its writing—typically arranged as month, day, year—as its title, which sets up the book to be read as a journal or memoir, especially when coupled with its autobiographical content. In the late '40s, Hoyleman wrote O'Donnell informing him that she wanted to "revise the Christopher MS by removing dates and making it into a running form";[82] had she done this, *Letters to Christopher* would be a very different text. Despite not making the change, Hoyleman still plays with the "running form" in certain parts, as can be gleaned from the following sequence:

> June, 1934
> Let Ponca burn!
>
> June, 1934
> All day there were impressions for his crown.
>
> June, 1934
> Our wilderness, no one has come to. The way is without bramble or tangle.
>
> June, 1934
> The water of patience has been drunk.
>
> June, 1934
> Courage has purpose like stone.

June, 1934
Flame is never lost to heaven or sky.

June, 1934
For a brief space you were real. Now, what shall I declare in the place of blood?

June, 1934
Carry festoons, broken by holly.

June, 1934
Spiral after spiral I shall wear these days, for you. Where is the home for preciousness?

June, 1934
Let us put our back to the sun and see whose voice first cries "Enough."

June, 1934
Fog, like hope, belittles the visage.

June, 1934
Report, as a whole, is thin.

June, 1934
Gleams of fleeing foam—lips do outmourn the stars.

June, 1934
Violets are here, and that should bring you.

June, 1934
Courage is a song unlost upon our lips. Now, I bow my head by every child of God.

June, 1934
Gold and dark escort the leopard home.

June, 1934
Business is quick and certain.

June, 1934
Immortal hope is fleeced by the tide.

June, 1934
I have come from the other side of creation.

June, 1934
Question is ribbon.

June, 1934
If you know how alone and dismal my day is, you would not ask for scr

June, 1934
Pretty head, what curls tumble your head?

June, 1934
Days that go, never return.

June, 1934
The sun shall conclude her heat–the wing the solitude of flight.[83]

While the decision to splice these lines with titles projects them as autonomous minimal poems, the use of the same month and year over and over has an eerily mimetic effect, highlighting the inherent fragmentation of the memoir via the obscurity of dates, speaking to what Mei-mei Berssenbrugge refers to as poetically "naturalistic": "If we sit here . . . and people walk by talking, and you record what we say and they say in patches, that's actually more representational than a single narrative line."[84] The disjunctive lines joined together by a duplicated—almost anonymous—time stamp exposes the problem of reading *Letters to Christopher* as a historical narrative. In lieu of a chronology, the "June, 1934" sequence presents something more organic to the writing process, allowing for the possibility of found or overheard snippets of language, erasures, palimpsests, or dates which may or may not be fixed.

That said, many of Phoebe's letters follow a traditional journal format, recording routine experiences and observations in straightforward prose. For instance, the first letter, "May 9, 1933," reflects on domestic life at the home she occupied with her brother Wayne during the winter of 1932–33, 7955 Susquehanna Street in Pittsburgh, on the cusp of her move to the Forbes Cottages, where *Letters to Christopher* started:

The great tree, east of the dining room is especially gay in its buffoonery. The leaves are humped like umbrellas. Rain is descending in very straight lines to the pavement. The Tall roofs are glossy black, and the sidewalks are a delicate gray. There are sputters in a shallow hole in front of the brick building across the street.

> Earlier in the morning I built a fire in the furnace by stuffing sheaves of last November's papers in its mouth.
> I thought I would write but have added but a couple of lines to my prose manuscript. My gratitude is unbecoming when I have no mood for writing.
> . . . .
> There are paper boxes by the tea table. Brother brought them for packing books and funny papers scattered about. I should be at work instead of adding nonsense.
> Shall I tell you I am baking crumbless muffins?—but I forget you have no particular taste for cornmeal.[85]

From the beginning, Phoebe trivializes her routine as "nonsense," even though she documents it and includes it in her "prose manuscript." That her letters often contain ostensibly banal activity is a clear departure from the gnarled language and fantastical imagery of her early work, such as "the white bull," but Hoyleman still describes *Letters* as a "mythology" and "legend."[86] What may be construed as chimerical or uncanny is, for the most part, only hinted at via the manifestation of certain observations. For example, Phoebe concludes the first letter with the following:

> Twin notes that terrify me:
> No one knows the names of trees unless they have gaudy blossoms or loud perfumes.
> Darker translation and morbid witches weave in the street—I refer to the traffic upon the globe of an interpreter.[87]

Although the concluding sentence may imply contexts of vision literature or channeling, one may still deduce an everyday image and encounter as their inspiration. Thus, *Letters to Christopher* is more subtle in its use of fantasy than *Asp of the Age*. As Ruby Mars observes of the latter, "[Hoyleman] is offering us, through the eyes of her personally developed mythological world, a filtered vision of the events of an intersecting plane."[88] In this case, Christopher enters Hoyleman's contemporary experience by way of physical and mental concordances marked by letter and dream, respectively.

That the ideal may be using Phoebe as a vector (i.e., by existing in Phoebe's dream-space and perhaps nowhere else) is indicated throughout *Letters* by Christopher's silence. Christopher does write back to Phoebe—albeit rarely—as she indicates in occasional entries, the first of which opens letter "July 15, 1933":

> Your message meant more to me than the face of a pansy. (I looked in the mirror for the image of its jewel but there was no reflection. The silver on the back had been dissolved by a sun.)
>
> . . .
>
> Each day I shall be searching for the pattern of your handwriting.[89]

Christopher's replies aren't accessible. Nor does Phoebe speak for Christopher; to the reader, the exchange is one-sided, and one can only know Christopher as an invisible listener, a constituent of Phoebe's creative fantasy. On the other hand, Christopher's letters inflate Phoebe's being, perhaps even craft it, as she is reliant on them for a kind of emotional and metaphysical sustenance ("Your beautiful message is still food").[90] She is tortured in their absence, telling Christopher that "Death would be superior to no communication."[91] Yet, Phoebe's fantasy space is constructed via correspondence, whether with an imaginary being who can't answer, or otherwise. One finds that Phoebe doesn't compose daily, which allows one to feel the slowness of the process, the time and labor it takes to write, send, and wait, all with no guarantee of reply. Of course, Christopher's silence between poems, and the gaps between dates—often for long periods of time—may imply possible return letters that Phoebe doesn't reveal to the reader, for whatever reason.

More important than Christopher's response is the world generated by Phoebe's correspondence and documentation of her life as more than everyday experience, which, again, she introduces as "nonsense" at the beginning of the text. *Letters* could easily be read as the (one-sided) exchange of lovers (e.g., "Beyond tomorrow shall we grow studious in keeping the tryst?") and possibly an extramarital affair (e.g., "How I love thee when the sun is least. . . . I would serve animal crackers to thy children") that by the end of the book is presented as unrequited love:[92]

> His heart I have never seen.
> It came and went away one day; and in its place a raindrop pursed my lips, and forever in my breast caused me to accept.
>
> . . .
>
> I kissed all that I had dreamed; and putting away him, I said I am acquainted with the cruelty he flaunts in my open face.
> I only know thou has pained me.[93]

However, it would be a mistake to view Christopher as a mere love interest. There are multiple Christophers that evolve and change throughout the text, encompassing various people, events, relationships, and romantic liaisons, all of which are projected by Phoebe onto her ideal.[94] Christopher becomes whatever Phoebe needs Christopher to be on any given day: a friend, a lover, a therapist, or perhaps most importantly, a vehicle for elevating everyday experience into myth. Letters that record ostensibly mundane activities—a trip to the library, the weather, something Phoebe overheard a classmate say—appear alongside letters passionately adulating Christopher: "Fair graciousness, you astound me with a knowledge of no import to the / universe. Time and space are without birth—and you earn the right to ascend and / reascend into the kingdom of the infinite."[95] Christopher is even rendered as a redeeming Christ-figure or personal deity: "Heal me now, O Christopher, by growth, by arcing white leopard's / fierce strategy—leaping velvet paws to eradicate the vision of swiftness / through the rainbow flowers of my dream."[96] One may consider the epistolary act a ritualistic communion, which allows Phoebe to touch an "intersecting plane"[97] or unknown territory, likewise constructing Phoebe and Christopher's symbiotic legend. Of course, one needs to be careful here, per O'Donnell: "Being private, the mythology cannot have the immediate, though complex, communicativeness that one finds, say, in Dante. And this defect is not one that glossing can remedy; for to offer an exposition of a private mythology is actually to do violence to it without really explaining it at all."[98]

Further complicating interpretations of Hoyleman's mythology is that she provided some (perhaps problematic) explanations later in life. In 1958, Hoyleman started writing a "Factual Outline" to *Letters*, and there are several slightly different versions of it in the archives. When read as a companion piece, it reveals that *Letters* is composed in sections governed by events taking place almost exclusively in Pittsburgh and Oklahoma. While this point could be gleaned from a close reading of the poems, Hoyleman gives us specifics that only she would know, like the dates of her attendance at the University of Oklahoma, and of her stays at various locations in Pittsburgh, chief among them "199 South Dithridge House," which appears on the cover of the self-published version of *Letters*, and where Hoyleman lived for much of 1938. Evidently, the "abode near one hundred years old" was in terrible shape and rat-infested, which sheds light on letters such as "May 19, 1938":[99]

> In the house Jack built, chimneys two strike moving to Mellon Institute, and wasp-spindles dazzle quaint last age.

> Be my Pied Piper? The rats are golden brown, their symphony is held by Pussy Bright.
>
> And while starlings lately barred from garden—robins, sir, bear permit to nip lettuce.
>
> Yet morning glory blue is for compositions lost to Bellefield, and declared our own on farthest Dithridge.
>
> The carrots are too busy growing to notice sister Iris or annual Rose about the fence.
>
> In the house Jack built, shake the floor from story two![100]

For certain explanations of the text the outline is invaluable, but it needs to be approached carefully. Hoyleman began writing it nearly a decade after the final letter, dated as "July 7 to October 7, 1949," and she had been through hell in the interim. Clearly, she was thinking differently about *Letters* later in life than she was when she was writing it in the '30s and '40s, as the outline quickly becomes a rather nightmarish autobiographical document, with the most detailed portions focused on her health (e.g., revealing the belief that her illnesses were caused by "biological warfare . . . to put [my] revolutionary mind out of complete & final order") and "systematic destructionist's attacks" from her brother Wayne and his partner. While it can be helpful, the outline is also a very sad addition to the project.

If read without its backstory, *Letters to Christopher* may cause a bit of confusion; the writing is simply too good to be so neglected. It truly is a "very singular work" in twentieth-century American literature, and certainly warrants more attention.[101] Of course, getting Hoyleman's poems in front of more readers is more difficult than it sounds. While *Asp of the Age* is somewhat accessible, available at twenty-eight libraries in the United States according to WorldCat, getting a look at the self-published version of *Letters* requires an appointment at the Poetry Collection at SUNY Buffalo or the archives at Pitt. The latter also contains a copy of the manuscript with Williams's (very minor) edits, and this is the closest one gets to what would've been the Jargon edition.

Despite the accolades Hoyleman received, especially early on in her writing career, *Letters to Christopher* remains "unfixed." This is mostly due to certain choices she made at the behest of her extreme wariness of publishers, which unfortunately included Williams. While they both expected the publication of *Letters* to garner the recognition that Hoyleman's writing deserved, at the end of the day she was more concerned with an unknown level of compensation that was apparently too difficult to match, especially for a small operation like Jargon. As O'Donnell writes to her in 1960, "Surely we both understand that a work like *Letters to Christopher* isn't going to make anyone a great deal of money. To think otherwise would be to live with a delusion. The job is to see it printed and appreciated by those who will appreciate it. . . . To see the whole thing decently printed and bound would be, I should think, a great satisfaction."[102] Hoyleman may have agreed with her friend, but not enough to trust Williams (or anyone else) to do the job.

Even though he knew publication was improbable by 1969, Williams let *Letters* linger in Jargon's planning for forty-eight years, a testament to his love for the maverick poet and her writing. That said, Williams didn't lose sleep over Hoyleman's refusal to work with him; he was already moving on to very different projects, as articulated by Jargon's photography and art books, which started to appear in the '70s. Of course, some of those are missing as well, including Richard C.'s "Notches along the Bible Belt," as discussed in chapter 3.

CHAPTER THREE

Notches along the Bible Belt (Jargon 98)

"You must be joking." That was the first thing Richard Craven (a.k.a. Richard C., a.k.a. Richard Canard) said when I cold called him to say I was an admirer of his work. Wanting to speak to the legendary correspondence artist about his unfinished book "Notches along the Bible Belt"—a curation of photos and clippings of bizarre evangelical materials, which Jonathan Williams had conceptualized in the mid-1970s and scheduled for publication with the Jargon Society—I telephoned the number of every "Richard Craven" I could find. I was fortunate to get Richard C. on the line after about a dozen tries. The connection was awful, but—generously—he offered to send me what he had related to the project. A few weeks later, I received a package of 35mm color slides along with an accordion file of ephemera; this is as close as one gets to the manuscript of "Notches along the Bible Belt," or at least what would've gone into it.

The story of "Notches," as discussed in this chapter, touches on a period when Williams was beginning to put out what he referred to as "picture books."[1] From Jargon's inception, most of its publications were composed of mélanges of text and visuals, in part due to the early influence of Kenneth Patchen and Williams's discovery of the English visionary tradition via William Blake.[2] As he tells Robert Dana in *Against the Grain*: "Blake was somebody I looked at a lot. Then I set about trying to learn how to do some of these processes like etching and engraving, which I studied with Stanley William Hayter in New York for a year. Then it seemed necessary to know even more. So then I went to Chicago to the Institute of Design and studied typography, briefly, and various kinds of graphic arts."[3] At the Institute Williams also developed an interest in photography, which led him to Black Mountain College to study with Harry Callahan and Aaron Siskind in July 1951.[4] Of course, he switched over to poetry after meeting Charles Olson, which was ultimately the spark needed to take his publishing activities to the next level. Although Jargon was born with the publication of *Garbage Litters the Iron Face of the Sun's Child* a month prior to his departure for Black Mountain, Williams tells Dana that "the reason, really, why Jargon started was to publish Olson."[5] This is an intriguing declaration, albeit a bit misleading. Williams had been talking about becoming a publisher well in advance of his time at Black Mountain, as Holly Beye documents in her memoir *120 Charles Street, The Village: Journals and Writings, 1949–1950*. One also learns from Beye (and elsewhere) that it was Patchen, not Olson, who initially inspired Williams to start publishing.[6]

While Williams's interest in the visual arts preceded his passion for poetry, it wasn't until the 1970s that he would publish proper photography and art books, commencing with *The Appalachian Photographs of Doris Ulmann* (Jargon 50). This move was anticipated by certain projects, such as Larry Eigner's *On My Eyes* (Jargon 36), which includes eight photographs by Callahan, and *Six Mid-American Chants* (Jargon 45), featuring poems by Sherwood Anderson and photos by Art Sinsabaugh.[7] But *The Appalachian Photographs of Doris Ulmann* was the first Jargon to be centered on photography, followed by Ralph Eugene Meatyard's *The Family Album of Lucybelle Crater* (Jargon 76) and Lyle Bongé's *The Sleep of Reason: Lyle Bongé's Ultimate Ash-Hauling Mardi Gras Photographs* (Jargon 77) in 1974, the same year that Williams started planning what would become "Notches along the Bible Belt." Although "Notches" was to be a very different book—consisting predominantly of newspaper and magazine articles and advertisements, alongside snapshots of whatever religious-themed toys and novelties Richard C. could get his hands on—it comes out of Williams's motivation to put visuals front and center, obviously coupled with his love for the work of Richard C.

Richard C. is perhaps best known as an early and central member of the New York Correspondence School (NYCS) and by his connection with its founder, Ray Johnson.[8] They began mailing each other in the early 1960s and continued to do so until Johnson's passing in 1995.[9] Beyond this, dates get a bit tricky, particularly as they relate to the elusive artist Richard C., the primary pseudonym that Craven used during his activity with the NYCS (and thereafter). The NYCS, as Johnson explains, was essentially a farce: "[Ed Plunkett] was the one who gave that name [i.e., New York Correspondence School] to the things I was doing, and I accepted it and adopted it since I thought that using that title would be an amusing vehicle or a joke."[10] While the NYCS essentially spoofed the mainstream art and gallery scenes of the day—with Johnson and his network doling out work for free and openly collaborating via the postal service—it ended up as an important group that figures prominently in various histories related to art movements in the mid-twentieth century, including pop art, neo-Dada, and Fluxus. That said, it's worth mentioning that Johnson took umbrage with historical chronologies. In "Should an Eyelash Last Forever: An Interview with Ray Johnson," Johnson says, "History is a very loose subject in which anybody can declare that anything happened at any time at all; and maybe that will be accurate information and maybe it won't be, and maybe that won't make any difference."[11] He's even more direct in another interview from 1968: "When I came to New York is of no interest to me because of my ideas of time and space. I think if I said 1912 or 1921 it doesn't really make any difference except for the fool who is going to start dissecting what the truth is, you know, exactly what year it was. I don't know whether you can do that."[12]

Similarly, dates and biographical snippets don't exactly serve Richard C., an artist whose work—like that of the NYCS—consciously eschews documentation, or at least insists on its transience. A reaction against establishment art collection and preservation is intrinsic to his primary medium (i.e., correspondence art), with each piece equipped with a sort of self-destruct mechanism. As the art writer and curator Huston Paschal explains in her catalog to the exhibition *A Richard C. Chrestomathy: Fine, Medium, and Coarse Art or, Decorative Doodads of Cosmic Significance*: "Loyalists hang onto the ephemeral postcard and vainly defy the artist's insouciance by matting and framing his script drawings, only to see the permanent marker fade and the poster paper yellow."[13] Deterioration, along with the limitations of space, size, and material of that which can be mailed, necessitates a sharpness in correspondence art—one's "message" must be quickly revealed before dissolving or being tossed aside (as one often does with one's mail). Richard C., among other mail artists,[14] embraces impermanence and restraint and uses it comically: "I think of myself as a visual comedian. These things are just jokes, and that's all they were intended to be."[15]

Tom Patterson refers to Richard C. as a "low-profile aesthetic prankster," which is well expressed in an anecdote he relates in his essay "A Polaroid Snapshot of the Artist as a Subversive, Populist Comedian":

> In the early '60s when Richard C. was an art student at [West Carolina University] . . . who should happen to drive into Cullowhee, North Carolina, one afternoon but Andy Warhol. The Pale One was in the midst of a cross-country automobile tour with cohorts Gerard Malanga and Wynn Chamberlain, and they were paying a visit to a friend who was on the WCU English faculty at the time. The English prof knew that Richard C. was particularly keen on Pop Art, so he invited him over for drinks and conversation with Andy and the guys. The young artist brought along one of his recent works . . . and Andy thought enough of it to ask if he could have it. But Richard wasn't willing to part with the piece, and he politely turned him down. He did,

however, present the Prince of Pop with another small work . . . signed in the distinctive manner which the young artist had already adopted (richard) . . . a single Bicycle brand playing card—(you guessed it) the joker.[16]

Richard C. has maintained a similar tongue-in-cheek aesthetic throughout his career, from his found art sculptures (e.g., "Still Life Landscape [1987 Version]," where a "sky" consisting of Sunshine Krispy saltine crackers resting on White Cloud toilet paper is raised over a panorama consisting of Mountain Dew, Bigelow Apple Orchard tea, James River chili Sauce, etc.) to his poetry (e.g., a Red Hots candy box flattened and tagged with the text "Poem by Richard C.") and his mail art (e.g., a cutout from a Stouffer's mac and cheese box: "I don't eat this stuff—but it is a 'classic' & will serve as well as most any commercial postcard").[17] While these works may be construed as anti-art or conceptual, Paschal suggests these terms be used only as a starting reference. She points to the necessity of the bricolage in his creative process—which is, to an extent, reminiscent of Williams's own found poetics—where "[Richard C.] uses the most direct means available," as reflected in his first and only book.[18]

Poems by Richard C., And/or Another Notepad for All Those Endless Lists was published by Nexus Press as an accompaniment to the exhibition *A Richard C. Chrestomathy*, which Paschal curated at the North Carolina Museum of Art (NCMA) in 1987. As she explains about the book: "Richard wrote poems on some of the pages, then left the rest blank (well, each page has the rubber-stamped heading: 'Poem by Richard C.') to be used for notes—and poems—by its purchasers."[19] This stems from a long-standing, recycling-based procedure within Richard C.'s repertoire—tagging found objects (e.g., soda cans and candy wrappers) and sayings with the phrase "Poem by Richard C." This became a sort of trademark for the artist, as Michael Crane notes, somewhat underwhelmingly, in *Correspondence Art: Source Book for the Network of International Postal Art Activity*: "[Richard C.'s] mailings, especially hand drawn postcard messages, poems, and rubber stamp *Poem by Richard C.*, are readily identifiable."[20] Richard C. explains that the motivation initially came from seeing one of e. e. cummings's self-portraits ("If cummings the poet can paint, then I can write poems"), and the book can be viewed as a culmination of this declaration.[21] In the catalog to the exhibition, Paschal summarizes the gist: "The artist as deadpan pundit converts the clichés of everyday conversation into one *Poem by Richard C.* after another. . . . Richard C. has a great ear for the standard excuses and hollow explanations in constant

"Red Hots," a poem by Richard C.

circulation, and with perfect pitch he sets these platitudes before us for our renewed attention and amusement. 'Think nothing of it.' 'Don't hold your breath.' 'Well, it's the thought that counts.' 'It's needless to say.' The stock phrase, thus isolated, jokingly encourages a literal interpretation."[22] It can be said that Richard C.'s found poems take a page from Williams's own poetics, yet differ in that they're mostly regurgitations of stale expressions, so mundane they seem to be drained of meaning, while Williams's found poems were supposed to result in "fresh lines."[23] Richard C. only reiterates what has been incessantly repeated by others; his preferred source material is the commonest of the common, overlooked due to its ubiquity.

Despite being only half-filled with clichés and random jottings, the book was printed as a spiral-bound tablet and sold as a notebook in the museum's gift shop. At first glance, its contents may draw parallels to the writings of the minimal poets of the 1960s and '70s such as Aram Saroyan and Robert Grenier, and even some of Williams's experiments from the '50s like "The

Jam of Sage Euhemerus" in "Jammin' the Greek Scene" ("Whoopee, Priape!"). But Richard C. provides another layer, in rendering minimalism to a kind of nothingness by giving up, and suggesting something more in line with the work of the NYCS, particularly its "on-sendings"—that is, delivering "a message to a party through an intermediary," typically with the expectation that the intermediary make changes/additions to the "message" before mailing it off again.[24] As Craig J. Saper explains in *Networked Art*, on-sendings were invented by Johnson in 1955 and gradually "evolved into more elaborate networks of hundreds of participants," shifting the audience away from its traditional role as passive observer toward dynamic participation, where the social trumps aesthetics.[25] Saper goes on to quote George Maciunas in relation to Fluxus, but it's no less relevant to Richard C.'s practice: "When the work has passed out of their [the producers'] possession, it is the responsibility of the new owner to restore it or possibly even to remake it. The idea of the work is part of the work here, and the idea has been transferred along with the ownership of the object that embodies it."[26] Richard C.'s use of the NCMA gift shop as an intermediary for inviting strangers to continue and potentially finish an incomplete list of sayings not only sheds light on the role that others play in his oeuvre but also relays a peculiar idea: even if one fills in the blank sections of *Poems by Richard C.*, each page is still titled "Poem by Richard C." As a proxy of its network, the artist is granted a unique spatial nature; not only can anyone write a poem, but they can write a poem by Richard C.

Richard C.'s apparent nonchalance, as glimpsed in his only published book, is complemented by a particular strain of attention. In his essay "The New York Correspondence School: Alternatives in the Making," which appeared in *Correspondence Art*, Craven quotes the art critic Barbara Rose: "The taste of the seventies is for a more personal art that is private sometimes to the point of introversion—an art that takes time to enjoy is often unpretentious and deliberately 'minor' as opposed to monumental and public. This art of the casual concentrates on the specific, literal quality of materials which often look . . . insubstantial and fragile."[27] Casual art, a designation that Richard C. apparently considers relevant to his own output, necessitates awareness and use of one's immediate surroundings: "I like to encourage people to just pay attention to what's around them. You don't have to go to museums and galleries to see art. All you have to do is look at whatever's in front of you, wherever you are."[28] Mail art is very much suited to this insight, with pretty much anything being potential fodder. Ray Johnson says of the NYCS, "It is secret, private, and without any rule."[29]

The only actual restriction is that it be transmittable via the postal service. Yet, ephemerality and prank are pervasive throughout the NYCS and Richard C.'s practice, which implies that one shouldn't be looking only for art in their immediate environment, but also for humor and perhaps even something juvenile. This isn't to denigrate the work. As Lucy Lippard reminds readers in *Pop Art*: "Far from constituting laziness on the part of the artist who chooses such new-born objects to depict . . . the present alone, takes both discipline and ingenuity."[30] Similarly, Paschal writes that "To isolate the commonplace is not easy, for the eye refuses to see it."[31] That said, Richard C. modestly offers a fundamental motivation: "I'm basically a little kid. . . . 'Gimme this. Lemme do that.' . . . I'm just doing this for fun, as a way of keeping myself entertained."[32]

The pseudonym itself, "Richard C.," is a throwback to childhood, taken from his earliest engagements with art while growing up in Thomasville, North Carolina, in the 1940s.[33] As Paschal shares: "In the early 1960s, when he was a fine arts major, he ran across a drawing he had done in elementary school . . . which he had signed 'Richard C.' and decided to use that version of his name.[34] One thing he liked about it was that he could adapt it to circumstances, for instance 'Richard Christmas.'"[35] His other pseudonym, "Richard Canard"—which he took on in correspondence with the artist John Evans—can be seen in a similar light: "Evans included ducks in his drawings and collages, and Richard began using 'Richard Canard' in his mailings to John. When Richard began doing the Faye Ache (fake Ray Johnson collages) pieces,[36] he thought 'Richard Canard' suited them. . . . He uses Canard when he thinks it appropriate to the particular work."[37] Although his pseudonyms are signed somewhat in jest, they're at least used in line with the general aesthetic of his work, particularly his correspondence art, where they seem to navigate postal anonymity and the accord of a group aesthetic.

The former evolved from a kind of necessity, as Saper points out in his essay "15 Minutes of Existence during a Pandemic: Pseudonyms in Mail-Art and Social Media": "The participants and artists-audiences know who and where the messages come from; it is only the spying eyes of the delivery person or governmental investigators or marketers who saw only the pseudonym without an identity."[38] Many correspondence artists continue to adopt aliases and, likely more relevant today, avatars that function simultaneously as a nod to like-minded confidants and as a cryptogrammatic veil. Furthermore, the New York Correspondence School—which may be considered a sort of collective pseudonym for Johnson, Richard C., and the network's postal activities over a given period[39]—is depicted with the mystique of a faceless crowd, as shown in Johnson's visuals of the network as a grid of identical cartoon bunny heads. As Thomas Albright writes in his essay "New Art School: Correspondence and Correspondence Art," "[The NYCS's] membership is a curious motley of individuals and largely fictitious or mythical 'companies,' 'banks' or 'schools' with cryptic names like A Space, Ace Space, Northwest Mounted Valise and Fat City School of Finds Art."[40] A similar theme may be gleaned from the subject matter of some of the events Johnson organized:

> At my fiftieth birthday party . . . [we] had a meeting of the—are you ready for this—Michael Cooper, Michael Cooper, Michael Cooper Club. There are two Michael Coopers who knew each other, and we had a third Michael Cooper meet, and all these Michael Coopers met the other Michael Coopers. Now, there might have been four of them, for all I know, I can't even, at this point, remember, because there was a possibility that there would be five at the next meeting. . . . Which brings us up to the Ray Johnson who streaked at the Vatican and was kicked out of Italy and had to go back to Trinity College in Hartford.[41]

Multiple identities may proliferate behind the proverbial curtains of a name or title. The artist Terry Reid writes, "For years everyone thought Richard C. and Ray C. Johnson were one and the same person speeding between mailboxes in North Carolina and New York."[42]

Of course, commonalities lofted at the NYCS are probably moot since the opposite can usually be applied. The look-alike bunny heads are often drawn alongside actual names, including those of established artists such as Cy Twombly, Nam June Paik, Dennis Hopper, and Yoko Ono. Thus, the NYCS's inconspicuousness, which is to an extent authentic, is also its own lark. Likewise, when Paschal is asked about the implicit obscurity of the name "Richard C.," she replies, "The anonymity strikes me as ironic, since Richard has succeeded in establishing a well-known identity for this anonymous artist."[43] This is an interesting point, as Richard C.'s "identity" is as versatile as Richard Craven's career, which in addition to correspondence art includes painting, drawing, sculpture, teaching,[44] and curation; and while Johnson considered Richard C. "one of [the NYCS's] superstars," it's Craven's career as a curator that established him as one of its primary chroniclers, albeit perhaps ironically, given Johnson's ostensible suspicions about dates.[45]

Craven started working as a curator in 1973 when he took a job with the Education Department at the NCMA.[46] Perhaps most notable is his 1976 curation of *Correspondence: An Exhibition of the Letters of Ray Johnson*, which

Notches along the Bible Belt 69

consisted of "some 550 letters sent by Ray Johnson."[47] Paschal, who at the time was an assistant curator at the NCMA, collaborated with Craven on the exhibition and shared their process: "We were pleased that Ray was so excited about it because you never knew how he was going to act. . . . We gathered a list of potential lenders. Some Ray gave and others Richard already knew. We wrote letters requesting the submission of ten letters they had received from Ray. . . . The idea was that we would choose what we wanted to show. There were so many responses to go through. It was like Christmas every day; it was loads of fun."[48] In addition to the exhibition, the NCMA published a catalog of the same name. Printed in an edition of 1,500 and sold for five dollars at the show, it contains "350 facsimile reproductions of correspondence," accompanied by an introduction from Moussa M. Domit and an essay by William S. Wilson.[49] Its non-book design—a 200-page built-up pocket portfolio slightly over letter size at 8½ × 11½—was lauded; not only did it win an AIGA award in the category of "Not Exactly Books," but it received praise from Johnson, who "was so pleased when he first saw [it] that he fell to his knees in gratitude," and from Andy Warhol.[50] Craven relays an anecdote where Warhol spotted Johnson walking in Soho and shouted to him across the street, "What a great catalog—catalog of the year!"[51] While *Correspondence: An Exhibition of the Letters of Ray Johnson* wasn't the first show related to Johnson and the NYCS, it established Johnson's early involvement with mail art and provided evidence for the NYCS origins in the 1940s.[52] As Johnson mentions in conversation with John Held Jr. the following year, "The North Carolina catalog had postcards from Arthur Secunda from the 1940s. So the Correspondence School had its beginnings in the 1940s, and it was a self-conscious activity in the '50s, and very self-conscious in the '60s, and, of course, now in the '70s."[53] Craven had already affirmed this in his 1973 essay "The New York Correspondence School: Alternatives in the Making," where he writes, "It is generally and correctly understood that Ray Johnson is the inventor and foremost proponent of the mail art movement."[54] However, the exhibition provided the actual materials, and it's typically cited to this day in reference to Johnson's role as the founder of correspondence art.[55]

Given Richard C. and Johnson's close friendship, one might assume that it provided a bridge for meeting Jonathan Williams, as Johnson and Williams moved in each other's periphery. While both went to Black Mountain College, Johnson was a student during the "Albers-Cage-Erik Satie Festival times" prior to the Charles Olson years, when Williams was in attendance.[56] Although Williams wasn't a member of the NYCS, he and Johnson (among other participants in the network) were correspondents. Williams's postal activities are themselves something of legend, typically related to his letter writing, but Williams was also a notable mail artist in his own right with respect to Jargon's postcard series.[57] Williams invited Johnson to contribute visuals for two Jargon books: drawings for Russell Edson's *What a Man Can See* (Jargon 37), and the cover for Harold Norse's translation of Giuseppe Gioachino Belli's poems *The Roman Sonnets* (Jargon 38), published in 1969 and 1960, respectively.[58] Despite the connection, Richard C. and Williams met independently of their mutual friend.

Throughout the 1960s and 1970s, when Williams wasn't on the move—on the road selling books door-to-door, hiking, and traversing the United States and the United Kingdom—he took on various residencies and taught at a number of institutions, including the Aspen Institute for Humanistic Studies, Maryland Institute College of Art, and several schools in North Carolina including North Carolina School of the Arts, Salem College, Winston-Salem State University, the Penland School of Crafts, and Wake Forest University.[59] It was during the mid-1960s, as a visiting poet at Wake Forest, that Williams gave a talk at the Southeastern Center for Contemporary Art (SECCA) in Winston-Salem, at which Richard C. was in attendance. Paschal writes, "Jonathan impressed Richard, and Richard added him to his mailing list. Richard's mailings obviously made an impression on Jonathan."[60] As the two corresponded over the following years, they invited each other to participate in various projects. Richard C. asked Williams to contribute to several exhibitions and readings at various galleries and institutions throughout the '70s and '80s. To this day, Richard C. merely considers himself "an admirer/fan of the writer/poet Jonathan Williams."[61] On Williams's end, he became interested in a certain strain running through Richard C.'s work and correspondence since their meeting, seen in this blurb from a letter from Richard C. to Williams dated "Januweary 26, 197One," which is exemplary of the subject: "'Lights' in Graham, N.C., is fun. . . . A very modest white frame house with tin roof with lights all around the front, side and back yard. . . . A couple of Santa Claues and alarge [sic] open bible on the roof, plus a large Manger scene to the left of the house. And a sign reading: Welcome to Christmas land U.S.A. attached to a tree with one of those Fluorescent Hardware 'No Trespassing' signs above that. And too sort of ironic was the wire fence topped with barbed wire."[62] These kinds of contradictory religious-themed juxtapositions are prominent in Williams's own photography and poetry as well, which include a 1954 photo of a boulder in Toxaway, Transylvania County,

North Carolina, crudely graffitied with "U NEED JESUS,"⁶³ and, from his found Appalachian poetry book *Blues and Roots / Rue and Bluets*:

U
NEED
JESUS
GOOD
BUDDY

and . . .

BEPREPA
REDTO
MEETGO
D

Both poems were lifted from signs found in North Carolina. But Richard C. took the hunt for bizarre evangelical ephemera and sayings to another level, and Williams respected him for it. In his interview with Dana, Williams refers to Richard C. as "a master finder of extraordinary things": "You wouldn't believe the things he finds. There are already evangelical billboards in North Carolina, for instance, that say, 'Jesus is the beef.' How can you believe it? But it's there. Richard Craven is the collagist, with a keen eye and a strong stomach."⁶⁴ To get a nod like this from the "truffle-hound of American poetry" is quite an achievement. Thus, it was Williams who came up with the idea for a book centered on Richard C.'s Bible Belt explorations and pitched it to him at some point during the mid- to late '70s.⁶⁵

The first reference to a possible Richard C. Jargon project appears in Williams's "An Attempt at a Complete List of Jargon Society Publications, including Titles in Press & Projected, as of January, 1974," where he writes, "Books by the following are being thought of: Guy Davenport, Ronald Johnson, Lorine Niedecker, Thomas A. Clark, Richard C., and Emmet Gowin."⁶⁶ Evidently, Williams spent 1974 mulling it over, as one finds the following mention in a January 5, 1975, newsletter titled "EPISTLE DE PROFUNDIS AD ASTRA FOR THE BOARD OF THE JARGON SOCIETY & SUBSCRIBERS & PARTICULAR FRIENDS": "We have a grant application in with the *National Endowment for the Arts* for $10,000 to let us move on Paul Metcalf's THE MIDDLE PASSAGE; Tom Meyer's THE UMBRELLA OF AESCULAPIUS; Simon Cutt's QUELQUES PIANOS; and Ronald Johnson's EYES & OBJECTS. . . . After that, there are books . . . [such as] a collection of objects, FROM THE BIBLE BELCH, by Richard C."⁶⁷ According to Williams, the book was to have an emphasis on "contemporary, mass-produced religious objects," with an emphasis on marketing and the commercialization of Christianity in the American South.[68] As Paschal explains, "[Richard C.] thought the ads and cheap approximations of religious trinkets for sale at various outlets were all a bad joke; he said he thought 'people should be more respectful of religion.'"[69] Thus, his spoofing seems to have targeted a fundamental corruption and greed all too familiar in his native North Carolina, as opposed to being a blatant mockery.

The idea for "Notches along the Bible Belt" was stewing for several years before Williams landed on the title. In the spring of 1977, he mentions that a "collection by Richard C. with a title like NOTCHES ALONG THE BIBLE BELT needs to happen to establish a more public reputation for this North Carolina sharp-shooter."[70] That same year, Williams got more serious about the project and included it in Jargon's budgetary planning at "$4000 required."[71] But when exactly he pitched the book to Richard C. is up for debate. Curiously, given references to a Jargon project for Richard C. as early as 1974, the artist doesn't remember hearing about the project until 1978 or later.

In 1977, Richard C. was awarded the National Endowment for the Arts / Southeast Center for Contemporary Art Southeastern Artist Fellowship and became part of the "Southeast Seven," named after the number of fellows SECCA took on each year.[72] During the fellowship he honed in on his religious-themed work, becoming a mail-order minister and crafting his "cross series," featuring works such as *Homage to the Christian Athlete*, where a crucifix is depicted as a complete basketball goal system, and *St. Duchamp*, where a single bicycle wheel protrudes from a stipes.[73] In 1978, the series was featured in the *Southeast Seven* exhibition, after which "Jonathan approached him about the 'Notches' idea. . . . Richard had been sending him mailings all along, many of which I gather related to religion and preachers. One thing in particular Richard told me about sending Jonathan was a poster for a 'wrestler-preacher.' Richard must have been delighted to come upon this; and Jonathan, to receive it."[74] Regardless of when Richard C. came into the picture, Williams was responsible for the concept and title, and was to be the book's editor and designer. Tom Patterson writes that "anything [Richard] C. produced could be fodder for the ms," in testament to how big a fan Williams was of his work.[75] Apparently, "Notches" was to include a flexible workflow, with Richard C. sending materials to Williams, who would arrange them into a book. But Richard C. was reluctant after learning about Williams's plans, as Patterson explains: "When I mentioned ["Notches"] to Richard he would kind of shrug and act sheepish, saying he wasn't sure what Jonathan had in mind. My sense of it is that JW would curate a selection of Richard's tongue-in-cheek religious-themed work, of which there was quite a lot. But the two of them never got together and made it happen."[76] Richard C. tells Paschal that he "never had any intention of doing a book," and that Williams was the "one pushing all along."[77] Paschal continues, "Richard hesitated because he was unsure of copyright laws and thought copyrights might be problematic with much of the material he was using if in book form. When I asked if Jonathan/Jargon couldn't have helped answer these questions, he said he just never pursued it.[78] I have the impression that Richard more or less let the matter drop, but I don't have that feeling about Jonathan. He often mentioned it to me, if only in passing, but enough to show it stayed on his mind."[79] That said, there was a period where Richard C. actually was interested in the project.

"Notches" gathered steam in the mid-'80s, though it fizzled out rather quickly. Patterson mentions that "there was a time in Jargon's history where it was thought that 'Notches' could bring in some money, mostly in relation to the financial success of *White Trash Cooking*" in 1986.[80] That year, the budget for "Notches" was set at a staggering $50,000. Of course, Jargon couldn't handle the demand for *White Trash Cooking* and had to sell it to a bigger publisher; the ensuing debacle turned out to be lucrative, but it was complicated, with various controversies, lawsuits, and much difficulty for Williams and Jargon's volunteer staff (i.e., Whitney Jones and Thorns Craven), to the point where Williams ended up not wanting a repeat of *White Trash Cooking*'s kind of success. In 1987, it was recommended that the budget for "Notches" be halved to $25,000, and the minutes of Jargon's annual meeting the following year called for further slashing:

> The Committee was uncertain whether or not ["Notches"] should be pushed forward into a bigger production budget since it had a certain sales potential following in the wake of *White Trash Cooking* and *St. EOM*.[81] Perhaps it should be kept fairly simple. There are a couple other projects that it might be more appropriate to support in a big way: *The Photographs of Art Sinsabaugh*, or even Jonathan Williams' own folk art book.[82] Jonathan Williams felt he would have to see what Richard C. had put together before he could really tell how big a production this book would entail. Perhaps all it needs is a colorful, eye-catching cover, along the lines of *White Trash Cooking*.[83]

But the notes from the Jargon Society executive committee meeting in the fall of 1988 tell a different story: "Still no coherent manuscript; perhaps this title should be either abandoned as too costly, or co-published with another press."[84]

In his lecture to the Hanes Foundation in 1989, which was published as *Uncle Gus Flaubert Rates the Jargon Society in One Hundred Laconic Présalé Sage Sentences*, Williams implies that Richard C. was dragging his feet: "When Richard figures out how to package this staggering collection of Fundamentalist art-schlock, it will be a sight to behold. George Sand asked me a funny riddle the other day. Question: 'What did Jim Bakker do with the first fifty-cent piece he ever made?' Answer: 'He married it.'"[85] It appears that Richard C., like Merle Hoyleman before him, was the primary reason that his Jargon book was never released, or even finalized for that matter, and there's some truth to that assumption, as he would be the first to admit. On the other hand, there's plenty of correspondence showing the opposite—that Richard C. was working on "Notches," particularly in the late '80s. According to Ted Potter, who was the director of SECCA and on Jargon's board of directors, the project was being held up by Jargon, not Richard C., at least at one point. Potter writes to Whitney Jones in June 1988, "[Richard C.] tells me that Roger Manley was to photograph the works he has put together for the book.[86] Roger hasn't been able to get the time to do it. So the project is stalled in Jargon's 'court.' Richard is willing to have David Roselli do the photo work. . . . He could work up a budget on what it would cost to photo the collection of works for the book. If you will okay this—he'll submit the proposal fee to you . . . and then this project can get moving again."[87] A month later, Richard C. writes to Jones, "The more that I think about it—the more I like the traditional book approach. Am really anxious to get going on this," and he even provides specs for the process:

> Enclosed is an estimate for photography. I still have a lot of questions regarding all this. I hope to utilize the services of 3 photographers (Roger Manley, Mark Clark & David Roselli). This estimate should cover the general costs of all three, however. This includes photographs for objects—not photos of the news clippings which are the basic book and to be photographed by the printer as I understand the process.
> Estimate on photographing:
> 125 items in Black and White
> 50 items in color
> B/W will be in 35mm negative
> Color will be in 35mm slides

(most of the items to be photographed are small object[s] in which a copy stand will be used. If the items are of more difficulty or size, then a higher fee may be charged)

The time estimated for shooting 50 items is one day. Total time is estimated at 31 [items] / 2 days.

Fee for shooting 50 items is $160.00. Total fee for shooting 175 items is $560.00

Cost of the film, processing contact sheets, and prints will be extra.[88]

In the end, Richard C. was able to secure the slides, photographs, and several files of ephemera; while there's no proper manuscript for the book, this is as close as one gets.

Richard C.'s "Notches" archives are arranged into six rough categories: "Various oddities," "Food-related items," "Advertisements," "Motorcyclists—Autos," "Christian athletes, pool players, etc." and a miscellaneous file. As he mentions in his letter to Jones, the most common format is newspaper clippings, which were to make up the majority of the book. As one might expect from the general theme, the articles contain strange headlines—such as "Bishop Responds to Fears of Chalice Spreading AIDS," "God Did It, Says the Fatty Who Lost 138 Lb," "Pope Marvel Is New Comic Hero," "The Bus That Was Driven by God," and "Eating by Scriptures Cited as Cancer Cure"—and many of the articles lead to advertisements. The last article promotes a cookbook titled *Eating to the Glory of God*, whose author claims that "eating according to the dietary rules set down in the Bible in Leviticus 11 and Deuteronomy 14" enabled her recovery from terminal illness.[89] Other ads include products such as "Genuine Sea of Galilee Water," "Nature's Mysterious Prayer Plant," "Last Supper Salt & Pepper Set," and "Scripture Cookies"—that is, fortune cookies that contain Bible verses. While some clippings were taken from tabloid papers like the *National Enquirer*, as their titles may suggest—for example, "Medical Examiner Says 30-Year Study Proves Holy Shroud of Turin Really Is the Burial Cloth of Christ" (which features a striking photo of a "Volunteer on simulated cross . . . examined by Dr. Zugibe in one of over 500 tests of this type he conducted")—many are odd stories from local newspapers, not all of them located in the Bible Belt. For example, "Woman 'Out of Key' with Church" tells the story of a Pittsburgh congregant who was banned from church for singing too loudly and subsequently found guilty of defiant trespassing, and "Religious Wives Enjoy Sex More, Survey Shows" lets readers know that for "the respondents who reported they prayed regularly, their enjoyment level jumped to 86 percent."

PRAISE THE LORD!!!
for
TWO CONSECUTIVE
RECORD BREAKING SUNDAYS
Help Us Make It
"3 IN A ROW"
by coming to our

Dorm "Quick-Draw" Landtroop
Pastor

ROUND-UP SUNDAY

Come dressed Western or Dude (20th Century) and hear Great Old-Fashioned Preaching and Western Singing.

A sample clipping from the "Various Oddities" folder, an ad for a cowboy-themed church service.

Other loose materials include comic books (e.g., one where Dennis the Menace is cast as David to take on Goliath), arts and crafts (e.g., instructions for how to fold a piece of paper to spell "HELL" or form a crucifix), and random testimony tracts, many of which are from ex-Hell's Angels. A small amount of the ephemera was combined or penciled into draft pages alongside articles, which shows that Richard C. was conceptualizing a design—for example, a crude drawing of a book with a title that reads like a concrete poem:

SOUL
The
Bible
FOOD
(Color photo)

Some spreads reveal that he was planning on incorporating handwritten found poems—similar to *Poems by Richard C., And/or Another Notepad for All Those Endless Lists,*—alongside ads and articles, with the headlines doubling as titles for both the story and the poem extracted from it.[90] "Snake Service in Field Broken Up by Deputies" tells the story of a snake-handling preacher whose snakes are confiscated by local authorities, and from it, Richard C. renders the following:

> i believe they ought
> to reinstate me them
> snakes or some of
> equal value said rev
> prince preacher & bait
> shop owner from canton
> the one that got the sheriff boy he
> was a good old big
> rattler boys it's real
> hard to get those

This poem comes from one of the more elaborate markups, a two-page fold-out containing multiple related articles revealing that the preacher later died from bites sustained during one of his services. "Plastic Jesus Freed by Thirsty Captors," relates a prank in Fitchburg, Massachusetts, where a baby Jesus is "kidnapped" from a Rotary Club's nativity scene, and from it, Richard C. appropriates this text:

> a note left in
> the empty manger sunday
> read we have jesus
> we will hang him
> unless the police leave
> five cases of budweiser
> here by jan first

Of the categorized folders, "Food-related items" has the most material, and Richard C. crafted several poems from the contents. "Housewives Turn to God to Lose Weight," is exemplary of this category in concluding with an ad for a dieting system:

> when all else failed
> i turned to his
> book to help shed
> my body of sinful
> pounds of ugly fat
> you too will bless
> the day that you

took up his way
to be slim send
$2.95 plus .25 postage

Other spreads are textless, indicating that Richard C. was undecided about the general layout of the book (which he admittedly was) and that he may have been mulling over several different designs, including construction paper overlays framing juxtaposed articles, ads, and ephemera.

In addition, the archives contain 35mm color slides and a series of 4"×6" black and white photographs, still in their 1 Hour Photo package. The contents follow the same general theme as the clippings and include images of toys like "Surprise Sponges: Birth of Jesus," which includes the instructions "Drop a capsule in warm/hot water and watch surprise appear," and a labyrinth marble maze with the text "JESUS NEVER FAILS" printed across its plastic cover; baking supplies such as "Anna Elizabeth WADE Imitation Vanilla Flavoring," whose label includes the end of 1 Timothy 6:17, "God . . . giveth us richly all things to enjoy"; and books like *If You Want Money, a Home in Heaven, Health, and Happiness, Based on the Holy Bible*, DO THESE THINGS, by Rev. Ewing, "Your Pastor-by-Mail," among other strange novelties. Perhaps the most shocking object is "THREE KINGS FRANK INCENSE & MYRRH OIL DRAWING POWER SPRAY"; its label boasts a detailed image of a bloodied and crucified Jesus.

Given how varied the materials are, it's certainly difficult to envision how Richard C. would've packaged the book, as Williams mentions in *Uncle Gus*. But this predicament speaks to Patterson's observation that Richard C. "wasn't sure what Jonathan had in mind." There's truth to this statement, as "Notches" was, to a degree, Williams's baby, even though he planned it around Richard C.'s work. Richard C. was initially reluctant to participate for reasons already mentioned, including possible copyright issues and the general feeling that his work didn't warrant a book; however, the project may have neglected certain qualities of his creative approach, which, as mentioned in relation to the NYCS, is "secret, private, and without any rule." His sole book, *Poems by Richard C., And/or Another Notepad for All Those Endless Lists*, was published because it evolved from his practice—essentially, it's a prank connected to an exhibition of other visual pranks. Williams understood, perhaps better than most, that Richard C. was "a master finder of extraordinary things"; but book production and the hunt for strange ephemera that could be sent out via the postal system are two different things. Clearly, Richard C. was less interested in the former than

His trusty Bible in his meaty hand, 330-lb. preacher-muscleman Paul Wrenn gets ready to read fire and brimstone to a congregation. The traveling evangelist call himself a "Bible-for-hire troubleshooter."

World's mightiest preacher is out pumping iron for God

PREACHER Paul Wrenn knows how to get a congregation's attention: First he lifts a 250-lb. man with his teeth. Then he has the man jump onto his stomach.

Only after all that does the 330-lb. giant, one of the world's strongest men, open his Bible. Wrenn describes himself as a traveling "Bible-for-hire troubleshooter" who combines his religious message with a career as a weightlifter. In fact, Wrenn will be competing for the world super-heavyweight power lifting championship in November. Last year he was runner-up. Until recently he held the world record for the squat lift — raising an incredible 954.5 lbs.

"My mixture of ministry and strength is a great attraction. It is very effective. It makes people listen to what I have to say," says the 33-year-old ordained Baptist minister. "When a pastor wants to increase the size of his congregation, he calls me in."

Wrenn says his massive show of strength also gets him the respect of convicts when he's called in to preach at prisons. "These people respect and admire strength and they really listen to my sermons," he says proudly.

Preacher Wrenn lifts weights as part of his pre-sermon show. Left, he has a 250 lb. man jump on him.

*his trusty bible in
his meaty hand 330
lb preacher muscleman paul
wrenn gets ready to
rain fire and brimstone*

One of Richard C.'s spreads from his "Christian Athletes" folder. This one includes the following found poem: "his trusty bible in / his meaty hand 330 / lb preacher muscleman paul / wrenn gets ready to / rain fire and brimstone."

the latter. For now, "Notches along the Bible Belt" turns out to be exactly what he's best known for—that is, an ephemeral artwork transported via the mail.[91]

Regardless of Richard C.'s apparent enthusiasm for the project during the late 1980s, Jargon 98 is left blank in the bibliographical checklist in *Jargon at Forty* composed in 1991, suggesting that Williams may have considered removing it from Jargon's schedule at one point. However, Williams brings it up again the following year: "Tom and I will spend a half hour showing some of the Jargon books and telling everyone about the next projects . . . [including] *Notches Along the Bible-Belt*."[92] It's easy to glean from Jargon board meeting notes and minutes from the late '80s how serious he actually was about putting "Notches" out in the '90s, when his publishing activities began to slow. Of course, one knows from its position in the bibliography that it was never axed, only brushed aside and left alone.

"Notches" flags a distinct shift in Williams's scouting practices, as the first in a line of projects dedicated to North Carolinians, whom he became increasingly interested in publishing during Jargon's later years. As he mentions to Leverett T. Smith in 1995,

> Jargon has never been regional or chauvinistic, but since I don't have the back muscles and energy that I used to, I don't drive 40,000 miles a year to try to know everybody everywhere. Thus, North Carolina looms larger than it did. And that means that every time I go in the bathroom I keep thinking I see Jesse Helms' shadow behind the shower curtain. Well, to hell with such early-flowering paranoia. Jesse couldn't care less about the outsiders we like. They include the photographers Elizabeth Matheson, Caroline Vaughan,[93] and Roger Manley. The artist Richard Craven. Poets Tom Meyer[94] and Jeffery Beam. These artisans are the focus of much of our attention.[95]

Curiously, "Notches" remained on his radar for thirty-four years, even if the chances of publishing it in 1995 were practically nil. Simply put, "Notches" was never completed because Williams and Richard C.'s enthusiasm for it came at different times; unfortunately, what apparently synced up in the end was a loss of interest and energy. But its story articulates certain aspects of Jargon's history, including its foray into religious-themed art books, North Carolinian writers and artists, and a continuation of its *art brut* projects. The subject of the next chapter, "The Lyrix of Col. Hampton B. Coles (Ret.)," shines further light on the latter, as expressed by the Southern Visionary Folk Art Preservation Project, arguably the Jargon Society's most ambitious initiative.

CHAPTER FOUR

The Lyrix of Col. Hampton B. Coles (Ret.)

Besides Jonathan Williams himself, few people were as involved with the Jargon Society in the mid-1980s as Tom Patterson, who served as its executive director from 1984 to 1987.[1] During that time, he managed its office in Winston-Salem, authored two books that were scheduled for publication under its imprint, and led its Southern Visionary Folk Art Preservation Project, a three-year, primarily grant-funded endeavor dedicated to the promotion and conservancy of contemporary self-taught artists practicing in the US South. Additionally, he pitched ideas for future projects and publications, including the subject of this chapter, "The Lyrix of Col. Hampton B. Coles (Ret.)," a selection of lyrics by the performance artist and bandleader Bruce Hampton, which was to feature drawings by the visionary folk artist James Harold Jennings and an introduction from Patterson. Williams slated it as Jargon 102 in 1984, but its numerical position was short-lived, as it was essentially axed from planning in 1987. While the manuscript was never published, "Lyrix" differs from the projects discussed in the previous chapters because its number was stripped and reassigned, and therefore, it doesn't appear in Jargon's book series.[2] But I wanted to take a closer look because it was the first "missing book" brought to my attention. Patterson refers to it, although not by title, during an interview I conducted with him for *Jacket2* in 2020: "One of the more interesting artist/characters I was involved with was the singer/performer Bruce Hampton (a.k.a. Colonel Bruce Hampton, a.k.a. Hampton B. Coles, Ret.). . . . When I introduced Jonathan to him and his work, Hampton was leading a band called The Late Bronze Age.[3] I brought Jonathan and . . . Thomas Meyer to several of their shows in Hampton's native Atlanta during the early 1980s. At my instigation, Jonathan launched plans to publish a small book of Hampton's unconventional lyrics under the Jargon imprint."[4] His mention of this is somewhat fortuitous, since one must really dig through the archives to find references to "Lyrix." It was occasionally mentioned during Jargon Society board meetings in the mid-'80s, but it doesn't appear in any prospectuses. It's a bit of an anomaly in Jargon's history, and unlike many of the other projects that Williams accepted and then nixed, it never found another publisher. Its contents, its lifespan as a proposed Jargon book, and Patterson's involvement

Tom Patterson *(left)* with Williams at St. Andrews College circa 1975. Photo by Charles McNeill, courtesy of F. Whitney Jones Papers, Special Collections, Appalachian State University.

place it within the vicinity of the Southern Visionary Folk Art Preservation Project, which provides context as to why "Lyrix" never made it very far.

When Patterson met Williams in 1974, the term "visionary folk art" hadn't yet been coined, but Williams had plenty of photographs to illustrate the type of self-taught artist's environments for which he and Patterson shared a fondness. Williams was visiting St. Andrews College (now St. Andrews University) in North Carolina as part of the Black Mountain College Festival that Patterson, then a senior at St. Andrews, helped organize.[5] Over several days, Williams met with students and faculty, held readings, and gave presentations on his travels, which included slides of Ferdinand Cheval's *Le Palais Idéal* in Hauterives, France, and Simon Rodia's *Watts Towers* in Los Angeles. These images prompted Patterson to tell Williams about Stephen Sykes's *In-Curiosity House*—a massive roadside sculpture that had intrigued him as a child when he passed it during trips from Georgia to visit family in Mississippi, where it was located.[6] Neither of them realized it at the time, but they had planted the seeds for a lifelong friendship and what would become the Jargon Society's Southern Visionary Folk Art Preservation Project.

The Lyrix of Col. Hampton B. Coles (Ret.)   83

Meeting Williams had a profound impact on Patterson, who shortly thereafter delved into a life of writing and publishing reminiscent of his influence. Relocating to Atlanta, he wrote poetry, supported himself as a journalist, and worked as an editor at Pynyon Press, a small letterpress operation based in downtown Atlanta, which he eventually took over as director. Falling in with the local art scene, he befriended many of its artists and musicians, including Bruce Hampton, whose music he had been following since the late '60s with the Hampton Grease Band. A 1983 feature on Hampton that appears in the Atlanta-based art periodical *Art Papers* quotes Patterson as saying, "I was in my late teens and living in Dublin, Georgia, when I first heard about the Hampton Grease Band. . . . The late '60s and early '70s was an outlandish era, but Hampton's peculiar brand of outlandishness made everything else going on seem boringly normal and unimaginative."[7] Their friendship was also unconventional, starting off with Hampton immediately guessing the birthdays and astrological signs of Patterson and his then-wife Ellen (the poet Ford Betty Ford) and then inviting himself over to their house for dinner.[8] Hampton was known for his appetite, and this would be the first of many meals he would enjoy with the Pattersons.

In 1979, Patterson reconnected with Williams to write an article about him for *Brown's Guide to Georgia*, a periodical dedicated to "stories about places to go, people worth paying attention to, and things to do in Georgia and the adjoining states."[9] Consequently, they rekindled their conversation on ad hoc artist environments, which they began referring to as "visionary folk art" alongside smaller-scale works by other self-taught artists, such as the pottery of Georgia Blizzard, the doll babies of Martha Nelson, and paintings by Sister Gertrude Morgan, among many others. Both Williams and Patterson were skeptical of labels and genres, but the term seems to have been developed out of necessity during their collaborative planning of the Visionary Project, as a means of defining its working parameters. As Patterson writes in the fourth installment of his memoir quartet, the designation of "visionary folk art" was created and used to "distinguish our focus from folk art as conventionally defined—objects handmade according to traditions passed through generations. Our interest was art made by autonomous, vernacular creators impelled by personal, visionary sensibilities. . . . We knew it when we saw it, especially when it spilled out into the artists' yards to form traffic-stopping environments."[10] It also differentiated this kind of work from the problematic category of "outsider art," a term that had been coined with Roger Cardinal's 1972 publication of the same name. Cardinal's initial title for the book was *Art Brut*, named for the art movement founded by Jean Dubuffet, which translates to "art in the raw" and refers to self-taught, typically socially or culturally marginalized artists.[11] "Outsider art" is essentially a corporate designation—pitched by Cardinal's publisher and adopted as the book's title—that neither Williams nor Patterson cared for; the latter later described it as stemming "from a false dichotomy that unfairly marginalizes the art and the artists who make it."[12] In *Reclamation and Transformation: Three Self-Taught Chicago Artists*, Patterson likewise expresses distrust for the term "folk," quoting the art critic Jenifer Borum as stating that both labels (i.e., "folk" and "outsider") "reveal more about those who use them than they do about the artwork and artists they tend to identify."[13] And there's no reason to think this skepticism can't be carried farther. For instance, Nek Chand, who constructed the illustrious sculpture park *Rock Garden* in Chandigarh, India, challenges the notion of even being referred to as an artist.[14] That said, Williams and Patterson occasionally use these words to describe and raise funds for their related projects, although they seem to do so with more consideration, awareness, and certainly broader context. For Williams, the work of self-taught artists speaks to his respect and appreciation for the homemade, the use of found materials, the noncommercial, and the strange. He refers to H. P. Lovecraft and J. R. R. Tolkien as his "first Outsiders" and considers many of Jargon's writers and artists (e.g., Alfred Starr Hamilton, Doris Ulmann, and Ralph Eugene Meatyard), as well his own writings (e.g., the found Appalachian poems of *Blues and Roots / Rue and Bluets*) to be in a similar vein.[15]

Williams's collaboration with Patterson illustrates a unique period in Jargon's history. Many volunteers worked with Jargon over the years, but the Visionary Project marks the first and only time that an individual other than Williams was given a salaried position.[16] While Patterson's compensation was modest, it came with health benefits and the impressive title of executive director. The nomination was tied directly to the project, which was unofficially conceived in 1980 when Williams and Thomas Meyer introduced Patterson to Eddie Owens Martin (a.k.a. St. EOM) at *Pasaquan*, his vernacular visionary environment near Buena Vista, Georgia, an event that set Patterson's life on a new course. After several visits and "offerings of cannabis" at St. EOM's request, the two became close friends, which eventually led to an interview that appears in the December 1981 issue of *Brown's Guide to Georgia*.[17] Two years later, St. EOM asked Patterson to help him write and publish a memoir. It was also during this time that Patterson arranged for a collaborative performance by EOM and Bruce Hampton at a fundraiser for *Art Papers*.[18] As he writes in *The Tom Patterson Years*: "It shouldn't have surprised me to learn . . . that Bruce and Saint EOM were old friends. They'd met years earlier, when a mutual acquaintance took Bruce to Pasaquan. . . . One of his enduring memories of his visit to Pasaquan was Eddie's spontaneous, improvisational chants performed while he strummed his randomly tuned acoustic guitar."[19] And this is essentially what EOM contributed, although the chanting was substituted with an ad lib autobiographical poem, while Hampton and The Late Bronze Age improvised percussive noisescapes to a receptive but rather "baffled" audience.[20] As noted in Jerry Grillo's biography on Hampton, *The Music and Mythocracy of Col. Bruce Hampton*, the event was filmed and edited for inclusion in the 1993 documentary *The Pasaquoyan: The Life and Works of Visionary Artist Eddie Owens Martin*, which features both Patterson and Hampton discussing EOM's work and their friendship with the artist.[21]

Patterson committed to working with EOM on his life story, and in 1983 he pitched the idea to Williams. Williams was already in the nascence of his own book that would include EOM, a travelogue in collaboration with the photographers Roger Manley and Guy Mendes, mostly made up of profiles on self-taught artists practicing in the rural South. Williams had mentioned this project, which at the time he referred to as his "Big Book of Southern (Folk) Art," and EOM in particular, to Patterson during their interview for the *Brown's Guide to Georgia* article.[22] In his memoirs, Patterson expresses that he was concerned that Williams might think he was stealing the idea to write about EOM, but Williams was more than supportive of the project, not only agreeing to put out Patterson's EOM book through Jargon but also proposing that he work on a second book about another one of Hampton's friends, the Reverend Howard Finster. Williams and Patterson had met Finster in the spring of 1980, visiting him at his visionary folk art environment *Paradise Garden* in Summerville, Georgia. As Patterson writes of the experience, "I had braced myself for meeting a fire-and-brimstone fundamentalist preacher determined to save our wayward souls. Instead, we found ourselves in the presence of this unselfconsciously hyper-manic, brilliant artist who delighted in regaling us with tales of his all-encompassing collection, his interplanetary travels, and his zealous pursuit of his creative vision."[23] Finster was relatively unknown at the time, but his fame was about to skyrocket, eventually placing him out of Jargon's league, at least according to Williams. Regardless, the Visionary Project was shaped by the prospective publications of the EOM, Finster, and Southern Folk Art books. Of course, this chapter also considers "The Lyrix of Col. Hampton B. Coles (Ret.)" in their periphery, even though it isn't mentioned in any documentation related to the Visionary Project. Its absence could very well be due to the manuscript being planned

The Jargon Society posing at *Art World* with the sign James Harold Jennings made for the Jargon offices in Winston-Salem, 1987. *Left to right*: Roger Manley, Whitney Jones, Thomas Meyer, Jonathan Williams, Otis Baby (one of several Jargon mascots created by Martha Nelson), Thorns Craven, Tom Patterson, and Jennings. Photo by Roger Manley.

out in advance of Patterson's employment with Jargon and initially slated for publication under the Pynyon imprint.[24] Although Hampton's lyrics arguably have a visionary quality, it's Williams's idea to use James Harold Jennings's drawings—which were to replace visuals by Hampton that Patterson had selected for the original manuscript—that flags a connection to the Visionary Project.[25] Jennings, whose artist environment *Art World* was located in Pinnacle, North Carolina, was a main focus of the Visionary Project.[26] Williams writes about and memorializes him in several collections, including the magnificent *A Palpable Elysium: Portraits of Genius and Solitude*, but "Lyrix" was the closest Jennings got to having his own collaborative Jargon publication.[27] Unfortunately, it never made it far enough in development for us to know which drawings Williams would have included.

The Lyrix of Col. Hampton B. Coles (Ret.)

The trajectory of the Visionary Project moved beyond its core books when Patterson proposed to Williams a broader mission: "Instead of just an effort to finance some new art books, I suggested framing the books as components in a larger project advocating preservation of the art they documented."[28] This approach was influenced by Seymour Rosen's SPACES (Saving and Preserving Arts and Cultural Environments), a Los Angeles–based non-profit dedicated to the preservation of visionary folk art, albeit in other parts of the country. As Patterson notes, he had Rosen's blessing: "Because [Rosen's] lone efforts were mostly focused in California and the western part of the country, he encouraged an application of his model in the South, a region where his opportunities and contacts were limited—and where there seemed to be an abundance of such places."[29] From Jargon's inception, Williams had emphasized preservation as being of personal importance to him as "the custodian of snowflakes," an ethic articulated by his impulse "to protect the Margins, because that's where I live."[30] SPACES, which is still active, refines a similar philosophy to focus on some of the most delicate art installations in the western and mid-western United States. Visionary vernacular environments and their creators are often situated in rural and impoverished areas with no community support, and among neighbors who not only lack an appreciation or understanding of the work but may be dangerously hostile and cruel—for instance, Finster had been shot at, and years of social ostracizing (among other factors) drove both EOM and Jennings to suicide in 1986 and 1999, respectively. Williams certainly saw the need for preservation, and he agreed to frame the Visionary Project around the protection of vulnerable artists and artwork; it was officially launched under Patterson's directorship at the annual Jargon Society board meeting in January 1984. Nobody was more surprised than Patterson at his new role, especially since Williams had been credited as executive director on the Jargon Society masthead since the late 1960s. Subsequently, Williams assumed the nominal title of "publisher," remaining very much at the helm of all things Jargon.

In addition to producing the three books at its center, the Project was to take on several other initiatives with the intention of raising awareness— with an eye to preservation—including organizing a visionary folk art exhibition,[31] providing support to artists and collectors, and founding a museum in Winston-Salem fixed around the work of the visionary folk artist Annie Hooper.[32] Hooper's environment—comprised of 2,500+ driftwood and concrete sculptures of biblical figures—was in Cape Hatteras, North Carolina, and one of the first targets of the Preservation Project. Roger Manley had unexpectedly met Hooper in the '70s, and the two became close friends.

He began "networking with the Jargon Society on Mrs. Hooper's behalf," well in advance of the Preservation Project.[33] His subsequent work with Williams as a photographer and folklorist led to his involvement on the Project as a consultant, and the museum was proposed essentially to house her massive collection.

It can be argued that the Project achieved its primary goal of raising awareness for the artists and their work despite meeting only a few of its objectives. Attempts to establish the museum proved too difficult and were halted due to a lack of funding. On the other hand, the Southern Visionary Folk Art exhibition, co-curated by Patterson and Manley, was a considerable achievement. It featured work by EOM, Finster, Jennings, Hooper, Bernard Schatz, Georgia Blizzard, Leroy Person, Sam Doyle, William Owens, Dilmus Hall, James Bright Bailey, John E. Queen, Clyde Jones, Raymond Coins, Reuben A. Miller, and Carl McKenzie.[34] For many of these artists, this was a first public showing, and for better or for worse, they received immediate national attention.[35] The exhibition even had the support of Robert Bishop, then-executive director of the Museum of American Folk Art in New York, who made the introductory speech on opening night. An accompanying publication, *Southern Visionary Folk Artists*, by Patterson and Manley, was published by the Jargon Society in an edition of 3,000 copies in 1984.[36] The Project also funded the fieldwork and research of Williams, Patterson, Manley, and Guy Mendes, and it inadvertently launched the curatorial careers of both Patterson and Manley, the latter going on to become the director of North Carolina State University's Gregg Museum of Art & Design.[37]

Although bittersweet—it would mark the end of the Preservation Project and Patterson's tenure as a Jargon employee—the most notable achievement was the publication of Patterson's EOM memoir, *St. EOM in the Land of Pasaquan (The Life and Times of Eddie Owens Martin)* (Jargon 64) in 1987. A singular work in the Jargon bibliography, it presents a transcribed oral history of St. EOM's extraordinary life alongside full-color photographs by Williams, Manley, and Mendes. In some ways, it represents a peak in Jargon's move toward publishing more visually oriented material, which, as mentioned in chapter 3, started in the early 1970s with *The Appalachian Photographs of Doris Ulmann*. Williams even told Patterson that *St. EOM in the Land of Pasaquan* was his favorite Jargon book. That isn't to say that Jargon stopped publishing beautiful "picture books" after 1987, but rather that *St. EOM* represented a culmination of many of Williams's interests— photography, visionary folk art, maverick artists, and preservation—and remains unlike any other Jargon book for that reason.[38] Of course, publishing photography, a medium far more expensive to publish than poetry, led to many projects never being released for lack of funding; the other two books at the heart of the Project unfortunately fall into this category.

Patterson's book on the reverend, *Howard Finster, Stranger from Another World: Man of Visions Now on This Earth*—which is very similar to *St. EOM in the Land of Pasaquan* in its presentation of dictated autobiography alongside photographs (including one by Williams and more than fifty by Manley)—was published by Abbeville Press in 1989.[39] Although Jargon had funded much of the work, Williams appears to have drastically soured on the book. In a letter to Patterson dated July 15, 1987, Williams writes, "The more I have seen of the Rev. Howard the more trouble I have had in swallowing the folk-art-dealer hardline that we are in the presence of a great artistic and spiritual figure. I smell snake oil, etc. . . . The fact that this curious old crock of shit and sublimity rather takes the heart 'out' of me is an important point. The idea of publishing a book on him leaves me cold."[40] Finster had garnered significant commercial attention, particularly after his appearance on *The Tonight Show* in 1983, and with his album cover for Talking Heads's *Little Creatures* selected by *Rolling Stone* as cover of the year in 1985.[41] By 1987, Williams doubted that Jargon could handle the production and sales that would likely result from the book, an anxiety that lingered from his experience publishing *White Trash Cooking* the year prior. In the same letter to Patterson, Williams shared similar misgivings regarding the budget required to publish his "Big Book of Southern (Folk) Art." *Walks to the Paradise Garden: A Lowdown Southern Odyssey*, as it came to be called, would have to wait over thirty years before coming out under Phillip March Jones's Institute 193 imprint in 2019.

Although not as planned under the auspices of the Preservation Project, the three core books were eventually published. "The Lyrix of Col. Hampton B. Coles (Ret.)," on the other hand, remained an outlier until axed from planning in 1987, presumably a victim of Jargon's full plate and the difficulties that came along with *White Trash Cooking*. Earlier that year, Hampton had sent Williams a typed manuscript containing a total of twenty-seven transcribed songs, including the lyrics from Hampton's two albums with The Late Bronze Age, *Outside Looking Out* and *Isles of Langerhan*, as well as some new material from his then-forthcoming solo record *Arkansas*, all of which came out with Landslide Records in 1980, 1982, and 1987, respectively. However, any arrangement for its release was suspended after Patterson left the Jargon Society.[42] In the minutes of the Jargon Society executive committee meeting held in January 1988, "Lyrix" is included in a section titled "Shelved Projects" alongside Bob Brown's *The Selected Poems* and Merle Hoyleman's *Letters to Christopher*, with a note reading, "At the moment no work is being done [on] these titles, and it is unlikely anything will before some time."[43] By 1991, "Lyrix" had all but disappeared, as conveyed by its former position being left blank in *Jargon at Forty*.[44]

While Patterson's departure may have been the final straw for the ouster of "Lyrix," publication was initially held up for a different reason: Williams simply didn't like the way it looked on paper, as articulated in Don B. Anderson's version of the minutes for the Jargon board meeting held on March 5, 1987. In a section called "Lacunae," the entry for "Lyrix" is crossed out, followed by a handwritten note: "Crazy! Don't make sense on the page, forget! (out)."[45] This seems to indicate that it was Anderson who rejected the manuscript, but Anne Midgette, Anderson's stepdaughter, confirms that it was, of course, Williams who made the call. The following month, Williams sent a letter to Patterson containing an ultimatum: "Dear Bubba Fieldhand,[46] I've written Col. Coles that I'm scratching my head trying to figure out if the high culture poem freaks that occasionally buy our austere products would think we were fucking with them or not if we brought out the delicate lyrics of the Colonel. I told him I was sending the script to you, and that if you knocked out a quick introduction/apologia, you might convince me this was for Jargon Society and not Pynyon or Tiolet.[47] Convince away."[48] Patterson couldn't sway Williams, who had pretty much already made up his mind. Regardless, transcription appears to have played a fundamental role in Williams's decision, which is indicative of something central to the conflict between poetry (ostensibly meant to be read) and lyrics (evidently meant to be sung) going back at least to the invention of the printing press, and bolstered by academia's long-standing exclusion of contemporary song lyrics, framed as not worthy of serious literary study. To be clear, this isn't to suggest that Williams rejected "Lyrix" based on any kind of academic elitism—to which Williams was very much opposed—but only to say that his preference for Hampton's lyrics in a performative and sonic context perhaps corresponds to an established division.

"The Lyrix of Col. Hampton B. Coles (Ret.)" would've been an unusual addition to Jargon's catalog. While Williams published Lou Harrison's *Three Choruses from Opera Libretti: Jargon's Christmas in 1960* as Jargon 41, "Lyrix" was the only project Williams considered that was centered on "rock" lyrics.[49] The genre is used loosely here, mostly to distinguish between libretto and the lyrics of more popular music genres that Williams detested. He was a passionate listener of classical and jazz but very much resistant to newer music, as he relates in an interview with Leverett T. Smith in 1995:

> I have a very bright young friend, Jay Bonner. . . . I ask him what he's listening to and he happily tells me: Liz Phair, Lipstick, Heavenly, Lilliput, Tiger Trap, Pere Ubu, Urge Overkill, PJ Harvey, U2, Digable Planets, Belly, and Mekons. . . . I have actually heard of U2—and R.E.M. and the Butthole Surfers before that. The rest come from the Asteroid Klutz, back of the Planet Mongo. Should I be declared certifiable and locked up out at the funny farm because I am still digesting all of Papa Haydn's trios and as many of Domenico Scarlatti's 555 harpsichord sonatas as I can get in my head?[50]

Despite Williams's curmudgeonly take on contemporary music, Patterson connected Jargon to the college rock scene of the early 1980s. In addition to Bruce Hampton, he introduced Williams to Michael Stipe and Kate Pierson too, and among the attendees at the Visionary Folk Art exhibition were Jeremy Ayers, Mitch Easter, and Ian McCulloch. Williams even appears in an episode of MTV's *The Cutting Edge* during a feature on the independent music scene in North Carolina.[51] Regardless of whether Williams enjoyed R.E.M., the B-52s, Let's Active, or Echo and the Bunnymen, Patterson imported a new generation of artists, and "Lyrix" would've been a manifestation of that network. That said, Williams didn't consider Hampton's work to be in the same vein as other acts of the day, and neither did Hampton, who shared similar tastes: "I can't listen to any of today's music. It bores me because it's all premeditated and calculated to reach other people rather than yourself."[52] In the same interview with Smith, Williams continues, "I've been listening to grown-up music since I was ten years old. Greasy Kidstuff never did it for me, though there are guys and groups on the wacko fringe that have always been great fun: Spike Jones, Slim Gaillard . . . Col. Hampton B. Coles (Ret.) and The Late Bronze Age." Williams maintained a fondness for Hampton's sound—even after deciding that "Lyrix" wasn't a good fit for Jargon—and that certainly has something to do with it being from the "wacko fringe."[53]

The kind of music associated with Hampton changed over his long career, but it's often described as blues / jazz / avant-garde rock, which has merit as it touches on several of his core influences, including Bobby "Blue" Bland, Little Richard, Ornette Coleman, and Sun Ra (who Hampton considered alongside EOM and Finster as one of his "Cosmic Southerners"), to name a small few.[54] That said, the description doesn't exactly account for the performance from which the music was derived. Hampton may have been equally influenced by stand-up comedy and professional wrestling, two fields that he briefly worked in during the 1970s, and some of that material made its way into his music. Although he had characteristic traits of a frontperson—smoking an invisible cigarette, checking an invisible watch, and screaming at the audience à la Classy Freddie Blassie—his theatrics were always improvised and often unhinged, which could send the band (usually in sync with his lead) to awkward, even "scary" places. Each performance, and the residual expression of sound, was unpredictable and strange; that said, it wasn't exactly an act but a reflection of who Hampton was offstage. A 2021 interview with Oteil Burbridge—who played with Hampton for many years, predominantly as a core member of the Aquarium Rescue Unit—sheds light on Hampton's aberrant personality:[55]

> They say DMT is endogenous. . . . It's supposedly released when we die or when something traumatic happens. I think, with Bruce, that gland was excreting it on a regular basis. . . . He regularly operated on a higher level of awareness. I saw him do so much psychic shit and freak people out completely—to the point where they started screaming. If he would sleep in close proximity to you at a certain time of the morning . . . he could see what was going on in your life. I'd roomed with him, so I always knew that I wasn't going to keep any secrets from him and I made peace with that.[56]

Music was secondary not only to performance but also to something perhaps extrasensory.[57]

Hampton's process, like Williams's, was reliant on a kind of magical attention and awareness. But Hampton took this a step farther with his creation of "Zambi," a philosophy/religion that emphasizes (among other things) the importance of "intention"—that is, one's motivation for doing anything.[58] Intention—which essentially must come from a place of selflessness—is the first step toward what he refers to as "platorum," a "state of attention where nothing happens," which may result in a Zen-like condition.[59] When achieved during performances, platorum may enable self-transcendence and certain spiritual connections, such as with one's instrument and bandmates. Played under its influence, Hampton's compositions were constantly subjected to impromptu arrangements. His bands never practiced in a conventional sense; rare rehearsals, if they could be called that, consisted of exercises that were geared toward an enhancement of awareness, such as walking up and down a stairway with intention.[60] This was apparently done in an effort to hone attention, and it would result in music that ultimately conveyed joy. Hampton remarks, "My goal is to heal myself through psychotherapy on stage and possibly heal others in the process."[61] His lyrics can be viewed as an expression of this symbiosis of attention and connectivity, as well as a way to break up a performative space.

In the 2012 documentary film *Basically Frightened: The Musical Madness of Colonel Bruce Hampton*, Hampton modestly sums up his writing practice: "I started writing about sixteen or seventeen and I really don't know how it came about. I never put anything together. I let it fall to where it might. It assimilates itself somehow. I have no master plan; it just collapses into place." This openness enabled him to gather language wherever it presented itself, but it also made the assemblages vulnerable to some misconceptions, as in this blurb from a review of the Hampton Grease Band's first and only record, 1971's *Music to Eat*, on its CD reissue in 2014: "As a non-instrumentalist, Hampton's role was to come up with lyrics, or at least something resembling them. . . . The often highly twisted structures frequently left him at a loss, and as a result he sometimes resorted to the recitation of preexisting printed material, much of it inherently banal."[62] That the use of found material—which Hampton employed throughout his career—signifies a half-assed approach to writing is a common slip that neglects certain writing practices that aren't only contemporary but date back at least to the "Alexandrian or late Roman method of making poetry out of tags and fragments of other people's verse, or . . . prose."[63] It does, however, introduce something in line with Williams's own poetics, or those of the poet John Clare, who "found the poems in the fields," a sentiment Hampton echoes during his 1983 performance with St. EOM when he tells the audience that "poetry . . . comes from the ground." Whether Hampton was lifting words from a paint can (e.g., "Hendon" by the Hampton Grease Band), collaging material from already existing songs (e.g., "Jack the Rabbit" by The Late Bronze Age), or using language gleaned from speech (e.g., "Raining in my Car" by the Fiji Mariners), his use of extant and overheard content was undoubtedly more haphazard than Williams's own practice. Even so, he viewed even the slightest discovery as fortuitous, and this wasn't limited to his lyrics. For example, the title for his first solo album came from the artist Flournoy Holmes mishearing Hampton's original title and repeating it back to him as "One Ruined Life of a Bronze Tourist."[64] In reply, Hampton said, "That's perfect. That's it. You know there are no accidents."[65] But according to Burbridge, Patterson, and many others, Hampton's process was also apparently visionary. It was typical for Hampton not only to accurately guess the birthdays and astrological signs of nearly everyone he met but also to provide his bandmates with special stage monikers, which he considered to be their "real" names. Harold L. Jones, percussionist for the Aquarium Rescue Unit, recalls when he first met Hampton and received the name Count M'butu: "[I asked him] 'Where did you get that name from?' He told me, 'It's written on your forehead.' Then he told me 'Your birthday is August 10th.' I just met him and I was feeling a little high."[66] M'butu was the name of a family Jones lived with years earlier, which Hampton couldn't have known. Hampton's process for discovery seems to have been well beyond "banal" appropriation, perhaps even drawing parallels with the practice of the poet Hannah Weiner, who also found words on people's foreheads and elsewhere.

Regardless, Hampton's lyrics continually drew criticism or at least condescension. Notable is a review of The Late Bronze Age's 1980 album *Outside Looking Out* in the *New York Times* in 1981. In an article titled "Recordings; POP ECCENTRICS REVISITED," the popular music critic Robert Palmer gives the record high praise but concludes with the following: "'Outside Looking Out' sounds like it was a lot of fun to make, and it's a lot of fun to listen to, as long as one doesn't pay undue attention to the lyric sheet."[67] Patterson appears to be the first to rescue Hampton's lyrics from the assumption that they were arbitrary, if not something worse. Fortunately, he not only paid attention to the lyric sheets but also included four songs in the third and final volume of Pynyon Press's Red Hand Book series: "Merged Moons" and "Farmers Earn Livings" from *Outside Looking Out*, and "Yonder Space" and "Celtic Annoyance" from *Isles of Langerhan*. The idea for "The Lyrix of Col. Hampton B. Coles (Ret.)" was derived from this publication, which situated "Hampton B. Coles (Ret.)"—one of Hampton's many stage monikers adopted during his stint as a stand-up comic—alongside an impressive lineup including Williams, Meyer, Larry Eigner, Jerome Rothenberg, and Allen Ginsberg. Patterson was aware of the dangers of pulling lyrics away from their sonic framework, stating that "the words of the best so-called 'rock poets' . . . rarely come off well as printed poetry"; nevertheless, he felt that Hampton's "hold up very well on the page apart from the musical accompaniment and . . . unique vocalizations."[68] *Red Hand Book III* offered a new context for the lyrics to be read as a kind of avant-garde literature and also provided Hampton with a calling card. As banjo player and frequent Hampton collaborator Jeff Mosier relates in *Basically Frightened*, Hampton was apparently proud of the publication: "[Hampton] said 'Some of my poetry is in this book.' . . . So I finally tracked down the *Red Hand Book* of poetry . . . and he's in there with these great poets. . . . I couldn't believe it was the same guy who wrote this stuff."

Billy McPherson (a.k.a. Ben "Pops" Thornton) on the left, and Bruce Hampton, made up to look like an old man, as they appear on the cover of *Outside Looking Out*, designed by Flournoy Holmes. Photo by Flournoy Holmes.

Red Hand Book III was the first time that Mosier (and many others) discovered that Hampton's words were worth paying attention to, and Mosier ended up an advocate, even reciting "Farmers Earn Livings" at Hampton 70, a concert organized to celebrate Hampton's seventieth birthday, on what would turn out to be the last night of Hampton's life:[69]

> by driving the wedges
> of huge stone into cradle-like bottoms
> ramps of earth triggered rope
> that prevented local circumstances
> from smelting paragraph texts
> in the crucibles expedition
>
> they bartered the mess of pottage
> and pile biled the magna charta

and dreadful taskmasters chop
composted straw materials

the barren shore will gain the fish
while the ocean will lose its gills
the air gains the birds' mental habits
while their wings will lose the hills
so you take care of your flock
farmers earn livings along valleys.[70]

"Farmers Earn Livings" is one of Hampton's more straightforward lyrical compositions, but it's still suggestive of something erratic in his writing. Many of the lyrics that appear in *Red Hand Book III* read like surreal historical fiction, collaging ostensibly lucid sentences alongside Dada-esque tongue twisters. As with his stage persona, Hampton teetered between something like a deranged history teacher and a hypnagogic prophet. Time appears to be disjointed in Hampton's songs—in this case, stuttered among references to the actual, historical Late Bronze Age, the thirteenth century, and a future where the oceans are apparently dead. In what is perhaps an (accurate) apocalyptic vision, or at least one that insinuates non-linear time, Hampton warns the listener/reader to "take care of your flock," even though he believed that the world ended a long time ago.

The transcriptions for "Farmers Earn Livings" and "Merged Moons" in *Red Hand Book III* appear in the same format as they do in the lyric sheet to *Outside Looking Out* that Palmer recommended ignoring, where they were already framed as poems with distinctive line breaks, spacing, lack of punctuation, and predominantly lowercase lettering; the latter is an important distinction, as it contrasts Hampton's boisterous stage presence and delivery and pulls the text away from the performative element from which it was generated. As songs that are to be read instead of sung, Hampton's language meanders through disembodied references and seems to follow its own structure. Indeed, Hampton believed that "lyrics develop themselves."[71] For example, when collaging lines with Ricky Keller (a.k.a. Lincoln Metcalf of The Late Bronze Age and other Hampton projects) for the song "Jack the Rabbit," "it was all random and miscellaneous, never a thought. . . . It was all random and it all worked."[72] However, the music writer Doug DeLoach observes that Hampton consciously "plays with words and phrases seeking a sharp sense of mellifluous combinations and humorous juxtaposition," and points to the apparently disjunctive fluctuations of "Merged Moons" as an example:[73]

> Merged moons perpetuated a resurgence of guesswork
> folklore splinters the five elements it's unseen
> it relaxed three geese in flight life creates itself
> dry earthworms look upon everything equally
>
> ornamentation is no stranger to fashion
> she is as old as her cousin if not older
> despite the myths contrary to unclean animals
> the woman welds cameos to impress the tourists
>
>> dramatic symptoms can be flawed by emptiness of policy
>> psychic flutters against the windows of agitation
>
> the splendor of the fungus culture burned within her
> while the present world moved in opposite direction
> the health care budget was toxic to actual needs
> and shortened forms of debate owed to the solemn appeal
>
> sensations of being stalked is illustrated
> by cannings in the courts devoid of jurisprudence
> so we took courses and devoted leisure hours
> into the condemned calendar dilemma
>
>> dramatic symptoms can be flawed by emptiness of policy
>> psychic flutters against the windows of agitation
>
> the separated gestures had no prior attention
> and were rejuvenated two hours a day
> the letters known to man as offset printing
> justified multidisciplinary therapy
>
>> dramatic symptoms can be flawed by emptiness of policy
>> psychic flutters against the windows of agitation
>
> relieved of her occupation as a gardener
> she took the threshing sledge and enhanced her memory
> relieved of her occupation as a gardener
> she took the threshing sledge and enhanced her memory

Again, Hampton indicates verbal and structural disjointedness, with multiple references to time, memory, and surreal past and future happenings.

But while this may connote a maniacal or schizophrenic episode when coupled with his intense stage presence and delivery, it's softened by its transcription, implying a more nuanced, perhaps even bucolic, delirium. The poet Tan Lin suggests that "a poem is just a space that is showing up somewhere else," a dictum that speaks to not only Hampton's use of found material but also how his transcribed lyrics seem to drift aimlessly across time and space and oscillate with allusions.[74] Lin also proposes that his own writing be approached in the framework of what he refers to as "ambient reading," which may likewise serve readers of Hampton's lyrics.[75]

Although Lin and Hampton's writings are substantially different, and there are a variety of interpretations related to what Lin terms "ambient," ambient reading often involves a text that is pocked with any number of interruptions on and off the page. Distraction, then, is embedded in the reading process and exacerbated by boredom, rather than anything manic. For example, in a 2010 interview, Lin recommends looking at his work with "the slightly bored *mood* of reading distractedly, while cooking, waiting for a subway, or watching TV,"[76] advice which perhaps fits Hampton's lyrical compositions more than a conservative reading would (e.g., to look at words or symbols and [ostensibly] understand what they mean). In assuming the either/or of disparate definitions, Hampton's words are themselves distracted, hinting that readers should follow suit as well. As the music writer Stanley Booth says while commenting on the song "Brato Ganibe" (a title that Hampton coined and which means either "World peace" or "Canoeist"): "This is the thing about Bruce. You can't ever catch him."[77] It's the presumptive search for "sense" that enabled Hampton to play with a listener/reader's attention. Palmer appears to have fallen into a trap when writing in his review of *Outside Looking Out* that "some of the lyrics do make some sort of sense," which is, of course, true, if not beside the point.

Patterson, on the other hand, refers to Hampton's lyrics on the page as reflections of "sound and associative connections." Also influencing his impression of how Hampton's lyrics might be read as poetry is that Hampton provided Patterson with his own transcriptions, in which they were presented with poetic spacing and line breaks. For instance, "Yonder Space" appears differently on the sheet for *Isles of Langerhan*—where the text is compressed without regard for its visual presentation—than it does in *Red Hand Book III*:

the kingdom nursed the resentment
great family loyalty stiffened
ordeals were pushed into the background
to add nine hours to the day

with the gentle, never at peace motive
the faceted wrath displaced motive
sterling customs granted the requests
tree victims had a hard stone to swallow

> the lone cloud showed the noble side
> looking out in yonder space!

penchant to overcome the hero
made the liquid wrath unbearable
the mercantile formed the core
clay tablets were the natural agents

> the lone cloud showed the noble side
> looking out in yonder space!
> the lone cloud showed the noble side
> standing on the motel steps
> the lone cloud showed the noble side
> I drove my child to school!

Hampton formatted "Yonder Space" similarly to the sheet for *Outside Looking Out*, which may be taken as a subtle nod to the lyrics themselves, which also throw back to the preceding album; the cloud's "noble side" is an edge that gazes outward into space (i.e., "outside looking out"). This ends up being a phrase that envelops The Late Bronze Age as a kind of motto, and it provides another clue for how one may engage with Hampton's writing (e.g., "when in doubt, go completely out").[78]

Additionally, "Yonder Space" highlights the importance of other people to his process—in this case, Billy McPherson (a.k.a. Ben "Pops" Thornton), multi-instrumentalist and Hampton's main partner in The Late Bronze Age. McPherson sings the majority of "Yonder Space," with Hampton occasionally interjecting with non-sequiturs like "I drove my child to school!" Collaboration goes back to Hampton's earliest lyrics, for "Halifax," for example, which were appropriated from an encyclopedia with Glenn Phillips, guitarist and co-founder of the Hampton Grease Band. Phillips holds that most of the lyrics on *Music to Eat* were a "collective effort," an assessment that Hampton didn't exactly agree with.[79] Nevertheless, at least half the songs credited to Hampton on *Music to Eat* have a second lyricist: "Halifax," "Six," and "Hey Old Lady and Bert's Song."[80] Although he was a singular (and oddly controlling) bandleader, Hampton thrived on collective and social energy, and this comes through in how his lyrics often include overheard snippets of language. Of course, anything that happened to be in Hampton's path could find itself in a song, including the paint can he used for "Hendon." As in ambient reading, one may also write while distracted by something else, such as "cooking, waiting for a subway," and so on.[81] The lyrics to "Celtic Annoyance," for instance, seem to have been penned while watching basketball:

> worst foot forward, absent again
> worst foot forward, concern pretend
>
> carved when at full length's focus
> his circle of life never relaxed
> remote paths of sensory time
> squander no more and panic resigns
>
> Celtic annoyance
> Celtic annoyance
> Celtic annoyance, remit overload
>
> Birmingham rumbles he's absent again
> muttered the concerns pretend
> required and contoured in epic's weave
> trampled swiftly with processed decree
>
> no tears waning and solitude bold
> Celtic abundance overloads
> protection left but granted though
> brandishing cables frozen hose
>
> imposing habits remain untouched
> when divesting the formula's fate
> through the progression of shadow's scorn
> rare half dreams intrude and born

It's difficult to ignore that "Celtic Annoyance" may refer to the Boston Celtics, a dominant team in the NBA around the time Hampton—an obsessive sports fan—would have been writing the song. The Celtics and Hampton's beloved Hawks had (and still have) a rivalry, which was certainly exacerbated when the top-seeded Celtics won the championship in 1981.[82] Hampton would have been quite annoyed with the Hawks's 31–51 record that year, while a young Larry Bird's "circle of life never relaxed." Of course, I may be falling into a linguistic trap. Hampton didn't care how his audience

The Lyrix of Col. Hampton B. Coles (Ret.)

engaged with his lyrics, and so one's reading of them may be as wide open as his writing process. Yet, it's also important to note that it's the conventional approach—a presumptive search for "sense"—that prompted their negative reception in the first place, at least until Patterson presented them in a different light.

Although *Red Hand Book III* includes only a small selection, it's the sole publication of Hampton's lyrics to this day, and "The Lyrix of Col. Hampton B. Coles (Ret.)" appears to be the only attempt to publish a full-length volume of Hampton's work. While his inclusion in the former established him as a poet, "Lyrix" would've revealed him as a kind of visionary lyricist in the vein of the "Cosmic Southerners" associated with the Visionary Folk Art Preservation Project. When asked if he had ever come across a textual equivalent to the vernacular visionary environments of St. EOM and Howard Finster, Patterson refers to Hampton's lyrics, and a Jargon Society book pairing Hampton with James Harold Jennings would've staked this connection. Oddly enough, it could be argued that this notoriety may have culminated on-screen in lieu of on paper, with the 1996 movie *Sling Blade*. Hampton essentially plays himself as the philosopher/lyricist Morris, a member of the antagonist Doyle's band. Billy Bob Thornton—the film's writer, director, and lead actor—was a fan and friend of Hampton's and wrote the part specifically for him. Hampton is spotlighted during an awkward scene where Morris recites his latest composition, "The Thrill," with classic Hamptonian delivery:

> I stand on the hill
> Not for a thrill
> but for a breath
> of a fresh kill
> Never mind the man
> who contemplates
> doing away with license plates
> He stands alone anyway
> Baking the cookies of discontent
> By the heat of a laundrymat vent
> Leaving his soul parting waters
> Under the medulla oblongata
> of mankind.[83]

Hampton didn't write this, but I include it for its implications. Hampton's on-screen role is comical, but it also ends up echoing an inaccurate assumption that Hampton's lyrics are half-assed and silly, and pretty much anyone can write them. Obviously, Thornton penned the piece in jest for his friend, but it's interesting to see someone try to emulate Hampton's voice and fall so far short.

Regardless, with practically no publications except for four songs in an obscure, out-of-print anthology from the early 1980s, getting more of Hampton's lyrics into book form is overdue. But one can't ignore his apparent disinterest here. Although he was motivated enough to send Williams the manuscript, he didn't pursue other publishers. That's not to say Hampton was indifferent, but only that he was more concerned with sound, especially by 1988 with the formation of the Aquarium Rescue Unit, which he considered to be his "1927 Yankees."[84] Oddly enough, the rejection of "Lyrix" in 1987 signaled a sea change in Hampton's career: The Late Bronze Age broke up that year, and he shedded the moniker "Col. Hampton B. Coles (Ret.)" in favor of "Col. Bruce Hampton," the stage name he would use the rest of his life. This is likely a coincidence; but Hampton believed there were "no accidents."

That Williams ended up not publishing "The Lyrix of Col. Hampton B. Coles (Ret.)" isn't particularly shocking, especially when considering the other titles that had their Jargon numbers stripped, which are documented in the following chapter. Of those eighteen prospective books, "Lyrix" is, appropriately, outside looking out, as the only one dedicated to strange "rock" lyrics. Given his particular sensibilities and tastes, it's surprising that Williams slated "Lyrix" at all, but not nearly as extraordinary as his appearance on MTV, the epicenter for music that he loathed. Both affirm Patterson's unique influence on the Jargon Society during the mid-'80s. Williams was stubbornly resistant to the advice of others, especially when it came to Jargon, but he clearly had a soft spot for Patterson, at least for a time.

As Jargon moved on from Patterson, the Southern Visionary Folk Art Preservation Project, and the *White Trash Cooking* fiasco, its publishing activities began to slow. In the 1990s it published only eight books, less than half of what it put out in the previous decade. This was due to a number of factors, not least of all, certain issues that Williams faced related to his health and personal life. Volunteer staff and some board members began to drift, including Whitney Jones, whose fundraising business grew over the course of the decade: "Thorns continued to watch over financial matters and Don Anderson and Philip Hanes remained involved, but I think that the energy was gone for the most of us for Jargon, as we were dealing with other priorities in our lives."[85] That said, Jargon never completely ceased activities, even though Williams assumed it would after his passing. As seen in chapter 5—which consists of lists of Jargon's published, prospective, and wished-for projects—books are still appearing in its series, the most recent being *The Tom Patterson Years*. Of course, with the imprint under the auspices of the Black Mountain College Museum + Arts Center, an active and dynamic institution, the publication of more Jargon books, including the missing ones, has very real potential.

CHAPTER FIVE

Bibliographical Checklists of the Jargon Society's Books including Prospective Titles and Authors

This chapter consists of two bibliographical checklists. The first records the books published as part of Jargon's book series—adapted from the most recent list assembled by Carissa Pfeiffer and found at the Black Mountain College Museum + Art Center's website, along with my own additions—spliced with prospective books that made it far enough along in planning to receive a Jargon number.[1] I provide my own notes where applicable. The second list contains every project I could find that Williams mentioned wanting to publish. How serious he was about some of these is difficult to tell. In many cases, he notes only potential authors (not titles), and I include those as well.

1. Jonathan Williams. *Garbage Litters the Iron Face of the Sun's Child*. Engraving by David Ruff. San Francisco, 1951.
2. Joel Oppenheimer. *The Dancer*. Drawing by Robert Rauschenberg. Black Mountain, 1951.
3. Jonathan Williams. *Red/Gray*. Drawings by Paul Ellsworth. Black Mountain, 1952.
4. Victor Kalos. *The Double-Backed Beast*. Drawings by Dan Rice. Black Mountain, 1952.
5. Jonathan Williams. *Four Stoppages / A Configuration*. Drawings by Charles Oscar. Stuttgart, 1953.
6. Kenneth Patchen. *Fables & Other Little Tales*. Karlsruhe, 1953.
7. Charles Olson. *The Maximus Poems / 1-10*. Calligraphy by Jonathan Williams. Stuttgart, 1953.

Prospective 8. Rainer Maria Gerhardt. "Poems, 1949-53."
Translated by Robert Creeley.

Rainer Maria Gerhardt was a poet and publisher from Karlsruhe, Germany. In 1949, he started the journal and writer's series *fragmente*, publishing works by Ezra Pound, William Carlos Williams, Olson, Creeley, André Breton, and Hans Arp, among others, some of which he and his wife Renate translated into German for the first time. Gerhardt and his family became friends with Williams while he was stationed in Stuttgart, Germany, with the Army Medical Corps. In a letter to Fielding Dawson dated April 5, 1953, Williams writes, "Things moving well on J-gon finally, after a great venting of spleen, bile, & energy in all directions & continents. . . . My stuff with Chas Oscar's graphics due in a week;[2] then the Patchen FABLES; then the Moby-O's new volume;[3] then a Gerhardt number, maybe translated by Creeley. Re/ Rainer, he's wonderful, one of the great people, but then so is Renate, his wife, & the kids, Titus & Ezra. We have great times together when I can get away from the Stuttgart Snakepit."[4] Sadly, Gerhardt took his own life the following year at the age of twenty-seven. "Poems 1949–53" was never published.

> 8. Robert Creeley. *The Immoral Proposition*. Drawings by René Laubiès. Karlsruhe, 1953.
> 9. Charles Olson. *The Maximus Poems / 11–22*. Calligraphy by Jonathan Williams. Stuttgart, 1956.
> 10. Robert Creeley. *All That Is Lovely In Men*. Drawings by Dan Rice. Photograph by Jonathan Williams. Asheville, 1953.
> 11. Kenneth Patchen. *Poemscapes*. Highlands, 1958.

Prospective 12. 100 Poems from the French.
Translations by Kenneth Rexroth.

Kenneth Rexroth, an early mentor of Williams's and the inspiration for the initial Jargon publication, was one of the first writers on Jargon's radar. That said, it wasn't until 1955 that Williams was able to slate *100 Poems from the French*. The 1958 prospectus PATCHEN REXROTH, which promotes Patchen's *Poemscapes* (Jargon 11) and *100 Poems from the French*, states that the latter was to be "one of the series of translations—Japanese, Greek and Latin, Chinese, French—which will comprise all of Kenneth Rexroth's work in this field." Curiously, in an article that appeared in the *Chicago Review* in 2006 titled "To Jonathan Williams," the intro erroneously mentions that Jargon published *100 Poems from the French* in 1955. Apparently, Rexroth retracted the manuscript due to his "dissatisfaction with post-war poetry in France" and replaced it with "100 Poems from the Greek & Latin."[5] *One Hundred Poems from the French* waited nearly twenty years to be published, coming out with Pym-Randall in 1972.

Prospective 12. "100 Poems from the Greek & Latin."
Translations by Kenneth Rexroth; drawings by Shirley Triest.

Rexroth's replacement for *100 Poems from the French* made it farther along in production. Williams included "line drawings by Shirley Triest," and "delivered [the manuscript] to Karlsruhe . . . to be ready in Summer of 1958" in an edition of 950 copies and 50 signed "Author's editions."[6] When the book didn't appear, Rexroth accused Williams of being "much too tardy in getting a book of his translations into print," and the two had a bit of a falling out. Williams returned the manuscript to Rexroth and expected "no further communication" anytime soon. In lieu, Williams offered subscribers "a return of $3.50 each, or $3.50 worth of books now available. I would prefer the latter, of course, my debts being what they are."[7] "100 Poems from the Greek & Latin" was never published, but *Poems from the Greek Anthology* came out with the University of Michigan Press in 1962.

12. Louis Zukofsky. *A Test of Poetry*. Published in association with Corinth Books. New York, 1964.

NOTE: *A Test of Poetry* was initially scheduled to be published in 1958 as Jargon 26 but was assigned to Jargon 12 after plans to publish Rexroth's translation series fell through.

13. Jonathan Williams. *Poems, 1953–1956*. In three volumes:
    13a. *Amen/Huzza/Selah*. "A Preface?" by Louis Zukofsky. Photographs by Jonathan Williams. Black Mountain, 1960.
    13b. *Elegies and Celebrations*. Preface by Robert Duncan. Photographs by Aaron Siskind and Jonathan Williams. Highlands, 1962.
    13c. Missing book, "Jammin' the Greek Scene." Note by Charles Olson. Drawings by Fielding Dawson. Karlsruhe, 1959. Never published.

NOTE: "Jammin' the Greek Scene" was never published due to a combination of factors; perhaps most surprising is that Olson played a role in quashing the project, which was explored in chapter 1.

14. Robert Duncan. *Letters: Poems 1953–1956*. Drawings by Robert Duncan. Highlands, 1958.
15. Louis Zukofsky. *Some Time*. A song setting on the cover by Celia Zukofsky. Stuttgart, 1956.
16. Joel Oppenheimer. *The Dutiful Son*. Frontispiece by Joseph Fiore. Highlands, 1957.
17. Stuart Z. Perkoff. *The Suicide Room*. Drawing by Fielding Dawson. Photograph by Charles Kessler. Karlsruhe, 1956.
18. Irving Layton. *The Improved Binoculars*. Introduction by William Carlos Williams. Highlands, 1956. A second edition, with thirty additional poems, was also published.

19. Denise Levertov. *Overland to the Islands*. Drawings by Al Kresch. Calligraphy by Jonathan Williams. Highlands, 1958.
20. Michael McClure. *Passage*. Calligraphy by Jonathan Williams. Big Sur, CA, 1956.
21. Kenneth Patchen. *Hurrah for Anything*. Drawings by Kenneth Patchen. Highlands, 1957.
22. Henry Miller. *The Red Notebook*. Drawings by Henry Miller. Photograph by Wynn Bullock. Highlands, NC, 1958.
23. Mina Loy. *Lunar Baedeker and Time-Tables*. Introductions by William Carlos Williams, Kenneth Rexroth, and Denise Levertov. Drawings by Emerson Woelffer. Highlands, NC, 1958.
24. Charles Olson. *The Maximus Poems*. Photograph by Frederick Sommer. Published in association with Corinth Books. New York, 1960.

Prospective 25. "Olson / 'By Ear,'" an LP recording of Charles Olson, reading from Maximus, The Kingfishers, In Cold Hell, in Thicket, etc. Cover by Fielding Dawson.

"To quote an unpresented television commercial: 'OLSON READS GOOD, LIKE A ZIGGURAT SHOULD!'"[8] Williams scheduled "Olson / 'By Ear'" for publication in 1958, and it had obvious potential—as a record—for changing Jargon's model. But Williams's interest in putting out recordings pre-dates Jargon's inception. As Thomas Meyer writes in our correspondence, Williams "had some connection with the recording business via 'poetry & jazz,' Patchen." In conversation with Connie Bostic, Williams mentions that in 1947 he approached John Cage about making a record of a Cage/Patchen radio play "which was broadcast . . . only once on CBS back in the . . . late '30s."[9] The LP "Olson / 'By Ear'" was never released, but Robert Creeley had already put out a record of Olson reading in 1954.[10] In a letter from Creeley to Robert Duncan dated September 24, 1955, he writes, "[Denise Levertov] had persuaded me to bring out a record Charles and I made [at Black Mountain College], a year ago, to play for [Mitch Goodman]; which we did, and clearly he was moved, by it."[11] Several other recordings were made available over the years, possibly the most notable being *Charles Olson Reads from Maximus Poems IV, V, VI*, which came out on vinyl with Folkways Records in 1975, cassette in 1992, and CD in 2012.[12]

25. Paul C. Metcalf. *Will West*. Asheville, 1956.
26. Robert Creeley. *The Whip*. Cover design by René Laubiès. Drawings by Kirsten Hoeck. Co-published with Migrant Press and Contact Press, 1957.[13]

Prospective 27. Lorine Niedecker. "Poems." Photographs by Harry Callahan. Karlsruhe/Baden 1959.

This was Williams's initial scheduling for a Jargon project related to the work of Lorine Niedecker, a poet that he held in the highest esteem: "Lorine Niedecker is the most absolute poetess since Emily Dickinson. She shuns the public world, lives, reads, and writes, very quietly, near the town of Fort Atkinson, Wisconsin, by the Rock River on its way to Lake Koshkonong. Her importance to—and remove from—the urbane literary establishment is of the rank of Miss Dickinson's. We are in the presence of a poet whose peers are the Lady Ono Komachi and Sappho. Few others come to mind."[14] That said, Niedecker was apparently "worried about how long it was taking for her book to come out."[15] Indeed, "Poems" became *Tenderness & Gristle: The Collected Poems (1936-1966)*, which was published ten years later in 1969 as Jargon 48.

27. Peyton Houston. *Sonnet Variations*. Photograph by Henry Holmes Smith. Highlands, 1962.
28. Irving Layton. *A Laughter in the Mind*. Photograph by Frederick Sommer. Highlands, 1958.
29. Bob Brown. *1450-1950*. Photograph by Jonathan Williams. Published in association with Corinth Books. New York, 1959. A facsimile reproduction of the book which was first published by the Black Sun Press of Harry and Caresse Crosby in Paris, 1929.
30. Jonathan Williams. *The Empire Finals at Verona*. Drawings and collage by Fielding Dawson. Highlands, 1959.
31. *14 Poets, 1 Artist*. Poems by Paul Blackburn, Bob Brown, Edward Dahlberg, Max Finstein, Allen Ginsberg, Paul Goodman, Denise Levertov, Walter Lowenfels, Edward Marshall, E. A. Navaretta, Joel Oppenheimer, Gilbert Sorrentino, Jonathan Williams, and Louis Zukofsky. Drawings by Fielding Dawson. New York, 1958.
32. Walter Lowenfels. *Some Deaths*. Introduction by Jonathan Williams. Photographs by Robert Schiller. Highlands, 1964.
33. Robert Creeley. *A Form of Women*. Photograph by Robert Schiller. New York, 1959. Published in association with Corinth Books.
34. Missing book, Bob Brown. "The Selected Poems." Introduction by Kay Boyle. Drawing by Reuben Nakian. Jargon 34 was projected but never published.

NOTE: Williams was trying to publish Bob Brown's selected poems well before reissuing Brown's *1450-1950* (Jargon 29) in 1959. The project even had several patrons, including Walter Lowenfels, Caresse Crosby, and Marcel Duchamp.[16] Complications arose when Bern Porter, who was already in the process of editing a selection of Brown's poems for his imprint Bern Porter Books, came into the picture.[17] In a letter from Williams to Brown dated April 7, 1958, Williams writes that Porter "suggests I might like to design a Selected BB for him and come in as co-publisher," next to which Brown wrote "No" in pencil.[18] Brown also mentions difficulties working with Porter in his reply: "Pay that Bern boy no heed. I don't remember how come he offered to do my Selected Pomes [sic], but I do know that I sent him a copy of every blessed thing I could lay my hands on. . . . I supplied him with books of mine I couldn't buy back today for $40.00 and evidently he sold them to the Calif. Lib. . . . Just a bit of modern piracy, but I don't mind."[19] Nevertheless, Brown apparently changed his mind in a letter dated the next day, suggesting that Williams and Porter co-publish the selected poems so that he and Walter Lowenfels can publish "a little collection of my short stories that I like as well or better than the pomes [sic]."[20] Williams replies, "Seems best not to fool with Bern the Porter. He has no funds and I'm sure things would get peculiar before long with him in on the deal."[21] By Brown's passing on August 7, 1959, Williams had a complete manuscript, which includes an introduction from Kay Boyle.[22] For unknown reasons, it appears to have been shelved and never picked up again some time after 1962.

Brown's life was remarkable, and certainly beyond the scope of this work. I highly recommend Craig J. Saper's *The Amazing Adventures of Bob Brown: A Real-Life Zelig Who Wrote His Way through the 20th Century* for further reading.

35. Irving Layton. *A Red Carpet for the Sun*. Photograph by Harry Callahan. Highlands, 1959.
36. Larry Eigner. *On My Eyes*. Introduction by Denise Levertov. Photographs by Harry Callahan. Highlands, 1960.

NOTE: Williams had initially slated a book called "Poems" by Larry Eigner, featuring a drawing by Karl Knaths, whom Williams studied under at the Phillips Memorial Gallery in Washington, DC. This likely became *On My Eyes*, sans the drawing.

37. Russell Edson. *What a Man Can See*. Drawings by Ray Johnson. Highlands, 1969.
38. Giuseppe Gioachino Belli. *The Roman Sonnets*. Translated by Harold Norse. Preface by William Carlos Williams. Introduction by Alberto

Moravia. Cover by Ray Johnson. Collage by Jean-Jacques Lebel. Printed by Igal Roodenko. Highlands, 1960.

39. Jonathan Williams. *Lord! Lord! Lord!: Traditional Funeral Music.* Hors de commerce, handset and printed "for the friends of the Jargon Press" by Igal Roodenko. Highlands, 1959.
40. Gilbert Sorrentino. *The Darkness Surrounds Us.* Introduction by Joel Oppenheimer. Collage and drawings by Fielding Dawson. Highlands, 1960.
41. Lou Harrison. *Three Choruses from Opera Libretti: Jargon's Christmas in 1960.* Hors de commerce and dedicated to Robert Duncan. Highlands, 1960.
42. Ronald Johnson. *A Line of Poetry, a Row of Trees.* Drawings by Thomas George. Printed by the Auerhahn Press, San Francisco. Errata sheet laid in. Highlands, 1964.

NOTE: This was originally titled *A Lap Full of Seed.*

43. Paul C. Metcalf. *Genoa: A Telling of Wonders.* Iconography by Jonathan Williams. Highlands, 1965.
44. Buckminster Fuller. *Untitled Epic Poem on the History of Industrialization.* Introduction by Russell Davenport. Highlands, 1962.
45. Sherwood Anderson. *Six Mid-American Chants.* Photographs by Art Sinsabaugh. Preface by Edward Dahlberg. Postface by Frederick Eckman. Highlands, 1964.
46. Guy Davenport. *Flowers and Leaves.* Photograph by Ralph Eugene Meatyard. Highlands, 1966.
47. Missing book, Merle Hoyleman. *Letters to Christopher.* Introduction by George Marion O'Donnell. Botanical pressings by A. Doyle Moore.[23] Jargon 47 was projected but never published by Jargon.

NOTE: *Letters to Christopher* was never published by Jargon because Merle Hoyleman refused to sign the contract that she insisted Williams provide her with; that said, its story—as explored in chapter 2—reveals personal conflicts that played a deeper role in stunting the book. Hoyleman self-published *Letters to Christopher* in an edition of twenty-five copies for distribution through James Lowell's Asphodel Book Shop in 1970, but she didn't view the book as official.

48. Lorine Niedecker. *Tenderness & Gristle: The Collected Poems (1936–1966).* Plant prints by A. Doyle Moore.[24] Penland, 1968.

49. Alfred Starr Hamilton. *Poems*. Introduction by Geof Hewitt. Drawings by Philip Van Aver. Photograph by Simpson Kalisher. Penland, 1970.

Prospective 50. Kenneth Patchen. But Even So.

"This is a wonder-book by the greatest exponent of literary expressionism that America has produced. The folio, again to be produced by Low's Inc., includes 44 picture/poems, a group that Patchen deems 'my most personal.'"[25] *But Even So* was published by New Directions in 1969.

50. Doris Ulmann. *The Appalachian Photographs of Doris Ulmann*. Introduction by John Jacob Nies. Preface by Jonathan Williams. Designed by Sam Maitin. Penland, 1971.

Prospective 51. Christian Morgenstern. Gallowsongs.
Translated by Jess Collins.

Williams met the artist Jess via his partner Robert Duncan in the '50s, and scheduled his translations of Morgenstern's *Galgenlieder* around the mid-'60s. The primary reason why he didn't publish it appears to have been financial: "I intend to pay off the Anderson/Sinsabaugh bill at Low's. Meaning, we can effect a beginning on the Gallowsongs. I'm determined, sir, all we have to do is survive and flourish. As I say, I am the last person not to get any help with publishing."[26] That said, one can imagine Duncan playing a role here, as he was reluctant to work with Williams again after the publication of his book *Letters: Poems 1953–1956* (Jargon 14) in 1958. As James Maynard explains, "At the height of his discontent, Duncan went so far as to confide to [Denise] Levertov a decision 'to strike Williams out of my world entirely.' . . . Although Duncan never quite cut out Williams 'entirely,' after 1960 his letters to JW became increasingly intermittent, with gaps of as many as three or four years in between the occasional short letter or Christmas greeting."[27] Jess's translation of *Gallowsongs* came out with Black Sparrow Press in 1970.

Prospective 51. Ian Hamilton Finlay. "The Selected Poems
of Ian Hamilton Finlay."

Ian Hamilton Finlay was one of Williams's primary mentors and essentially responsible for his foray into concrete and visual poetry. In Monty Diamond's documentary *Jonathan Williams: By Eye and by Ear*, Williams puts Finlay on the same level as Olson in terms of influence: "My first mentor was Charles Olson. One of his preachments was 'by ear.' . . . Ian Hamilton Finlay, my second mentor, said exactly the opposite. He said the important thing about poetry was not its sound at all but its appearance. . . . These are two diametrically opposed views; both of them are true." Williams published Finlay's *The Blue and the Brown Poems* (Jargon 68) in 1968, but his idea for a selected poems isn't referenced until the mid-'70s. It seems to be an odd choice, as Gael Turnbull had already published Finlay's *The Dancers Inherit the Party: Selected Poems* under his imprint Migrant Press in 1962. Of course, Williams's selection would've been quite different; nevertheless, a Jargon version was never published, and this is likely due to certain complications that soured their friendship in the '70s.

51. Thomas Meyer. *A Valentine for L. Z.* Highlands, 1979.
52. Peyton Houston. *Occasions in a World.* Drawings by Bob Nash. Penland, 1969.
53. Mina Loy. *The Last Lunar Baedeker.* Edited and introduced by Roger Conover. Designed by Herbert Bayer. Highlands, 1982.
54. Missing book, Mason Jordan Mason. "The Selected Poems." Introduction by Judson Crews.[28] Drawings by Jorge Fick. Jargon 54 was projected but never published.

NOTE: Williams wanted to publish this very early on, and surprisingly, he even mentions that he "might just try to dust it off and do it" during Jargon's twilight years, when his publishing activities were minimal.[29] Mason Jordan Mason was one of many pseudonymic alter egos of the poet and publisher Judson Crews, to whom Williams was introduced via Robert Creeley in the '50s.[30] But things get problematic when one discovers Crews's background for Mason: "Is he a psychotic Black poet in a hospital in India? Is he fighting for S.W.A.P.O. in the jungles of Namibia? Is he the remarkable persona of Judson Crews?"[31] Indeed, Mason was supposed to be an African revolutionary poet from Zambia, who Crews claimed was a friend.[32] While Mason was part of Crews's broader system of fantasy characters, the mythology is difficult to swallow, with Crews, a white man, writing as an African Black man in extraordinarily challenging circumstances, including imprisonment and institutionalization. In addition, Mason's publications typically came with cutouts from heterosexual porno magazines. Crews was a proponent and publisher of Henry Miller and an activist against censorship—it appears that Williams's interest in maverick and eccentric writers is the reason why he wanted to publish Mason for so long.[33] Williams claimed to have a completed manuscript for Mason's "The Selected Poems," although it isn't found in any of Jargon's archives. However, the Beinecke has a 462-page typescript of poems, with ninety-four of them marked "Jargon 54" in what appears to be Crews's handwriting. More than half of them have the word "ass" in the title, e.g., "The Ass and the Nudist Convention" and "The Ass and the Under-Developed Cock"; apparently, the book was to have a tongue-in-cheek sexual theme.

    55. James Broughton. *A Long Undressing: Collected Poems, 1949–1969*. Photograph by Imogen Cunningham. New York, 1971.

NOTE: This was initially planned as a selected poems.

    56. James Broughton. *High Kukus*. Preface by Alan Watts. Drawings by Hak Vogrin. "Rainbow edition" printed on multicolored, accordion-folded pages. New York, 1968.

    57. Joel Oppenheimer. *Just Friends / Friends and Lovers (Poems 1959–1962)*. Photograph by Bob Adelman. Highlands, 1980.

    58. Paul C. Metcalf. *Patagoni*. Iconography by Jonathan Williams. Penland, 1971.

Prospective 59. Spike Hawkins. "Spike Hawkins versus the Bat-People & Other Bloody Poems." Note by Jonathan Williams.

Williams discovered the poems of Spike Hawkins via Ian Hamilton Finlay and met him in 1966 at the Trent Bookshop in Nottingham:[34] "I found myself compère at a Friday night poetry & jazz session, which included a sloshed Spike Hawkins."[35] This book was the first of two by Hawkins that Williams slated. While he ended up not publishing either, Williams includes text from what was to be his introduction to "Spike Hawkins versus the Bat-People & Other Bloody Poems" alongside some of Hawkins's poems in a brief essay titled "We All Live in a Yellow Submaroon," which appears in *Blackbird Dust*. In the piece, Williams writes that the book was to be "a wee volume to follow upon *Spike Hawkins Poems* (Tarasque Press, Nottingham, 1966) and *The Lost Fire Brigade* (Fulcrum Press, London, 1968). Somehow it never happened. If video took away literature and its audience, it was because we were too careless, too meagre, too reluctant to get bloody thumb out, mate." However, he mentions that the poet's increasing reclusiveness was a barrier to publishing: "Mr. Hawkins still hangs on. . . . I don't see him; nobody sees him. I can get no poet to knock on his door and ask for the poems since 1968. The fragility of the whole thing is more than enough to bring tears to the eyes."[36]

59. Joel Oppenheimer. *Names & Local Habitations (Selected Earlier Poems, 1951-1972)*. Accolade by Hayden Carruth. Introduction by William Corbett. Illustrated by Philip Guston. Designed by Thomas Meyer. Winston-Salem, 1988.

NOTE: *Names & Local Habitations (Selected Earlier Poems, 1951-1972)* was initially referred to as "Collected Poems" and "Uncollected Poems" at different times. Williams also wanted to publish a sequel, "The Selected Later Poems of Joel Oppenheimer (1973-1988)," but it never received a Jargon number, nor was it published elsewhere.

60. James Broughton. *75 Life Lines*. Designed and produced at the Arion Press, San Francisco. Winston-Salem, 1988.
61. Jonathan Williams. *Lullabies Twisters Gibbers Drags*. Cover by R. B. Kitaj. Highlands, 1963.
62. Jonathan Williams. *Emblems for the Little Dells, and Nooks and Corners of Paradise*. Highlands, 1962.
63. Simon Cutts. *Seepages (Poems 1981-1987)*. Winston-Salem, 1988.

Prospective 64. Jonathan Williams. "NC 64."
"In 1964 [Lyle Bongé] and Williams drove across North Carolina with the aim of collaborating on a book inspired by their travels. The project was eventually shelved, but Williams still has a couple of the photographs Bongé made during their travels, including one that eventually made its way into the Jargon-published collection *The Photographs of Lyle Bongé*."[37]

64. Tom Patterson. *St. EOM in the Land of Pasaquan (The Life and Times of Eddie Owens Martin)*. Photography by Jonathan Williams, Roger Manley and Guy Mendes. Foreword by John Russell. Highlands, 1987.
65. Edwin Morgan. *The Siesta of the Hungarian Snake*. Designed and printed by students of A. Doyle Moore at his Finial Press in 1971.

NOTE: Curiously, there are several bibliographical checklists stating that *The Siesta of the Hungarian Snake* was "never officially published," which led me to include it in my list of missing Jargon books early on in this project; however, its publication is confirmed by James S. Jaffe, one of the few authorities regarding Jargon's bibliography.[38] While the title is printed as *The Siesta of a Hungarian Snake* on the cover, it's recorded in most checklists as *The Siesta of the Hungarian Snake*. I've maintained the latter since I'm not entirely sure which is the official title. Even more confusing, there are multiple mock-ups with differing titles (and even authors) in the archives at SUNY Buffalo. I recommend Kyle Schlesinger's musings on the subject in his essay "The Jargon Society" in *Jonathan Williams: The Lord of Orchards*.

Prospective 66. Jonathan Williams. "Slab." Photo-silkscreen cover and design by Nicholas Dean.

"Slab" was planned as a collaboration with the photographer and graphic designer Nicholas Dean and focused on the composer Carl Ruggles. Dean taught at the Penland School of Crafts in North Carolina when Williams was active there, and the two worked together on several projects.[39] Notable is Williams's 1971 edition of *Blues and Roots / Rue and Bluets: A Garland for the Appalachians*, which includes photographs by Dean.[40] According to their correspondence, Dean had sent Williams at least one proof copy of "Slab" and was in the process of printing an edition of 220 or 225 copies: "I am running 200 copies on Strathmore cover stock (white) silkscreen, with an additional 20 or 25 on very good rag paper."[41] The cover stock versions were to be folded into 11″ × 14″ envelopes. Why "Slab" never came out is unclear, especially considering that it was apparently printed, at least according to Dean's letters.

66. Jonathan Williams, editor. *Madeira & Toasts for Basil Bunting's 75th Birthday*. Designed by A. Doyle Moore. Cover portrait by R. B. Kitaj. Highlands, 1977.
67. Guy Davenport. *Do You Have a Poem Book on E. E. Cummings?* Drawings by Guy Davenport. Designed by A. Doyle Moore & R. E. Chapdu. Penland, 1969.
68. Ian Hamilton Finlay. *The Blue and the Brown Poems*. Prefaces by Michael Weaver and Jonathan Williams. Notes by Stephen Bann. Calendar design by Herbert M. Rosenthal. Published in association with the Atlantic Richfield Company and Graphic Arts Typographers, Inc. Large format 1968–69 calendar of twelve concrete poems. Aspen, 1968.

Alternate 69. Jonathan Williams. The Plastic Hydrangea People Poems. Drawings by Claes Oldenburg.

"Stay clear of the Plastic Hydrangea People. . . . Asheville's Woolworth's has the finest display of plastic hydrangeas I have seen anywhere. The electric orange ones at two ninety-eight are particularly engrossing."[42] As Jeffery Beam notes in *Blue Darter*, *The Plastic Hydrangea People Poems* was originally published as Jargon 69.[43] In our correspondence, Beam explains, "I'm sure [Williams] wanted *The Bang Book* (being his first publication . . . of his new main man, Tom) to be sixty-nine. Either he lost track of *Plastic H.* or just decided to ignore it! I suspect that he just forgot that *Plastic* had a Jargon number since I think there were only about 15 copies printed." Of course, the books of the two lovers entwined in position 69 appears to be purposeful. Williams also announced that *The Plastic Hydrangea People Poems* was going to be published by Black Sparrow Press; it never was, and it remains quite rare.[44]

69. Thomas Meyer. *The Bang Book.* Designed and illustrated by John Furnival. Highlands, 1971.
70. Richard Emil Braun. *Bad Land.* Photograph by Fredrick Sommer. Penland, 1971.
71. Ross Feld. *Plum Poems.* Drawings by Dan Rice. Accolade by Gilbert Sorrentino. New York, 1972.
72. Ronald Johnson. *The Spirit Walks, the Rocks Will Talk.* Drawings by Guy Davenport. Penland, 1969.
73. Douglas Woolf. *Spring of the Lamb.* "Broken Field Runner: A Douglas Woolf Notebook" by Paul Metcalf appended at back. Photographs by Ralph Eugene Meatyard. Highlands, 1972.
74. Jonathan Williams, editor. *Epitaphs for Lorine.* Frontispiece by A. Doyle Moore. Back cover by Ian Hamilton Finlay. Photograph by Diane Tammes. Penland, 1973.
75. Thomas A. Clark. *Some Particulars.* Photograph by Bart Parker. Highlands, 1971.
76. Ralph Eugene Meatyard. *The Family Album of Lucybelle Crater.* Texts by Jonathan Greene, Ronald Johnson, Ralph Eugene Meatyard, Guy Mendes, Thomas Meyer, and Jonathan Williams. Highlands, 1974.
77. Lyle Bongé. *The Sleep of Reason: Lyle Bongé's Ultimate Ash-Hauling Mardi Gras Photographs.* Texts by James Leo Herlihy and Jonathan Williams. Highlands, 1974.
78. Paul C. Metcalf. *The Middle Passage (A Triptych of Commodities).* Highlands, 1976.
79. Jonathan Williams and Thomas Meyer. *EPitaph.* Designed and printed by Asa Benveniste. Corn Close, 1972.
80. Jonathan Williams. *Pairidaeza: A Celebration in Lithography & Poetry for the Garden at Levens Hall, Westmoreland.* Lithographs by Ian Gardner. Dentdale, 1975.

81. Simon Cutts. *Quelques Pianos*. Accolade by Ian Gardner. Highlands, 1976.
82. Jonathan Williams. *Who Is Little Enis?* Photograph by Guy Mendes. Corn Close, 1974.
83. Thomas Meyer. *The Umbrella of Aesculapius*. Introduction by Robert Kelly. Drawings by Paul Sinodhinos. Designed by A. Doyle Moore. Highlands, 1975.

Prospective 84. Baron Corvo, Baron von Gloeden, and Baron von Plüschow. "Boys." Historic photographs. Introduction by Robert Chapman. Preface by Jonathan Williams.

"Boys" was to be a collection of nudes by the Uranian photographers Wilhelm von Gloeden and his cousin Guglielmo Plüschow, alongside the writer Frederick William Rolfe (a.k.a. Baron Corvo), who started taking photographs in the vein of Gloeden and Plüschow in the 1890s. Williams mentions wanting to speak to the photographer Clarence John Laughlin about "Baron Corvo, Baron Von Gloeden, Baron Von Plüschow" in a 1973 essay;[45] however, the only published reference I spotted for "Boys" appears in "An Attempt at a Complete List of Jargon Society Publications, including Titles in Press & Projected, as of January 1974."

84. Ronald Johnson. *Eyes & Objects (Catalogue for an Exhibition: 1970–1972)*. Foreword by John Russell. Highlands, 1976.
85. William Anthony. *Bible Stories*. Drawings and texts by William Anthony. Introduction by Gilbert Sorrentino. Highlands, 1978.
86. Thomas A. Clark. *A Still Life*. With *Six Variations on a Chrysanthemum of William Morris* by Ian Gardner. Dentdale, 1977.
87. Peter Yates. *The Garden Prospect: Selected Poems*. Introduction by Peyton Houston. Silverpoint illustrations by Susan Moore. Highlands, 1980.
88. Thomas Meyer. *Staves Calends Legends*. Emblem by John Furnival. Designed by Jonathan Greene. Highlands, 1979.
89. Lyle Bongé. *The Photographs of Lyle Bongé*. Introduction by A. D. Coleman. Afterword by Jonathan Williams. Text by Lyle Bongé. Highlands, 1982.

Prospective 90. John Kingsley Shannon, editor. "Eyes in Leaves: A Tribute to Guy Davenport."

This was initially titled "Festschrift for Guy Davenport's 50th Birthday" and scheduled in 1976 to be published for Davenport's birthday on November 23,

1977. Shannon was soliciting contributors for a deadline of December 15, 1976, and had assembled a "tentative outline," so one gets a good idea of what the book's structure would've looked like:

I. EXHIBITS — A Selection of Work by Davenport
   a. A story
   b. A selection of poems, edited by Karl Young
   c. An Essay
   d. Set of Drawings
   e. From his Letters
II. INTERVIEW, Discussion of Colloquy with Davenport
III. Reminiscences, notes on the man himself
IV. A photographic view of Lexington & Davenportiana — [Ralph Eugene] Meatyard and Son
V. Critiques — Depthy essays on Davenport's work
VI. Field Notes — Short items on specifics, by hands: two paragraphs on the metre in [Flowers & Leaves], Part IV; one paragraph on Max Ernst's Spirit and Davenport's Phantasm; 200 words on Plato, Caves & TATLIN! Specifics: tributes, observations, digs, visual gifts, limericks, and such. NO BLURBS!
VII. Checklist of Work
VIII. Editor's Afterword
IX. Notes on Contributors
X. Contents/Index

Shannon also includes the motivation for the book: "The basis of this fest is a symposium on Davenport edited by JKS and published in MARGINS, Aug. 1974. Contributors included: Stan Brakhage, Lukas Foss, Peter Jay, R. Johnson, R. Kelly, Hugh Kenner, Paul Metcalf, John Peck, Sister Bernetta Quinn, Richard Taylor, Jonathan Williams, and Karl Young."[46] Meyer speculates that Davenport may have quashed the project after learning about it. According to Jonathan Greene, a festschrift was assembled for the event, but it wasn't published by Jargon. I wasn't able to track down a copy.

90. William Anthony. *Bill Anthony's Greatest Hits*. Foreword by Robert Rosenblum. "Flapdoodle" text by Jonathan Williams. Highlands, 1988.

91. Jonathan Williams. *Elite / Elate Poems (1971–1975)*. Photographs by Guy Mendes. Highlands, 1979.

Bibliographical Checklists 119

Prospective 92. Paul Kwilecki. "Decatur County: Photographs by Paul Kwilecki."
In the mid-'70s, Williams wanted to put out a collection of Paul Kwilecki's documentary photography, which was focused exclusively on Decatur County, Georgia. An article that appeared in *SF Camerawork Quarterly* in 1987 explains, "Kwilecki was born in Bainbridge, Georgia, the county seat of Decatur County in 1928, and with the exception of five years at Emory University in Atlanta, he has not left the county for any length of time. For most of his adult life, he owned and ran a large hardware store."[47] Williams held Kwilecki's photography in the highest esteem: "I have been to Bainbridge twice in the past two years to see Paul's photographs. As a publisher and as a poet, I would venture to say he is one of the really primary figures in his craft working now in the entire nation."[48] The book was budgeted at $12,500 in 1977.[49] Aside from the assumed financial challenges he likely faced when considering the price tag, it's not entirely clear why this project was abandoned, although Meyer suggests that Kwilecki may have been "a little uneasy [about] the Jargon brand."[50] Several collections eventually came out with other publishers; arguably the most notable is *One Place: Paul Kwilecki and Four Decades of Photographs from Decatur County, Georgia*, published by The University of North Carolina Press and CDS Books of the Center for Documentary Studies in 2013.

92. Paul C. Metcalf. *BOTH*. Highlands, 1982.
93. Thomas A. Clark. *Ways through Bracken*. Kendal, Cumbria, England, 1980.

Prospective 94. Simon Cutts. Feuilles Albumesques: Selected Poems of Simon Cutts. Edited by Thomas Meyer.
"Mr. Cutts strikes me as the most ingenious and appealing of the younger English poets. This will be edited in 1981 by Tom Meyer."[51] Williams met Cutts in the mid-1960s via the latter's connection with Tarasque Press and its founder, Stuart Mills.[52] The three of them became close friends and collaborators, going on to publish each other under their respective imprints.[53] Cutts's *Pianostool Footnotes* came out as Jargon 94 instead of *Feuilles Albumesques*, which was published via Cutts's imprint Coracle Press in 1981. That said, as Cutts notes, the Coracle edition is a different project, "much more [a] slight piece of ephemera really, like a little 19thC momentum album, with a few tipped-in poems and a marker ribbon."[54]

94. Simon Cutts. *Pianostool Footnotes*. Edited by Thomas Meyer. Kendal, Cumbria, England, 1982.

95. William Innes Homer, editor. *Heart's Gate (Letters Between Marsden Hartley and Horace Traubel 1906-1915)*. Edited and introduced by William Innes Homer. Designed by A. Doyle Moore.[55] Highlands, 1982.
96. Peyton Houston. *Arguments of Idea*. Highlands, 1980.
97. John Menapace. *Letter in a Klein Bottle: Photographs by John Menapace*. Introduction by Donald B. Kuspit. Afterword by Jonathan Williams. Highlands, 1984.
98. Missing book, Richard C. (a.k.a. Richard Craven or Richard Canard). "Notches along the Bible Belt." Jargon 98 was projected but never published.

NOTE: "Notches along the Bible Belt" was to be a collaboration between Williams—who conceptualized the project, came up with the title, and was to edit and design the book—and Richard C.—who was to provide clippings and photos of odd evangelical materials found in the Bible Belt and elsewhere. As explored in chapter 3, it was never published because the manuscript was never finalized, mostly due to waning interest from Richard C. and Williams at different times.

99. Thomas Meyer. *Sappho's Raft*. Frontispiece drawing by David Hockney. Designed by Ken Carls. Highlands, 1982.
100. Lorine Niedecker. *From This Condensery: The Complete Writings of Lorine Niedecker*. Edited by Robert J. Bertholf. Highlands, 1985.
101. Ernest Matthew Mickler. *White Trash Cooking*. Photographs by Ernest Matthew Mickler. Highlands, 1986.

Prospective 102. Col. Hampton B. Coles (Ret.). "The Lyrix of Col. Hampton B. Coles (Ret.)." Introduction by Tom Patterson; drawings by James Harold Jennings.

As discussed in chapter 4, Tom Patterson planned to publish "The Lyrix of Col. Hampton B. Coles (Ret.)" at the Atlanta-based Pynyon Press, after he included a selection of Bruce Hampton's lyrics in *Red Hand Book III*. During Patterson's employment with the Jargon Society, he introduced Williams to Hampton and suggested that Jargon take on the project. Williams became a fan of Hampton and his then-band The Late Bronze Age and agreed to publish the book. On receiving the manuscript from Hampton, Williams decided he didn't like the way the lyrics looked on the page, and the manuscript was never published.

Alternate 102. Thomas Meyer and Jonathan Williams. "Acrostical Birthday Poem for Large Chorale, Sorghum & Grits." Highlands, February 8, 1989.

The short poem "Acrostical Birthday Poem for Large Chorale, Sorghum & Grits" was written as a birthday gift for DeWitt Hanes, one of Jargon's veteran patrons, and published on a single sheet of paper in two versions identified by the colors fuchsia and yellow. It's marked as Jargon 102 but doesn't appear in any of the checklists. Meyer notes, "The 1989 number 102 . . . time swallowed entirely. *At Dusk Iridescent* takes the number ten years later because at the time it was (we thought) unassigned." He also mentions that he had nothing to do with the piece, and that his name was added as a courtesy to Hanes, like signing a birthday card.

> 102. Thomas Meyer. *At Dusk Iridescent: A Gathering of Poems, 1972–1997.* Photograph by Reuben Cox. Designed by Jeff Clark. Production Supervision by Jonathan Greene. Winston-Salem, 1999.

Prospective 103. Spike Hawkins. "Poems of Spike Hawkins."

This was Williams's second attempt at a book by Spike Hawkins, which, of course, he never published. An unrelated book with a similar title, *Spike Hawkins Poems*, came out with Tarasque Press in 1966.

> 103. Jonathan Williams, editor. *DBA at 70: A Festschrift*. Photographs by Jonathan Williams. Designed by Jonathan Greene. Winston-Salem, 1989.

Prospective 104. Art Sinsabaugh. "The Photographs of Art Sinsabaugh." Introduction by David Travis. Preface by Jonathan Williams. Design by Eleanor Caponigro.

Williams met the photographer Art Sinsabaugh during his very brief, yet formative stint as a student at the Institute of Design in Chicago.[56] As he details in *Blackbird Dust*,

> I knew [Art Sinsabaugh], now and again, over 32 years. We met one evening in the spring of 1951 at Hugo Weber's studio on North Avenue, Chicago. I was nicely loaded with J. W. Dant's bourbon . . . and was ranting on about the collective deficiencies of the faculty of the Institute of Design to a select number of these worthies, lined up waiting to take abuse. A. R. Sinsabaugh, next in line, got redder and redder and was about to slug this haughty, southern, freshman apostate, when

J. Williams had the wisdom to leave the room, throw up, and pass out on a bed covered with coats.[57]

Nevertheless, they were friends off and on, and Williams published some of Sinsabaugh's photographs alongside poems by Sherwood Anderson in 1964's *Six Mid-American Chants*, which Vic Brand notes "was one of only a few publications . . . to feature Sinsabaugh's work in his life-time."[58] Williams had hoped to publish a full-length monograph on his work for "nearly forty years."[59] In the late 1980s, he tried to co-publish the book with the Art Institute of Chicago, but mentions that "negotiations . . . have been slow moving. . . . It is now believed that The Art Institute . . . did not expect to provide any major funding."[60] Additionally, Meyer relates that the book was most likely never published due to "definite cooling of the relationship and enthusiasm," and later possibly due to it being "a posthumous project that the Sinsabaugh estate shied away from."[61] Hudson Hills published *American Horizons: The Photographs of Art Sinsabaugh* in 2004.

104. Mark Steinmetz. *Tuscan Trees: Photographs*. Text by Janet Lembke. Winston-Salem, 2001.
105. Reuben Cox. *The Work of Joe Webb: Appalachian Master of Rustic Architecture*. Text by Reuben Cox. In association with the University of Georgia Press. Highlands and Athens, 2009.
106. Peyton Houston. *The Changes Orders Becomings*. Drawings by James McGarrell. Designed by William E. Loftin. Highlands, 1990.
107. Richard Emil Braun. *Last Man In*. Photograph by Ron Nameth. Highlands, 1990.
108. Williams, Jonathan. *A Hornet's Nest*. Quotes compiled by Jeffery Beam. Drawing by James McGarrell. Frontispiece by Sandra Reese. Photograph by Dobree Adams. Published in association with Green Finch Press (Green Finch Keening 71). Highlands and Chapel Hill, 2008.
109. Paul C. Metcalf. *Araminta and the Coyotes*. Cover painting by Mary T. Smith. Highlands, 1991.
110. Lou Harrison. *Joys & Perplexities: Selected Poems of Lou Harrison*. Accolade by Ned Rorem. Winston-Salem, 1992.
111. David M. Spear. *The Neugents: "Close to Home."* Afterword by Jonathan Williams. Highlands, 1993.

112. Elizabeth Matheson. *Blithe Air: Photographs from England, Wales, and Ireland*. Illuminations and pyrotechnic display by Jonathan Williams. Accolade by Thomas Meyer. Winston-Salem, 1995.
113. Jeffery Beam. *Visions of Dame Kind*. Accolade by Thomas Meyer. Designed by Jonathan Greene. Winston-Salem, 1995.
114. Phillip March Jones. *Points of Departure: Roadside Memorial Polaroids*. Foreword by Thomas Meyer. Designed by Carly Schnur. Winston-Salem, 2011.
115. Blake G. Hobby, Joseph Bathanti, and Alessandra Porco, editors. *The Anthology of Black Mountain College Poetry*. Published by The University of North Carolina Press.
116. Reuben Cox. *Corn Close: A Cottage in Dentdale*. Essays by Thomas Meyer and Anne Midgette. Preface by James S. Jaffe. Portraits by Mike Harding. Published by Green Shade (Salisbury, CT), 2015.
117. Tom Patterson. *The Tom Patterson Years: Cultural Adventures of a Fledgling Scribe*. Designed by Jonathan Greene. Published by Hiding Press (Philadelphia), 2021.

Prospective titles and authors that never received a Jargon number

This list, which is by no means comprehensive, is composed of projects that Williams mentioned wanting to work on but which didn't make it far enough in planning to receive a number. I only include potential Jargon projects, not ones from Jargon spin-off imprints such as DBA editions, Skywinding Farm, the Press of Otis the Lamed-Vovnik, and so on. Entries appear in alphabetical order by author, and I provide notes where applicable.

1. Sigmund Abeles. [Unknown project].
2. Sam Abrams. [Unknown project].
3. A. R. Ammons. [Unknown project]. "I hoped to publish [A. R. Ammons] as early as 1959."[62]
4. Sherwood Anderson. *Honeymoon Journal & Other Early Writings*. "This is a possible collaboration with the Sherwood Anderson Foundation. Anderson has always been one of the veritable freshets in our literature. Back in the 1960s we published his *Six Mid-American Chants*, with remarkable banquet-camera photographs by Art Sinsabaugh. Anything by Sherwood Anderson should interest us. As Arnold Schoenberg said: 'I should even have liked to observe how Gustav Mahler knotted his tie. . . .' We feel like that.

One thousand copies in cloth, circa $15,000.00."[63] *Honeymoon Journal* was featured in "the inaugural issue of the *Sherwood Anderson Review* in 1998."[64]

5. William Anthony. "Drawings of Truth & Beauty." Introduction by Robert Hughes. This turned into *Bill Anthony's Greatest Hits* (Jargon 90).
6. Glen Baxter. [Unknown project].
7. William Benton. *Marmalade (Drifts, Gists, Versions, Drafts & Takes from the Poems of Stéphane Mallarmé)*. Prints by James McGarrell. This was published by Elephant's Foot Press in 1993 and George Adams Gallery Press in 1997.
8. Pete Brown. *Brown's Black Greenhouse*.
9. Lucinda Bunnen and Virginia Warren Smith. *Scoring in Heaven*. Discussing the publication of a book of graveyard photos by Lucinda Bunnen and Ginny Smith, Williams recalls:

When I first looked through several thousand slides and several hundred prints spread over the refectory table here at Skywinding Farm, I asked: "Lucinda and Ginny, don't you think Scoring in Heaven is too strange even to be a Jargon Society book?" They thought that was the nicest question anyone had ever asked them. I was, of course, just kidding. I love to visit the Strange like some people love to visit the Country, as I say over and over again.[65]

Williams had planned on publishing this but pulled out once he "saw the design mock-up, its rather jokey treatment."[66] *Scoring in Heaven: Gravestones and Cemetery Art of the American Sunbelt States* was published by Aperture in 1991.

10. Basil Bunting, editor. [an anthology of poetry in English]. "Jonathan has asked us to commission Basil Bunting to edit an anthology of poetry in English. This is a project which Basil has been working on over the last two decades, and one which is as important in his work as Louis Zukofsky's *A Test of Poetry* was in his. It would be a very appropriate title in the Jargon series, and would add greatly to the understanding of poetry in English. We would like to propose to the directors of the Jargon Society that we pay Basil the sum of up to $5,000 per year, not to exceed a three-year period, as a commission for the work. While we have sought both legal and accounting advice on this, I would like the directors to express their support (or disagreement) with this project. In anticipation of this project,

the Jargon Society has already received some $3,000 in contributions from supporters of Basil. (Basil is now 80 and would use whatever income he might receive to pay for rent of an apartment.)"[67]

11. William S. Burroughs. *Naked Lunch*. While Williams bragged a bit about rejecting *Howl*, he was apparently interested in publishing *Naked Lunch* but backed off out of fear of legal troubles.[68]
12. CAConrad. "Frank." Drawings by Hak Vogrin. "New 'Frank' poems emerge regularly from the wild and woolly pen of this 29-year-old Philadelphian. We will do a large, bleeding hunk. . . . Mr. Conrad has read his Patchen and his Edson and his Spicer and reaches their zany heights easily, with as much energy as Bette Midler and Mojo Nixon between them. One thousand copies in paper will cost about $8,000.00. I hope to get Henrik Drescher to do a few drawings of Frank in action."[69] Williams was introduced to CAConrad through the poet Jim Cory. "Frank" was the last book that Williams took on for Jargon, but as Meyer writes in a personal communcation, "[Williams] simply ran out of steam when faced with raising the funds." *The Book of Frank* was published by Wave Books in 2010.
13. John Cage. [Book on Pierre Boulez]. This was from a series Williams proposed to work on with Larry Walldrich called the Music Pocket-Book Series. It wasn't specifically intended for Jargon, but Williams wasn't opposed to it: "You [Larry Walldrich] would of course be credited as editor. I, assuming I'm not publisher, will be Director of Series, or something like that."[70]
14. Catullus. Translated by Celia and Louis Zukofsky. *Gai Valeri Catulli Veronensis Liber: Catullus Poems* was published by Cape Goliard in 1975.
15. Blaise Cendrars. [Unknown project].
16. Jim Cory. [Unknown project].
17. Robert Creeley, editor. "The Black Mountain Review #8." "These were to be Jargon's next titles: . . . Black Mountain Review #8. . . . However, I am using my thirtieth birthday, March 8, 1959, to declare a moratorium on the press."[71] This was to be the last issue of the *Black Mountain Review*, but it was never published. As mentioned in chapter 1, Olson wanted Williams to become Black Mountain College's publisher, which Williams accepted, but the school closed shortly thereafter. As Williams tells Robert Dana in *Against the Grain*, "I think I'm listed as publisher of the *Black*

Mountain Review in the last issue.⁷² But that just meant that I was left with, you know, a garage full of it. Nobody wanted it."⁷³

18. Edward Dahlberg. *Alms for Oblivion*. Introduction by Allen Tate. Drawing by James McGarrell of Hart Crane "looking rather like Jack Kennedy," Stephen Crane, Marsden Hartley, Sherwood Anderson, and William Carlos Williams.⁷⁴ This was published by University of Minnesota Press in 1964 sans the intro and drawing, and with a foreword by Herbert Read. Dahlberg was one of Williams's early and principal mentors. He never received his own Jargon book, likely due to having a problem with pretty much everything that Jargon published. Nevertheless, he contributed to *14 Poets, 1 Artist* (Jargon 31) and wrote the preface to *Six Mid-American Chants*, although he disdained the outcome of the latter: "[*Six Mid-American Chants*] is utterly monstrous. Your emphasis on photography, a lazy stepmother art, is nonsensical. Both the Mid-American Chants and my 'Note' are buried now beneath snows of mere camera-work. So much money spent, and for what?—to put into the ground two doomed writers."⁷⁵ Williams edited the encomium *Edward Dahlberg: A Tribute*, which was published by David Lewis in 1970.

19. Edward Dahlberg. "Oracular Essays."

20. Fielding Dawson. "The Stories of Fielding Dawson." Dawson and Williams met at Black Mountain College, where they were fellow students under Olson's tutelage. They remained close friends and collaborators over the years, but while Dawson contributed visuals for numerous Jargon publications, he never received his own book.⁷⁶ Curiously, Williams designed and oversaw publication of two of Dawson's early books, neither of which were considered Jargons. *Elizabeth Constantine* was published through Biltmore Press in Asheville,⁷⁷ and *Krazy Kat and One More* was published via David Ruff's Print Workshop in San Francisco. Of the latter, Williams writes, "If I weren't committed to seven books previous to yours, I'd publish it in my series."⁷⁸ Black Sparrow Press published Dawson's short story collections from the '60s through the '90s.

21. Baby Dodd. "Baby Dodd's Book of Drumming." Edited by William Russell. From Williams's proposed Music Pocket-Book Series (see 13. John Cage).

22. Robert Duncan. *Derivations*. As mentioned in the entry for Jess Collins's translation of *Gallowsongs*, Duncan and Williams had a bit of a falling out after the publication of Duncan's *Letters: Poems*

1953–1956 in 1958, which is likely why Jargon never put this out. *Derivations: Selected Poems, 1950–1956* was published by Fulcrum Press in 1968.

23. Kay DuVernet. "The Color Photographs of Kay DuVernet."

    "Kay DuVernet's ancestors were Huguenots who settled around Albany, Georgia, and became nurserymen, supplying seeds and plants. It is an isolated place to work in, just as Bainbridge, Georgia, is for Paul Kwilecki, another excellent photographer out of the public eye. But Kay DuVernet also makes visits to New Orleans and that is where she began making these extraordinary images derived from the surfaces of barges, boxcars, industrialized waste, and abandoned buildings. She didn't know of Aaron Siskind when she started (some 15 years ago), but they both find themselves and other worlds in their materials. These images are in color. Sultry and complex likes rugs from Persia. And very beautiful. They will make a book that will astonish people. A thousand copies in cloth will cost circa $25,000."[79]

    Rain from Nowhere: Poems and Photographs by Kay DuVernet was independently published in 2009. Sadly, she passed away during the book's production and never got to see the edition.

24. Glen Eden. [Unknown project].
25. John Ferren. "The Notebooks of John Ferren."
26. Ian Hamilton Finlay. [A portfolio of pure concrete poems]. This likely ended up as *The Blue and the Brown Poems*, published as Jargon 68 in 1968.
27. Ian Hamilton Finlay and Dom Pierre-Sylvester Houédard, editors. [A concrete anthology]. This didn't pan out as Finlay "distanced himself" from Houédard over the latter's support for younger and emerging concrete poets during the Mimeograph Revolution. As Ross Hair writes in *Avant-Folk*, "Finlay's position on the new wave of concrete poetry is especially apparent in his critique of the Polluted Lake Series of concrete poetry booklets published by d. a. levy's Renegade Press in Cleveland. 'The important point is that everyone ought now to be able to SEE the clear divergence between concrete and NEW BANDWAGON GUTTER CONCRETE.'"[80]
28. Sandra Fisher. [Unknown project]. The painter Sandra Fisher was close with Williams and Meyer, and did several collaborations with the latter, including *Sonnets & Tableaux* (Coracle Press, 1987) and

Days on the Water and Other Pictures (Odette Gilbert Gallery, 1989), among others. Williams memorializes her in *Palpable Elysium: Portraits of Genius and Solitude.*

29. John Furnival. [Unknown projects]. In the mid-'60s, the artist Barbara Jones introduced Williams to John Furnival and recommended him as the illustrator for Williams's *The Lucidities: Sixteen in Visionary Company,* which was published by Turret Books in 1967. They collaborated on numerous projects over the years, including *Letters to the Great Dead,* which they worked on together for nearly thirty years. Furnival considered the project to be "on-going" even after Williams's death in 2008.[81] Although Furnival never had his own Jargon book, he comes very close with his design of Meyer's *The Bang Book,* which features his drawings on nearly every page. Furnival's wife, the artist Astrid Furnival, was also very close with Meyer and Williams, and while Williams never planned a Jargon project for her, she knitted a number of intricate and beautiful sweaters for the couple, including one with a portrait of Samuel Palmer on the front, which Williams can be seen wearing in several photos.
30. LaVerne George, editor. "The Notebooks of Arthur Dove."
31. Paul Goodman. "Ballads of New York."
32. Wallace Gould. [Unknown project]. In *Blackbird Dust,* Williams writes about working with Bill Harmon to track down poems by Wallace Gould. He came across a reference to Gould's poetry while reading William Carlos Williams's *Autobiography* in the late 1950s and thought he might have "a genuine snowflake on the line." In 1973 he was still waiting for "some back-water scholar [to] enlighten us with a horde of good Gould poems," which apparently never happened.[82]
33. Emmet Gowin. [Unknown project].
34. Mike Harding and Jonathan Williams. [Project related to Corn Close]. "I always hoped to unearth bits of the Corn Close book Jonathan was going to write, but haven't ever found it. I think . . . a lot of his later books remained merely castles in the air."[83] See Anne Midgette's epilogue, which follows this chapter.
35. Lou Harrison. "Carl Ruggles." Cover by Cy Twombly. From Williams's proposed Music Pocket-Book Series (see 13. John Cage).
36. Friedrich Hölderlin. [Unknown project translated by Robert Payne].
37. Homer. [Unknown project translated by Herbert Schaumann].

38. Dom Pierre-Sylvester Houédard. [Unknown project].
39. Charles Ives. "Excerpts from Essays before a Sonata." Edited by Lou Harrison. From Williams's proposed Music Pocket-Book Series (see 13. John Cage).
40. Mahalia Jackson. *Movin' On Up.* From Williams's proposed Music Pocket-Book Series (see 13. John Cage). Jackson's autobiography was published, with the same title, by Hawthorn Books in 1966.
41. R. B. Kitaj. [Unknown project].
42. R.E.F. Larsson. [Unknown project].
43. Roger Manley. "Root & Flower: The Photographs of Roger Manley." "I often say to myself, and anyone else who will listen to my wild talk, that Roger Manley is the most useful citizen of his age (roughly 40) now living on our continent: folklorist, anthropologist, photographer, curator, and barbecue connoisseur. His photographs document the Aborigines, Navajo, Gullah, and Outsider people all over. Fifteen hundred copies in cloth, circa $30,000."[84] Manley frequently collaborated with Williams and briefly worked as a consultant with the Jargon Society on the Southern Visionary Folk Art Preservation Project. Williams often talked about a book dedicated to Manley's photographs up until his passing in 2008, but it never happened, mostly due to his dwindling enthusiasm for fundraising in the '90s and aughts. In correspondence, Manley mentions that this book may still come to fruition.[85]
44. Edward Marshall. "Poems." "The Edward Marshall is a real mystery, though he'd be a perfect Jargon find since he's renown for having been neglected."[86]
45. Ann McGarrell. [Unknown project].
46. Stuart Mills. [Unknown project].
47. Charles Mingus. "Beneath the Under-dog: The Autobiography of Charles Mingus." Williams and Mingus were friends, and Williams included him on the advisory board of the Nantahala Foundation, Williams's first attempt at a non-profit and what essentially became the Jargon Society. Williams also contributed to the liner notes for the 1959 release of *Mingus Ah Um*. That Jargon was an early candidate to publish Mingus's autobiography is somewhat surprising considering how big a project it was[87] and the bidding war around it in the '60s.[88] *Beneath the Underdog: His World as Composed by Mingus* was published by Alfred A. Knopf in 1971.
48. Raymond Moore. [Unknown project].

49. Hilda Morley. [Unknown project].
50. Charles Olson. "The Maximus Poems (Expanded Edition)." "The Maximus Poems; archive of material relating to an aborted edition of The Maximus Poems, including the original annotated paste-ups, correspondence and other documents relating to an expanded edition of Olson's *The Maximus Poems*, which was ultimately abandoned."[89]
51. Charles Olson. "Maximus Poems Vol. 3."
52. Joel Oppenheimer. "The Selected Later Poems of Joel Oppenheimer." Photographs of New York City pavements by Lyle Bongé.

> STOP PRESS!!! Jargon will not be doing this edition. The word is that the Oppenheimer Family has located (in the glorious words of William Claude Dukenfield) a "Ubangi in the Fuel Supply" on the shores of beautiful Lake Erie, ready and eager to step in with resources and a firm publication date. We will believe it when we see it, etc. For Joel's sake, we hope for a book free from sloppiness and drab design. Jargon has to look under lots of rocks to find any resources at all. It seems unfortunate that the Oppenheimer Family did not make a serious effort to help us find some money, instead of being finagled by the UFS. I have a stack of letters about this book addressed to the Rauschenbergs and Twomblys and Chamberlains and Hockneys and Kitajs of this world. But they never respond. Nor did seven foundations and some 50 individuals. It is galling to be scorned as a publisher because of lack of money. An affluent (but amiable) Bostonian like David Godine will always chide us that we are simply too poor to try to publish books. Well, that's as may be. . . . I am writing this newsletter not long after a Reunion at Lake Eden in Buncombe County, NC of some 200 people who were at Black Mountain College. It was always said, then and now, that the College had no business to exist—it was too poor. One year it operated on a budget of $25,000.00! Because almost everyone there took a vow of involuntary poverty, it continued. And now consider the achievement of those poor American artists—including Joel Oppenheimer! Excuse me if I sound bilious. It's only because I am.[90]

53. Bart Parker. [Unknown project].
54. Kenneth Patchen. "Like Fun I'll Tell You."

55. Tom Patterson. "Howard Finster, Man of Visions." As discussed in chapter 4, Williams asked Patterson to work on a book about the visionary artist Howard Finster in addition to Patterson's book on St. EOM. The Finster project was largely funded by the Jargon Society, but Williams soured on it by the end of the Southern Visionary Folk Art Preservation Project. *Howard Finster, Stranger from Another World: Man of Visions Now on This Earth* was published by Abbeville Press in 1989. The story surrounding Patterson's work on it is currently being explored in Patterson's memoir quartet.
56. Kenneth Rexroth, editor. "New American Poets." This was to be "an anthology of American avant-garde poets from Lowenfels to Creeley, selected and introduced by Kenneth Rexroth."[91]
57. Bill Russell. "New Orleans Brass Bands and Bunk Johnson." From Williams proposed Music Pocket-Book Series (see 13. John Cage).
58. Erik Satie? [A play of Satie]. From Williams's proposed Music Pocket-Book Series (see 13. John Cage).
59. Erik Satie. "Selections from Writings by Erik Satie." Translated by John Cage or Robert Motherwell. From Williams's proposed Music Pocket-Book Series (see 13. John Cage).
60. Henry Holmes Smith, editor. ["A series of monographs on American photographers under the editorship of Henry Holmes Smith"].[92]
61. Keith Smith. [Unknown project].
62. Stevie Smith. "Novel on Yellow Paper."[93]
63. Jack Tworkov. "The Notebooks of Jack Tworkov."
64. [Unknown]. [Book on Thelonious Monk]. Part of Williams's proposed "Music-Pocket Series (see 13. John Cage).
65. [Unnamed anthology featuring Mina Loy, Stevie Smith, Lorine Niedecker, Louis Zukofsky, Joel Oppenheimer, Philip Whalen, Edgar Rice Burroughs, Pamela McFram Gleese, and Ruby Jewel "Big Mother" Flucker (with an introduction by George Wallace)].
66. [Unnamed collection of prose by Fielding Dawson, Russell Edson, Douglas Woolf, and Jonathan Williams].
67. Minor White, editor. "Substance & Spirit (Photographs and Articles from Aperture)."
68. Jonathan Williams. *Blues and Roots / Rue and Bluets* (paperback edition). "Jonathan Greene . . . is obtaining estimates for a Jargon Society paperback edition of my BLUES & ROOTS / RUE & BLUETS, now out of print from Grossman Publishers. This seems an ideal project for support from the North Carolina Arts Council and

several foundations within the State that have viewed us either with alarm or snoring for kalpas of eternity."[94] The paperback edition was published by Duke University Press in 1985.

69. Jonathan Williams, editor. "Chasing El Lobo (Festschrift for Douglas Woolf (1921–1992)." "Douglas Woolf died awhile back and there needs to be a *Festschrift* for this formidable and touching writer. We will call it *Chasing El Lobo*."[95]

70. Jonathan Williams. "Franklinia Alatamaha (An Herbal & Theogony)." "In 1957 Jonathan Williams was a Fellow of the Guggenheim Foundation in poetry, and much of the research done under the auspices of the grants has now been published in the book, Franklinia Alatamaha."[96]

71. Jonathan Williams. "Gists from a Presidential Report on Hardcornponeography."

72. Jonathan Williams. "Hikes up Helicon Creek (Notes toward an Autobiography)."

73. Jonathan Williams. "A History & Guide to Highlands."

74. Jonathan Williams. "Is / Or / Might Be /."

75. Jonathan Williams, editor. "An Olson Miscellanea." Featuring Curtius, WCW, Katue Kitasono, René Laubiès, and others. "Have been meaning to ask you if you'd like to write a piece on Olson, as part of the forthcoming Miscellanea? . . . Any aspect of his work wld be ok, certainly, tho I hope the emphasis to stay on Maximus. . . . Cld be a useful little book. Pocket format probably."[97]

76. Jonathan Williams. "Slow Owls."

77. Jonathan Williams. [Untitled journals project and "book on the British literary scene"]. "In October I hiked the Lake District which will be published in 1963 with sketches by Barry Hall, of London. I want to also hike the Cornish coast, the Wye Valley, Offa's Dyke in Wales, the Pennine Path, and the Highlands. These journals will be interludes in a book on the British literary scene."[98]

78. Jonathan Williams. *Walks to the Paradise Garden: A Lowdown Southern Odyssey*. Photographs by Roger Manley and Guy Mendes. As mentioned in chapter 4, this was Williams's "Big Book of Southern Folk Art," which he began in the '70s. It was scheduled as part of the Southern Visionary Folk Art Preservation Project, but Williams ultimately deemed it too expensive to publish. It was shelved for over thirty years before being edited and published by Phillip March Jones under his imprint Institute 193 in 2019.

79. Stefan Wolpe. "Essays." From Williams's proposed Music Pocket-Book Series (see 14. John Cage).
80. Caroline Vaughan. "Photographs of Caroline Vaughan."

> Duke Press published the book . . . with an introduction by the late Reynolds Price in 1996. *Borrowed Time: Photographs by Caroline Vaughan.* . . . When I asked Reynolds Price to write the introduction to my book . . . he said he would do it on one condition—that I not use Jargon Press because they had no system of distribution. I told him I'd been trying for 18 years to find a publisher and if he wanted me to change he'd have to find me one. He said Duke Press had asked him numerous times to write something for them and he refused. He said he'd give them a call and within 4 days an editor from DP called me and said they'd like to see my manuscript. They liked it and Reynolds agreed to write the introduction. That's how it happened.[99]

81. Hak Vogrin. "The Adventures of Pebble, Rock, and Stones."
82. Peter Yates. "Essays on American Music."
83. Louis Zukofsky. "55 Anew."
84. Louis Zukofsky, editor. "A New Objectivist's Anthology."
85. Louis Zukofsky. *All: The Collected Shorter Poems of Louis Zukofsky.* Charcoals by Esteban Vicente. *All: The Collected Shorter Poems of Louis Zukofsky* was published by Jonathan Cape in 1965.

Epilogue
Corn Close

BY ANNE MIDGETTE

Jargon 116, *Corn Close: A Cottage in Dentdale*, was published in 2015, seven years after Jonathan Williams's death. The title never actually appeared on any list of forthcoming Jargon books. But it did exist for years, in some form, in Williams's head.

For someone who had spent so much time documenting the place-names and found observations of his home turf in Appalachia and the rural South, it was only logical to produce a book about the other locale that captured his heart and where he spent so much of his life. Williams and Tom Meyer found Corn Close after Donald B. Anderson, for years an indefatigable Jargon patron, saw Williams's claim on a jacket bio that he spent half the year in the Yorkshire Dales, and offered to make the fiction a reality. Williams had been spending considerable time in England already. One close friend, the poet Basil Bunting, pointed him to Dentdale, saying it was the bonniest of the Dales, and Corn Close (the name means "grain field") was purchased and subsequently fixed up with Williams's vision—including hand-blocked William Morris wallpaper and hand-forged hardware for the window latches—and Anderson's money.

Williams approached the United Kingdom, and Europe, with the same blend of truffle-hound curiosity and grouchy disdain that he brought to all his Jargon endeavors, most particularly his "begging letters." Self-styled as "Lord Stodge" or "Lord Nose" in his Corn Close correspondence, he played the lord of the manor to the hilt, holding court by inviting friends—Bunting, David Hockney, R. B. Kitaj and Sandra Fisher, Lou Harrison, Simon Cutts and Erica Van Horn, John and Astrid Furnival, Mike and Pat Harding, and many others—to come and stay; patronizing those local pubs he deemed to have met his exacting culinary standards; and developing the garden and landscaping (somewhat in opposition to Anderson, who liked wide-open spaces as much as Williams liked enclosed ones). He followed his passion for walking, with a complete collection of the works of Alfred Wainwright, who documented the walks of the Dales and nearby Lake District in breathtaking detail; he amassed a library of British authors and reference works;

and he delighted in the words and names of northern England as much as he did those of the American South, collecting them in compendia such as "The Concise Dentdale Dictionary of English Place-Names," a slender but properly dust-jacketed book sent out to 175 friends as a kind of holiday card in 1987, produced by Meyer on their heavily used Apple computer, "Mangel Wurzel."

But having resources at his disposal, at least in the form of a fully funded second home, may have fulfilled Thomas Lask's long-ago prophecy that "prosperity would be the ruin" of Williams (see introduction). Age, too, may have tempered his appetite for the kind of ceaseless travel, fundraising, and struggles to publish that marked Jargon's early years. No longer quite as central a figure in the world of poetry as he had been in his prime, he was grumpy at his lack of recognition, grumpy at the English, grumpy about his health, even grumpy about his patrons—who grew a little grumpy at him, in turn. In the early 1980s, Anderson and Philip Hanes spearheaded an attempt to establish an endowment so that Jargon could operate somewhat more freely, but as Anderson drily observed at one meeting, "We had an endowment, but the officers spent it." The flood of Jargon books slowed to a trickle, and Williams's own output shifted to quote books, limericks, clerihews, and discursive, sometimes dyspeptic introductions to other people's work. The writing style of his later years is displayed in *Walks to the Paradise Garden*, with text by Williams and photographs by Roger Manley and Guy Mendes, which, as mentioned in chapter 4, sat unpublished for thirty years: the writing is as whimsical and idiosyncratic as Jonathan himself.

The Corn Close book was another project that was, as envisioned, too big to succeed. The idea was for Williams to document the people and places that defined England for him, along with the incomparable cottage he and Meyer had created. His partner for this book was Mike Harding, the British comedian, writer, folk musician, and activist, who was nationally famous at the time he moved down the road from Corn Close and became one of Williams's closest friends. For a few years, Harding, an accomplished photographer, documented many of the comings and goings at Corn Close; he still has in his personal archive a wonderful portfolio of unpublished portraits of Hockney and Harrison and others of their ilk. The Corn Close book, however, never came to fruition—a failure that can't be blamed on lack of funding but simply on the author's inability to finish it before he plunged rapidly, even prematurely, into old age, around the time he returned to North Carolina for good. The book that was ultimately published documents an absence: rather than the center of hospitality and conversation that the cottage was in its heyday, we see Reuben Cox's beautiful, evocative pictures of rooms and artifacts, the things Williams left behind in a now often-empty house.

Whether the Corn Close book would have had a place in the Jargon catalog, had Williams finished it, is forever hypothetical. But Williams gave a taste of what it might have been like in *Eight Days in Eire,* another small publication, brought out by North Carolina Wesleyan College Press, that documented a trip to Ireland Williams took with Harding in 1990. "I have allowed myself . . . to reflect . . . on my having lived in England on and off for 26 years," he wrote.

> From what follows, you may well want to ask why the hell do I stay there if I dislike it so much? Poets are touchy, ornery folks and shooting their mouths off is just part of the job. . . . Well, I stay because Tom Meyer and I have put 18 years into the restoration of a 17th century stone cottage, Corn Close, and the making of a garden in Dentdale, Cumbria, one of the most sublime landscapes under the (occasional) sun. Dentdale offers endless footpaths and walking in every direction. It offers conversation with local shepherds; Theakston's bitter beer; a chance to breathe the same Dales air that Frederick Delius once knew; a place to entertain our friends from America, from Europe, and even from England. Despite my ravings about England and the English, how could one have better friends than John Sandoe or Arthur Uphill or John and Astrid Furnival or Mike and Pat Harding? I name only a few. Anyway, five months a year is just right. By the time October ends, I have burnished and polished my Anglophobia to astonishing brightness. . . . Then, we pack up and head back to the Carolina Blue Ridge for a winter of Jesse Helms and his pals. Which, in turn, makes us happy to flee to shambolic England every middle of May, time of the bluebells, bear garlic, and thorn blossoms.[1]

Afterword
Channeling Bibliography
BY NICOLE RAZIYA FONG

The archivist takes as subject matter the omissions and absences procured by history as surplus. Focusing on the unsent letters, shared correspondence, and ephemera locating the Jargon Society's missing and unpublished books in absence, *Shy of the Squirrel's Foot* proposes a signifying structure meant to referentially contain that which history excludes. Only by outlining the means through which these omissions become permanent fixtures does the archive tangentially permit us access. Any such representation fails to be determinate, as these missing books are in constant movement within (and through) time. As spectral presences indicated in the archive as material, that we cannot track their movement doesn't mean they aren't there; as Martrich notes, perhaps the books are yet to arrive, and will arrive.

Archives are essentially mediums in search of a vessel—the active possession of their content, as well as one's ability to access the work within them, requires an acting corporality. In acting upon the archivist, the archive is both in motion and bound to the constraints of its own methodology. Whether by combing geographically distant locales, locating archives drawn from various sources, or the exertive efforts of cold-calling a previously undisclosed name retrieved in a phone book, the archivist both searches for and acts as a channel through which these books may manifest a kind of completion within their contextual disappearance. This "replacement in absence" functions as an ordinal point or cipher from which the Jargon Society's missing or otherwise absent books may be peripherally accessed, revealing the moment in which a perceptible silhouette begins to take shape as a kind of contextual locus. In delimiting the space existing on the outskirts of this central omission, the "contentless-ness" of its vanishing becomes less of a slip and more of a channel through which we begin to see the outline of certain recognizable forms; as through a curtain, what is revealed can only iterate some variation on an outline which categorically disallows complete understanding of it by way of its constitutive parts. The archive, then, functions as a kind of stand-in for the subject, as well as for the projects which were never completed.

THE CHANNELING BETWEEN *fictive* and *actual* relative to one's work within an archive is mirrored in the varied approaches taken by the Jargon authors under discussion. Artist and curator Richard Craven's / Canard's usage of the pseudonymous signature Richard C. is itself referential of a lack of—or interchangeability between—meaning and source material. The open-endedness of signifier and pseudonym beget a series of potential fabrications whereby any number of names, nouns, or adjectives might be substituted in. In tagging commonplace materials—a crushed soda can, cutouts from a mac and cheese box—with overused expressions or the pseudonymous signature "Poem by Richard C.," Craven is engaging in a kind of epigrammatic indexing. Pastiche and methods of accumulation are all relevant to the practice of mediumship, channeling, and misattribution. One thinks of the remaining verses of Sappho, Homer, Ovid—fragments of referentially indistinct works signaling toward the edges of what may or may not form a complete picture were its parts to be joined. It is likely that any such cohesion would only serve to raise additional questions about the texts situating an author within their oeuvre.

WHAT CONTROL IS EXERTED beyond that which is excluded from the reader's immediate range of reference? How can one claim authorship over the commonplace, toward that which our referential knowledge excludes, so becoming an unquestioned (or conversely, unquestionable) aspect of the disembodied "speaking" composing the tenets of our assumed language? In general usage, a series left incomplete is archived not only to preserve it, but, in a way, to function as its completion. Where the archive acts as a kind of stand-in to missing text and author, it necessarily becomes inclusive of both, acting as a substitute or third function to these missing texts. Perhaps both are simply two sides of the same coin—that which is so commonplace that it necessarily fades from appearance, and that which is so rare that its existence within the world is predicated on its disappearance.

CALLING INTO QUESTION the very nature of the archive—what is a placeholder for what?—Merle Hoyleman's "Imaginary" opens onto that which is categorically untouchable, exposing a personal mythology, subterranean dream, undisclosed memory, or sequence of correspondences to take place within the waking world. In Hoyleman's text *Letters to Christopher*, the character of Phoebe writes to a myriad of Christophers who may or may not be (inter)related—an exchange meant to serve a protective purpose. Intentionally or not, Phoebe constructs her "ideal Christopher" as stand-in to whatever role is desired by Phoebe in the moment, providing an enumeration of the ways absence itself might be switched in as a kind of compensative material.

ALL ARCHIVE FUNCTIONS are in various states of incompletion. In a case of misplaced signifiers, one meaning might be substituted for another, to no ill effect. In this sense, the archive functions as a kind of mistaken identity. Singular in its attempts at representation, any adoption of a visage is necessarily incompatible with true appearance. This transitory state or transfer between affectations is apparent in Jonathan Williams's title "Jammin' the Greek Scene," which partakes in an improvisatory method of composition. Like Bruce Hampton's indexed title "The Lyrix of Col. Hampton B. Coles (Ret.)," it invokes a kind of material transition or channeling between the immateriality of text and the physicality of sound—in transposing a poem onto an aural landscape, a previously non-existent form begins to crystalize.

RICHARD C.'S WORK in the New York Correspondence School is immediately distinguishable through the artwork's separation from objective use value or *ready-to-handedness*. This inversely mirrors Jonathan Williams's desire for "fresh lines" or distillations of meaning—a flipped or opposing image of some fundamentally shared intention or concern. Drawing on Williams's convictions about the custodial or preservational duties of the poet and publisher, capturing that which is, by its very nature, impermanent, artistic networks of human relation and care invoke an attempt to relate oneself to a process of attention. To be attentive to time is a way of being in the world, alongside others, in proximity—perhaps relating an extrasensory perception soon to be archived in memory (the "living archive"), book, or bibliography.

ARTICULATION, VIBRATION, TENOR, SILENCE—I wonder about the missing books indicated only by name in bibliography. Where have these texts relocated to? As a project that collected rarity, the Jargon Society publications aimed to preserve that which would otherwise vanish by way of exclusion or lack of attention. It seems a foregone conclusion that we are left with fragments, representations of a representation—one cannot, after all, capture a snowflake using the same method one might use to procure a less materially evasive form. With such incomplete access to the subject's "living archives," what we are able to access by way of the sources at hand necessarily excludes us from it, even as that which is omitted peripherally acts on our understanding. Can such a history (center excluded) be anything but epigrammatic, composed of excursions from the main current of thinking, the seamless and totalizing narrative of "history?"

IN PURSUING HISTORY by way of an archive, one opts to believe that human experience can be located in time at all, much less functionally reconstructed. The crumbling Parthenon of the Black Mountain College and ephemera of its networks and communities still exist and can be accessed in and by way of the archive. A monumental unbrokenness permeates history's conception of linear time as both unchangeable and constantly advancing, yet such a force necessarily exudes exceptions. As with our human and therefore necessarily imperfect grasp on time—being, by nature, a leviathan to the same degree—memory, as our "living archive," also exudes exceptions: displaced fragments constituting lost time. That which differentiates *missing* from *apparent* is subjective; it all comes down to the direction in which one is facing.

Notes

Preface

1. William Fitzgerald, *Martial: The World of the Epigram* (Chicago: University of Chicago Press, 2007), 2.
2. Fitzgerald, 1; Martial, *Epigrams, with an English Translation*, trans. Walter C. A. Ker (London: W. Heinemann, 1919), 22–23.
3. Craig Dworkin, *The Perverse Library* (York, England: Information as Material, 2010), 12–13.
4. Thomas Meyer, "Introduction: Ach, Du Liebe! Mein Herr Williams, Du Bist Buddhist!" in *The Magpie's Bagpipe: Selected Essays of Jonathan Williams*, by Jonathan Williams (San Francisco: North Point Press, 1982), xv.
5. Tom Patterson served as executive director of the Jargon Society from 1984 to 1987.
6. Guy Davenport, introduction to *An Ear in Bartram's Tree: Selected Poems 1957–1967*, by Jonathan Williams (New York: New Directions, 1972).
7. Ten Speed Press.
8. James S. Jaffe is considered by many, including Thomas Meyer, to be Jonathan Williams's bibliographer; however, Jaffe modestly notes that he views his bibliographical work related to Jargon and Williams as "a natural side-line to . . . collecting. 'Bibliographer' is a misnomer; too grand a word for what I did" (personal communication with author).
9. Richard Owens, "In Conversation with Jonathan Williams, 1 June 2007," in *Jonathan Williams: The Lord of Orchards*, ed. Jeffery Beam and Richard Owens (Westport, CT: Prospecta Press, 2017), 355. Jargon's archives aren't only scattered but also still surfacing. The Poetry Collection at SUNY Buffalo holds the largest collection of Jargon Society materials, while the Beinecke at Yale holds Williams's photographs, Meyer's papers, and the James S. Jaffe Collection of Jonathan Williams and the Jargon Society. The F. Whitney Jones Papers, which span Jones's tenure as president of the Jargon Society, are held in the Belk Library at Appalachian State University in Boone, North Carolina. Then, it's about a two-hour drive to Asheville, where the Black Mountain College Museum + Arts Center, which took over the Jargon inventory and rights in 2012, has its collections. Thorns Craven, who served as Jargon's treasurer and lawyer from the late 1970s onward, donated his collection to his alma mater Washington and Lee University in 2021. Tack on the papers of Williams's correspondents, authors, and benefactors—as well as the network, which Williams claims went all the way back to Hesiod—and things start getting very deep.
10. Williams, *Magpie's Bagpipe*, 116.
11. Donald B. Anderson was a painter, a patron of the arts, and a principal benefactor of the Jargon Society. In 1969, Anderson financed Williams and Meyer's search for

a house in the English countryside, resulting in Anderson's purchase of Corn Close, the seventeenth-century cottage that he and his family shared with Williams and Meyer. In celebration of Anderson's seventieth birthday in 1989, Williams published *DBA at 70* (Jargon 103).

12. Ken Chute, personal communication with author, May–August 2022.

13. Merle Hoyleman was born Hoylman; she added the *e* later in life.

Introduction

1. Thomas Meyer, "JW Gent & Epicurean," in Beam and Owens, *Lord of Orchards*, 251.

2. James S. Jaffe, "Jonathan Williams, Jargonaut," in Beam and Owens, *Lord of Orchards*, 295.

3. William Gaddis, *The Recognitions* (London: Penguin Classics, 1993).

4. Jacques Derrida, *Archive Fever: A Freudian Impression* (Chicago: University of Chicago Press, 1996), 9.

5. Fredson Bowers, *Principles of Bibliographical Description* (New York: Russell, 1962), 113.

6. Philip Gaskell, *A New Introduction to Bibliography* (New Castle, DE: Oak Knoll, 2009), 315.

7. Millicent Bell, *The Jargon Idea* (Providence, RI: Brown University, 1963), 4.

8. Robert Dana, *Against the Grain: Interviews with Maverick American Publishers* (Iowa City: University of Iowa Press, 1986), 215.

9. Rexroth was an early mentor of Williams, the inspiration behind Jargon 1, and one of the first writers whom Williams planned on publishing. The first volume of Rexroth's translation series was forecasted at different times as both *100 Poems from the French* and "100 Poems from the Greek & Latin." Although the series was to consist of translations from the Japanese, Greek and Latin, Chinese, and French, and would "comprise all of Kenneth Rexroth's work in this field," the other volumes were never officially scheduled (Jonathan Williams, PATCHEN REXROTH [Jargon, 1958]). Williams tells Robert Dana in his interview for *Against the Grain* that he wanted to publish Rexroth but "couldn't raise the money" (210), but this was likely part of a deeper issue. In "Issue #2 of an Occasional Jargon Newsletter," dated February 25, 1960, Williams writes, "Mr. Kenneth Rexroth and I are currently having one of those feuds which seem the order of business since some mad publicist invented a generation yclept beat. Mr. Rexroth feels I have been much too tardy in getting a book of his translation into print. And while this is true, let it be said that Mr. Rexroth is not a paragon of Eager-Author-Cooperation-With-His-Publisher. He seems to feel that JARGON has been publishing quantities of trash, by a nefarious gang of debauchers, thieves, arsonists, addicts, and Black Mountain College graduates. I hope I am not behaving simply as a Southern Gentleman in stating my anger at this baronical accusation. . . . In any event, I have returned the manuscript of 100 POEMS FROM THE GREEK & LATIN to Mr. Rexroth and I expect no further communication from him until perhaps we meet at the YMHA Poetry Center in New York when he reads there in early April."

10. Ross Hair, *Avant-Folk: Small Press Poetry Networks from 1950 to the Present* (Oxford: Oxford University Press, 2016), 134.

11. Donald B. Anderson and R. Philip Hanes (of Hanesbrand, Inc.) were businesspeople, patrons of the arts, and key members of the Jargon Society's board as its primary financial supporters. Both Hanes and Anderson met Williams "at a seminar pairing commerce and art" while Williams was a writer-in-residence at the Aspen Institute in the 1960s. Thorns Craven, "Poetry, Photography, and White Trash Cooking: Talk to the Friends of Washington and Lee University on the Occasion of Thorns Craven's 50th Reunion" (unpublished manuscript on file with author).

12. Jonathan Greene, "Jonathan Williams: Taking Delight in Two Worlds," in Beam and Owens, *Lord of Orchards*, 201.

13. Thomas Lask to Jonathan Williams, January 27, 1976, Thomas Lask Papers, 1920–1980, Kislak Center for Special Collections, Rare Books and Manuscripts University of Pennsylvania.

14. Jonathan Williams, *Further Tired Fried Homilies* (Highlands, NC: Jargon, 1959).

15. Lask to Williams, January 27, 1976.

16. F. Whitney Jones, personal communication with the author, May 2021. Jones was a core member of the Jargon Society's volunteer staff, serving as its president from 1977 until Williams's passing in 2008, although his work with Jargon dipped in the 1990s as its publishing activities began to wane.

17. Diana C. Stoll, "Jonathan Williams—More Mouth on That Man," in Beam and Owens, *Lord of Orchards*, 44–46.

18. David Ruff is often credited as the co-founder of Jargon, but I think this is a bit misleading. Ruff collaborated with Williams on what would become Jargon 1, *Garbage Litters the Iron Face of the Sun's Child*, contributing an engraving and printing it at the Print Workshop, which he ran in San Francisco; his involvement with Jargon ended there.

19. Holly Beye, 120 *Charles Street, The Village: Journals and Writings, 1949–1950* (Kindle Edition) (Huron, OH: Bottom Dog Press, 2006).

20. Neal Hutcheson, "Inclemented That Way—Jonathan Williams—Final Script—Talk about Writing: Portraits of North Carolina Writers," in Beam and Owens, *Lord of Orchards*, 410.

21. This was something Patchen apparently enjoyed doing with his younger friends, as Holly Beye also transcribed work for him.

22. When asked about the name "Jargon," Williams responds: "It was . . . Paul Ellsworth, fellow student, painter, at the Institute of Design. He was barely articulate at all. He would throw words around, and he kept talking about jargon. 'Life's jargon. Jargon.' I said, 'What do you mean?' and he'd say . . . 'I mean in my own speech. My language, as opposed to the tribe's language.' . . . And then I happened to be checking in a big dictionary, and there was the word 'jargonelle,' a kind of spring pear in France. And jargon in psychiatric jargon is the language of the infant before it learns social conventions. And, also, in French *jargon* means twittering of birds. So when you add all these things up, it seems just fine" (Dana, *Against the Grain*, 203).

23. Beye, 120 *Charles Street*.

24. Williams, *Magpie's Bagpipe*, 25.

25. *Jonathan Williams: By Eye and by Ear*, directed by Monty Diamond, 1975. YouTube video, 14:00, https://www.youtube.com/watch?v=H9mvYo3AoUo&t=55s.

26. Beye, 120 *Charles Street*.

27. *Jonathan Williams: By Eye and by Ear*.

28. Williams, *Magpie's Bagpipe*, 65.

29. Williams writes, "I always tell the gullible and the gormless that Allen [Ginsberg] offered Jargon Society a look at HOWL and NAKED LUNCH back in 1955. It is, oddly, the truth; and it figures that a budding Black Mountaineer like myself would hiply say: 'No way, José.'" Jonathan Williams, *Dear World, Forget It! Love, Mnemosyne: A Range of Letters, 1984–85: Plus a Few Elusive Items* (Roswell, NM: DBA/JCA Editions, 1985). At first glance, his mention of Black Mountain here may suggest a reactionary attitude replete with Olson's biases; however, Jargon was publishing writers against Olson's wishes from its inception, and while Williams is often affiliated with New American Poetry and the Black Mountain poets, his role as a conservator of the overlooked meant challenging what he considered to be fashionable poetic movements, e.g., the Beats, the San Francisco renaissance, the New York school, and, a bit later, L=A=N=G=U=A=G=E poetry. That said, his aversion to these groups was by no means dogmatic, and he had close friendships and correspondences with many of their practitioners (including Ginsberg). In Kyle Schlesinger's *A Poetics of the Press: Interviews with Poets, Printers, & Publishers*, Jonathan Greene says Jargon wasn't "'foolishly consistent'—we both published Robert Duncan's poems . . . and would never think not to publish him because he was associated with the San Francisco poetry scene" (Brooklyn, NY: Ugly Duckling Presse, 2021). While Williams did reject *Howl*, he and Ginsberg were close, and he included his writing in several Jargon publications, including *14 Poets / 1 Artist* (Jargon 31) and *Epitaphs for Lorine* (Jargon 74). Surprisingly, Williams was interested in publishing *Naked Lunch* but was afraid of the legal troubles it would cause. James S. Jaffe, *Jonathan Williams / The Jargon Society* (Deep River, CT: James S. Jaffe Rarebooks, 2022), x.

30. Tom Patterson, *The Tom Patterson Years: Cultural Adventures of a Fledgling Scribe* (Jargon 117) (Philadelphia: Hiding Press, 2021), 162.

31. *Black Mountain College: A Thumbnail Sketch*, directed by Monty Diamond, 1989.

32. Hutcheson, "Inclemented That Way," 384; Jeffery Beam, "The Truffle-Hound of American Poetry," *Asheville Poetry Review* 15, no. 1 (2010): 18, https://ashevillepoetry review.com/2010/issue-18/the-truffle-hound-of-american-poetry.

33. Anne Midgette, "Substantiating the Cottage," in *Corn Close: A Cottage in Dentdale* (Jargon 116), by Reuben Cox (Salisbury, CT: Green Shade / The Jargon Society, 2015), 47.

34. Greene, "Taking Delight in Two Worlds," 201.

35. Via the Print Workshop, Ruff would also print the first book in the City Lights Pocket Poet Series, *Pictures of the Gone World* by Lawrence Ferlinghetti, among other works.

36. Dana, *Against the Grain*, 205.

37. Dana, 208.

38. Jargon 1–3 and 5 are folded single-sheet objects of varying length. Jargon 4 "consisted of loose sheets in a decorated folder" (Bell, *Jargon Idea*, 3).

39. Michael Adno, "The Short & Brilliant Life of Ernest Matthew Mickler," *The Bitter Southerner*, accessed November 22, 2021, https://bittersoutherner.com/the-short-and-brilliant-life-of-ernest-matthew-mickler.

40. Kyle Schlesinger, "The Jargon Society," in Beam and Owens, *Lord of Orchards*, 302. Whitney Jones writes, "Jonathan often said that he wanted each title to be a surprise, similar to a well-wrapped gift, and one looked forward to each publication wondering not only what it would be, but also what it would look like." F. Whitney Jones, "Jonathan Williams, the Jargon Society, and Black Mountain College," *Appalachian Journal* 44/45 (2017/2018): 246–52.

41. Hair, *Avant-Folk*, 14.

42. By "foundational," I mean that most later checklists refer to Edelstein's list as the primary reference.

43. That said, Jaffe's compilation *Jonathan Williams: A Bibliographical Checklist of His Writings, 1950–1988*, and Beam's *Blue Darter* are good places to start. While the latter was never completed, Beam includes a version of it in *Lord of Orchards*.

44. Kenneth Patchen is the exception.

45. Williams and Johnson were together from 1958 to 1967. Peter O'Leary, "Am Sparked to Write Again—a Selection of Letters from Ronald Johnson to Jonathan Williams 1958 to 1979," in Beam and Owens, *Lord of Orchards*, 65–87.

46. Rae Beamish's attempts to publish *Asp of the Age* and *Letters to Christopher* under his imprint Black Faun Press were unsuccessful, as explained in chapter 2. *Asp of the Age* was published in 1967 by Ron Caplan and distributed by James Lowell's Asphodel Book Shop in Cleveland; it's a singular production.

47. Very little was known about Hoyleman's life until the 2002 publication of Lisa A. Miles's *This Fantastic Struggle: The Life and Art of Esther Phillips*, which discusses Hoyleman's close friendship with the artist Esther Phillips. Today, Hoyleman's papers are accessible thanks to the efforts of her friends Ken Chute and Mike Vargo, who saved them from destruction in 1984 and paid for their storage until Chute was finally able to find a home for them at the University of Pittsburgh in 2015.

48. Hoyleman didn't consider it to be an official publication.

49. Meyer and Williams met on September 27, 1968, at Robert Kelly's house in Annandale-on-Hudson.

50. When, exactly, is up for debate, as discussed in this chapter.

51. Ernest Matthew Mickler's *White Trash Cooking* was Jargon's only true financial success, and while it saved Jargon from going under in the mid-1980s, it caused a lot of problems for Williams and Jargon's volunteer staff, especially Thorns Craven and Whitney Jones. At first, the book's popularity had Williams looking at other projects in a similar light, including "Notches along the Bible Belt," which he thought had sales potential. But things turned messy—mostly due to burdensome negotiations with commercial publishers, copyright issues, and lawsuits—leaving Williams and company burned out and not eager to relive the experience. *White Trash Cooking* signaled a sea change for Jargon, and it was never quite the same afterward (Craven, "Poetry, Photography").

52. Jargon 102 was eventually reassigned to Thomas Meyer's *At Dusk Iridescent: A Gathering of Poems, 1972–1997*, a personal favorite of mine.

53. Beam assembled *A Hornet's Nest* specifically for the memorial service held for Williams on June 1, 2008.

Chapter One

1. During an interview in 1977, Williams mentions that he didn't write a poem until he was nineteen (Jaffe, *Jonathan Williams*, viii). In his late teens, literature was secondary to an interest in art and art history. As Ronald Johnson explains, "Consecutively, without taking a degree, [Williams] studied art history at Princeton, painting with Karl Knaths at the Phillips Memorial Gallery in Washington, etching and engraving with Stanley William Hayter at Atelier 17 in New York, and the whole range of arts at Chicago's Institute of Design." Ronald Johnson, "Jonathan (Chamberlain) Williams," *Jacket* 38 (2009), http://jacketmagazine.com/38/jwb11-johnson-ronald.shtml. At the latter, he learned about Black Mountain College from M. C. Richards, and shortly thereafter, he enrolled in a summer photography course to study with Harry Callahan and Aaron Siskind. After meeting Olson, Williams switched his focus to poetry.

2. Martin Duberman, *Black Mountain: An Exploration in Community* (Evanston, IL: Northwestern University Press, 1972), 405.

3. Dana, *Against the Grain*, 207.

4. Michael Rumaker, *Black Mountain Days* (Brooklyn, NY: Spuyten Duyvil, 2003), 355.

5. Duberman, *Black Mountain*, 376.

6. Dana, *Against the Grain*, 207.

7. Dana, 205–6.

8. Williams attended three semesters at Princeton in 1947 to 1948, and one semester at the Institute of Design in 1951.

9. Jonathan Williams, letter to the editor, *The Times* (London), January 20, 1970.

10. Duberman, *Black Mountain*, 404–5.

11. Charles Olson, "Projective Verse," in *The New American Poetry*, ed. Donald M. Allen (New York: Grove Press, 1960), 389.

12. Jonathan Williams, *Blues and Roots / Rue and Bluets: A Garland for the Southern Appalachians* (Durham, NC: Duke University Press). Williams was born in Asheville, North Carolina, and raised in Washington, DC. His family kept a summer home in Scaly Mountain, North Carolina, that his father named "Skywinding Farm," which Williams eventually inherited.

13. Hutcheson, "Inclemented That Way," 380.

14. Christer Henriksén, *A Companion to Ancient Epigram* (Hoboken, NJ: Wiley-Blackwell, 2018), 119.

15. Henriksén, *Companion to Ancient Epigram*, 4.

16. Eric Mottram, "An Introduction: Stay in Close and Use Both Hands" in *Niches Inches: New & Selected Poems, 1957–1981*, by Jonathan Williams (Corn Close, Dentdale, [England]: Jonathan Williams, 1982).

17. Jonathan Williams, *Blackbird Dust: Essays, Poems, and Photographs* (New York: Turtle Point Press, 2000), 10.

18. Williams, *Blackbird Dust*, 11. Getting the words right, or, to quote Williams quoting Jonathan Swift, "the right syllable in the proper place," is key to Williams's poetics. As a teacher, he often uses the writings of Sappho to stress this point. In an

essay titled "Colonel Colporteur's Winsome-Salami Snake Oil (JW to His Students)," he writes: "Sappho is just as interesting now as she was to the poets on her isle of Lesbos in the B.C. Greece of her day. Because she got the words right. Every generation with eyes and ears has been retranslating her fragments into the language and light of its day. Sappho is more interesting than any man or woman now living, probably, even though she is older than your 1970s Dodge Polara and never got it from the Colonel or Burger-Chef" (*Magpie's Bagpipe*, 68). Williams believed that there were "many wrong ways" to write (*Dear World, Forget It!*), an idea he seems to have picked up early on as a student at St. Albans School in Washington, D.C., where he served as editor for the *St. Albans News* under the auspices of Ferdinand E. Ruge, a teacher whom he considers having been vital to his development as a writer.

19. Olson, "Projective Verse," 387.

20. Allen, *New American Poetry*, 425.

21. Paul Christensen, *Charles Olson: Call Him Ishmael* (Austin: University of Texas, 2012), 34.

22. Gary Grieve Carlson, "At the Boundary of the Mighty World: Charles Olson and Hesiod," *Mosaic: An Interdisciplinary Critical Journal* 47, no. 4 (2014): 135–50.

23. Duberman, *Black Mountain*, 383.

24. Ross Hair, "'Hemi-demi-semi barbaric yawps': Jonathan Williams and Black Mountain," *Journal of Black Mountain College Studies* 3 (September 2012), https://www.blackmountaincollege.org/volume3/3-2-ross-hair/.

25. Duberman, *Black Mountain*, 383.

26. Rachel Blau DuPlessis, "Manhood and Its Poetic Projects: The Construction of Masculinity in the Counter-cultural Poetry of the U.S. 1950s," *Jacket* 31 (October 2006), http://jacketmagazine.com/31/duplessis-manhood.html. Apparently, suppressing poetic voices was common among some of Olson's mentors; for example, as H. D. reflects on Pound, "My poetry was not dead but it was built on or around the crater of an extinct volcano. Not *rigor mortis*. No, No! The vines grow more abundantly on those volcanic slopes. Ezra would have destroyed me and the centre they call 'Air and Crystal' of my poetry." H. D., *End to Torment: A Memoir of Ezra Pound* (New York: New Directions, 1979), 35.

27. Hair, "Hemi-demi-semi barbaric yawps."

28. Hair, *Avant-Folk*, 117.

29. Edith Sitwell, "Experiment in Poetry," in *Tradition and Experiment in Present-Day Literature* (New York: Haskell House, 1966), 84.

30. Edith Sitwell, *Taken Care of: An Autobiography* (London: A&C Black, 2011), 35.

31. Sitwell, 133.

32. Guy Davenport, introduction to *Jonathan Williams: A Bibliographical Checklist of His Writings, 1950–1988*, by James S. Jaffe (Haverford, PA: James S. Jaffe Rare Books, 1989), viii.

33. Christensen, *Charles Olson*, 185.

34. Johnson, "Jonathan (Chamberlain) Williams."

35. Allen, *New American Poetry*, 107.

36. A comprehensive list of the poems associated with "Jammin' the Greek Scene" is provided at the end of this chapter.

37. Jonathan Williams, "American Society of the Loon Poultry Division" (Asheville, NC: Jargon Society, 1969).

38. The proofs were printed in 1959, although the title page and colophon state 1956.

39. Jaffe, *Jonathan Williams*.

40. Jonathan Williams, "JARGON (in conjunction with the MACON COUNTY MESHUGGA SOUND SOCIETY) offers its Xmas Mish-Mosh Message and Winter-Solstice Jeremiad to the Citizens of Tophet, Gehenna & Beulah Land" (Jargon Society, 1957).

41. While the drawing has since been lost, brief descriptions of it are found in correspondence. In a letter to Williams dated February 18, 1956, Dawson writes: "Have spent all day on the collage & have finished it. Will send it early next week. As I look at it now I think it's fine. Very abstract, but jagged & very jumping. . . . It took me forever it seemed, to get the sense of the thing knowing nothing abt the [Greeks]" (The Jargon Society Collection, 1950–2008, The Poetry Collection of the University Libraries, University at Buffalo, The State University of New York). On March 21, 1956, Williams replies: "It's great that you made [the drawing] so well. Reproduction will be jet black on glossy orange paper, with red-type saying Jammin' the Greek Scene—which should put everybody way out of it; that is, into the book. I'm hopeful" (Fielding Dawson Papers, Archives & Special Collections, University of Connecticut).

42. Jeffery Beam, personal communication with author, June–July 2021.

43. "Poems: 1953–1955" was the original title; Williams, "JARGON."

44. Williams refers to it as his first "proper book" in *An Ear in Bartram's Tree*.

45. Jonathan Williams, *Uncle Gus Flaubert Rates the Jargon Society in One Hundred Laconic Présalé Sage Sentences* (Rare Book Collection, The University of North Carolina at Chapel Hill, 1989), 8.

46. Johnson, "Jonathan (Chamberlain) Williams."

47. Williams also contributed to the liner notes for the 1959 release of *Mingus Ah Um*.

48. Jonathan Williams, "Jammin' the Greek Scene" (unpublished proof, 1959).

49. Eric Sneathen, "Utopian Gossip: 'The Homosexual in Society' from Robert Duncan to New Narrative," *Sillages critiques* 29, no. 2 (2020), http://journals.openedition.org/sillagescritiques/10651.

50. *Oxford English Dictionary Online*, s.v. "jazz," accessed October 2021, https://www.oed.com/dictionary/jazz_n?tab=meaning_and_use#40332881.

51. Tom Vitale, "The Musical That Ushered in the Jazz Age Gets Its Own Musical," NPR, March 19, 2016, https://www.npr.org/2016/03/19/470879654/the-musical-that-ushered-in-the-jazz-age-gets-its-own-musical.

52. *Oxford English Dictionary Online*, s.v. "jazz"; this is also a definition of "jargon."

53. This is how the poem appears in *An Ear in Bartram's Tree*; the proof version is slightly different. Williams tinkered with the "Jammin'" poems at least until the publication of *An Ear in Bartram's Tree* in 1969.

54. Christensen, *Charles Olson*, 185.

55. Hair, "Hemi-demi-semi barbaric yawps."

56. Classical Youth Society Ireland, "Conversing the Classics (Series II)—Martial," YouTube, March 31, 2019, 27:36, https://www.youtube.com/watch?v=E3b5maKPjw8.

57. Beam, personal communication with author.

58. Hair, "Hemi-demi-semi barbaric yawps"; John Browning, "Interviews Jonathan Williams and Thomas Meyer," in *Gay Sunshine Interviews*, vol. 2, ed. Winston Leyland (San Francisco: Gay Sunshine Press, 1982), 282.

59. Kenneth Irby, "America's Largest Openair Museum," *Jacket* 38 (2009), http://jacketmagazine.com/38/jwb10-irby-kenneth.shtml.

60. Maria Damon, *The Dark End of the Street: Margins in American Vanguard Poetry* (Minneapolis: University of Minnesota Press, 1993), 187.

61. For example, when telling Michael Rumaker to "stop sucking the cock of your own experience," as Rumaker writes in *Black Mountain Days* (138).

62. Beam, personal communication with author.

63. Cody Carvel, "USA: Poetry Episode Denise Levertov and Charles Olson," YouTube, September 14, 2017, 29:00, https://www.youtube.com/watch?v=uYOirCmgvpg&list=PLFvKUhH5M1d7SKoeSz2ehPZACgoiIwgPJ&index=6.

64. Browning, "Interviews," 285; Tom Clark, *Charles Olson: The Allegory of a Poet's Life* (Berkeley, CA: North Atlantic Books, 2000); Hair, "Hemi-demi-semi barbaric yawps."

65. "Funerary Ode to Charles Olson" was written in the late '60s, well after the "Jammin'" poems.

66. Olson, "Projective Verse," 389.

67. Williams, "Jammin' the Greek Scene" (proof).

68. Christensen, *Charles Olson*, 175.

69. Allen, *New American Poetry*, 425.

70. Lauren Davis, "A Latin Poem So Filthy, It Wasn't Translated until the 20th Century," *Gizmodo*, June 11, 2014, https://gizmodo.com/a-latin-poem-so-filthy-it-wasnt-translated-until-the-2-1589504370.

71. Williams, "Jammin' the Greek Scene" (proof).

72. Charles Olson, "Nota" in "Jammin' the Greek Scene" (proof).

73. Christensen, *Charles Olson*, 207.

74. Duberman, *Black Mountain*, 383.

75. R. Michael Johnson, "Mediation of 'Paideuma,'" *The Overweening Generalist*, August 18, 2011, http://overweeninggeneralist.blogspot.com/2011/08/meditation-on-paideuma.html.

76. Ezra Pound complicates the word further in *Guide to Kulchur*, where he defines it similarly to Frobenius as "the tangle or complex of the inrooted ideas of any period" but uses it with shifting implications.

77. Jane Ellen Harrison, *Myths of Greece and Rome with Emphasize on Homer's Pantheon* (Prague: e-artnow, 2021).

78. Edith Fowke and Joe Glazer, *Songs of Work and Protest* (New York: Dover, 1973), 156.

79. Williams, *Blackbird Dust*, 119.

80. Fitzgerald, *Martial*, 3.

81. George MacDonald, *Lilith Annotated* (Independently published, 2021). The use of *Lilith* here nods to the influence of Robert Duncan, who was a big fan of the novel, as articulated in *The H. D. Book* and other writings.

82. The title is also a pun of the "Beat Scene," which carries certain implications about Williams's contention with the Beats. That said, he held many friendships with those affiliated with the Beats, and he was even considered by some to be peripheral to the school, with his work featured in related journals and anthologies of the day, including—somewhat ironically—the 1960 anthology *The Beat Scene*.

83. Rumaker, *Black Mountain Days*, 355.

84. Dana, *Against the Grain*, 208.

85. Dana, *Against the Grain*, 211–12.

86. In a letter to Williams from 1953, Olson writes, "i wondered how you have planned to define yourself, on such books as . . . this [Maximus] frankly, my own verse is such . . . that if you call it 'Jargon,' i shall feel uncovered" (The Jargon Society Collection, 1950–2008). He goes on to suggest that Williams use a different name for the publisher.

87. Hair, "Hemi-demi-semi barbaric yawps."

88. It's worth noting that Orpheus was murdered with "penis-shaped wand[s]" (Damon, *Dark End of the Street*, 193).

89. Williams, *Magpie's Bagpipe*, 7.

90. Duberman, *Black Mountain*, 395.

Chapter Two

1. The poet and founder of New Directions, James Laughlin, published a selection from *Letters to Christopher* in the 1937 edition of *New Directions in Prose & Poetry*. Laughlin and his mother Marjory were also financial supporters of Hoyleman.

2. Hoyleman's ashes are actually in Calvary Cemetery in Pittsburgh.

3. Williams, *Uncle Gus Flaubert*, 17.

4. In a letter to Williams, Hoyleman writes that she submitted the manuscript at 4:45 P.M. on October 4, 1960. Hoyleman to Jonathan Williams, October 8, 1960, The Jargon Society Collection, 1950–2008.

5. Hoyleman succumbed to a kidney infection at Western Pennsylvania Hospital in Pittsburgh on July 16, 1984.

6. Miles, *This Fantastic Struggle*, 354.

7. Robert J. Bertholf was the curator of the Poetry Collection at SUNY Buffalo from 1979 to 2004.

8. Jonathan Williams to James Lowell, July 21, 1984. James R. Lowell Papers, Kent State University Libraries, Special Collections & Archives.

9. Ken Chute and Mike Vargo were friends with Hoyleman and provided much-needed support to her later in life. For a time, they served as the only chroniclers of her life. Their knowledge and research related to Hoyleman were foundational to the construction of this chapter. Of particular use was a thirty-one-page timeline that Chute assembled on Hoyleman's life, "Merle Hoyleman: A Tentative Timeline" (unpublished document on file with author).

10. Mike Vargo, "Memories of Merle Hoyleman—How We Met, Made TV, and the Rest" (unpublished document, 2022).

11. Miles, *This Fantastic Struggle*, 445. With the help of the librarian Michael Dabrishus, Chute was finally able to secure a home for the papers at the University of Pittsburgh in 2015, more than thirty years after he and Vargo saved them from being destroyed.

12. There's some speculation here, as the Kansas 1905 census lists January 10 as the birth date; however, Hoyleman's grandnephew Rhese S. Hoylman III provided numerous records stating that Merle was born on January 18.

13. While Hoyleman worked for a time as a teacher, and as a writer employed by the Works Progress Administration (WPA), among other short-term jobs, she was on public assistance for most of her adult life.

14. It should be noted that Hoyleman's relationship with her brothers as presented here was assembled from various resources found in her papers, especially a document titled "Factual Outline to *Letters to Christopher*," which I talk about later in the chapter. Rhese S. Hoylman III, Hoyleman's grandnephew, contests that her characterizations of her brothers are often unfair and/or misleading.

15. Hoyleman studied English at the University of Oklahoma and gained local recognition as a poet. Consequently, her work is featured in *A Handbook of Oklahoma Writers*, edited by Mary Hays Marable and Elaine Boylan in 1939. She eventually received a bachelor's degree in education from Duquesne University in 1948 (Chute, "Merle Hoyleman," 4, 16).

16. Ken Chute, personal communication with author, May–August 2022.

17. Merle Hoyleman to George Marion O'Donnell, July 17, 1951, George Marion O'Donnell Papers, Julian Edison Department of Special Collections, Washington University Libraries.

18. Hoyleman observes that "Pennsylvania law requires a ten-day observation period to declare one insane," which was apparently overlooked in her case (Miles, *This Fantastic Struggle*, 274).

19. Hoyleman was released from Mayview State Hospital in August 1951 (Miles, 275).

20. Rachel Blau DuPlessis, *The Pink Guitar: Writing as Feminist Practice* (New York: Routledge, 1990), 38.

21. Miles, *This Fantastic Struggle*, 275.

22. Chute, personal communication with author.

23. Merle Hoyleman to George Marion O'Donnell, April 15, 1953, O'Donnell Papers.

24. Miles, *This Fantastic Struggle*, 57.

25. Hoyleman worked on several writing and research projects related to Pittsburgh, including a study of the folklore surrounding the steel industry in Pittsburgh.

26. Chute, personal communication with author.

27. Miles, *This Fantastic Struggle*, 354.

28. The poet CAConrad—one of the few contemporary advocates of Hoyleman's work—writes that Williams told them about the experience: "[Hoyleman] stood in the middle of the room screaming at apparitions that only she could see that she claimed swirled in the upper corner above the table and chair. . . . Then she calmed and said, 'Okay, I hear you, yes I hear you,' and sat at the table for the next

few hours to write down exactly what the spirits told her to write. Jonathan said she referred to these spirits as The Scum, and while she had a tumultuous relationship with these spirits, they were where her poems came from." CAConrad, "Occult Poetics & (Soma)tic Rituals," *Ignota*, October 4, 2019, https://ignota.org/blogs/news/occult-poetics-somatic-rituals.

29. Megan Shay, "Passion for Paint: The Life of Esther Phillips," *Pittsburgh History* 74, no. 3 (Fall 1991): 118.

30. Chute, personal communication with author.

31. Jonathan Williams to Jack Shoemaker, March 15, 1977, J. M. Edelstein Collection, Stuart A. Rose Manuscript, Archives, and Rare Book Library, Emory University.

32. Chute, personal communication with author.

33. Williams, *Magpie's Bagpipe*, 3.

34. Miles, *This Fantastic Struggle*, 361.

35. Williams, *Blackbird Dust*, viii. Williams's preservation efforts are further explored in chapter 4.

36. George Marion O'Donnell to Merle Hoyleman, May 18, 1960, O'Donnell Papers.

37. Merle Hoyleman to George Marion O'Donnell, September 18, 1960, O'Donnell Papers.

38. George Marion O'Donnell to Merle Hoyleman, October 6, 1960, O'Donnell Papers.

39. O'Donnell's introduction would instead appear in *Asp of the Age*.

40. Jonathan Williams, "Parson Weems & Vachel Lindsay Rent a Volkswagen and Go Looking for Lamedvovnik #37; Or, Travails in America Deserta," *Arts in Society: The Institutions of Art* 3, no. 3 (1965): 379.

41. Jargon's first publishing contracts were for its collaborations with Corinth Books. Jonathan Greene writes: "JW was not business-minded and so I think mostly never did anything with contracts. But Ted Wilentz, the literary half of Corinth Books, was more of a business person. . . . When Ted started to collaborate with Jargon . . . I imagine there were contracts written up by Ted. Which was important in probably only the one case—Olson's *Maximus*" (personal communication with author, June 2022).

42. Gordon Roysce Smith was another major advocate of Hoyleman's work. He was also well established in the book trade and worked for the American Booksellers Association from 1971 to 1984, first as educational project director and then as executive director.

43. Chute, "Merle Hoyleman," 27.

44. *Asp of the Age* is often described as having been published in 1966, which is the copyright year. The book was released on March 14, 1967 (Chute, 26).

45. ULS Archives and Special Collections, "Guide to the Merle Hoyleman Papers, 1918–1982" (collections guide, University of Pittsburgh, 2021), 19.

46. *Asp of the Age* was initially titled "Projections into the Abstract," and then "Withering Fruition" (Chute, "Merle Hoyleman," 4).

47. Chute, 4.

48. ULS Archives and Special Collections, "Guide to the Merle Hoyleman Papers," 5. A later version of this essay appeared in the 1949 winter issue of *Delta* as "A Note on Merle Hoyleman & *Letters to Christopher*" (Hoyleman, *Letters to Christopher*).

49. Rae Beamish to George Marion O'Donnell, March 17, 1941, O'Donnell Papers.

50. Twenty-six copies were supposed to be "specially bound and contain original prints by margaret cray brown, numbered and signed by the author & artist," but it's doubtful they exist (Chute, personal communication with author).

51. Ruby Mars, "8th Annual Napomo 30/30/30 ::Day 3:: Ruby Mars on Merle Hoyleman," *The Operating System & Liminal Lab*, April 3, 2019, https://medium.com/the-operating-system/8th-annual-napomo-30-30-30-day-3-ruby-mars-on-merle-hoyleman-4b62c138fa5a.

52. I imagine that for most readers this will be their first time reading one of Hoyleman's poems, since they're not exactly easily accessible. It's also important to note that this is not how the poem appears in the 1967 version of *Asp of the Age*; I use the New Directions version, as the typeface translates better to transcription than the poet's handwriting.

53. There's a line missing from the New Directions version which precedes this one: "As moist breasts lift in the contusion of white waste." It's unclear whether this omission was intentional, but judging from the line, it may have been censored.

54. "Olive yard," in *Asp of the Age* by Merle Hoyleman (Toronto: Ron Caplan, 1967).

55. "Scale knife," in Hoyleman, *Asp of the Age*.

56. Awkward to make this a fragment, but it was most likely done out of necessity due to page size.

57. George Marion O'Donnell, "The Work of Merle Hoyleman, and the 1940s," in Hoyleman, *Asp of the Age*.

58. O'Donnell, "Work of Merle Hoyleman."

59. Mars, "8th Annual Napomo."

60. Charles Olson, "Projective Verse," in Allen, *New American Poetry*, 387.

61. CAConrad, "Merle Hoyleman," *Kesey Occult Poetics Workshop* (blog), January 8, 2019. https://keseyoccultpoetics.blogspot.com/2019/01/merle-hoyleman.html.

62. James Laughlin, ed., *New Directions in Prose & Poetry* (New York: New Directions, 1937).

63. Letters featured in *New Directions in Prose & Poetry* (1937): June 6, 1933; July 6, 1933; August 7, 1933; October 4, 1933; September 1, 1934; October 28, 1934; November 3, 1934; December 7, 1934; September 15, 1936; September 20, 1936.

64. Chute, "Merle Hoyleman," 13. Bishop was apparently a fan of *Asp of the Age* but not *Letters to Christopher* (Chute, personal communication with author).

65. ULS Archives and Special Collections, "Guide to the Merle Hoyleman Papers," 21.

66. Chute, "Merle Hoyleman," 11.

67. Merle Hoyleman to Jonathan Williams, date unknown, The Jargon Society Collection, 1950–2008.

68. Merle Hoyleman to George Marion O'Donnell, December 12, 1957, O'Donnell Papers.

69. Merle Hoyleman to George Marion O'Donnell, December 4, 1955, O'Donnell Papers.

70. Vargo, "Memories of Merle Hoyleman."

71. Merle Hoyleman to Jonathan Williams, April 30, 1973, The Jargon Society Collection, 1950–2008.

72. Merle Hoyleman to Jonathan Williams, December 16, 1972, The Jargon Society Collection, 1950–2008.

73. Most of *Letters to Christopher* was written during the 1930s and '40s, but Hoyleman continued to tinker with and add new letters to the manuscript throughout her life.

74. Hoyleman, "Factual Outline"; Merle Hoyleman to Alpha Colvard, March 27, 1969 (Chute's personal archives).

75. O'Donnell, "Work of Merle Hoyleman."

76. Hoyleman includes snippets about immediate family in *Letters to Christopher*. She also addresses Mary Adelaide Strong, her maternal grandmother in "October 29, 1933," but the book's relationship to her ancestors is abstract.

77. In our correspondence, Chute points out that Hoyleman alludes to this connection several times in her "Factual Outline to *Letters to Christopher*."

78. Hoyleman, "Factual Outline."

79. Helen Vendler, *Invisible Listeners: Lyric Intimacy in Herbert, Whitman, and Ashbery* (Princeton, NJ: Princeton University Press, 2007), 1.

80. Vendler, 1.

81. Hoyleman, *Letters to Christopher* (self-published, 1970), 2–3. I've tried to maintain the shape as distinguished by the self-published version of *Letters to Christopher*.

82. Merle Hoyleman to George Marion O'Donnell, December 9, 1947, O'Donnell Papers.

83. Hoyleman, *Letters to Christopher*, 38–41.

84. Laura Hinton, "Three Conversations with Mei-mei Berssenbrugge," *Jacket* 37 (2003), http://jacketmagazine.com/27/hint-bers.html.

85. Hoyleman, *Letters to Christopher*, 1.

86. Hoyleman, "Factual Outline."

87. Hoyleman, *Letters to Christopher*, 1–2.

88. Mars, "8th Annual Napomo."

89. Hoyleman, *Letters to Christopher*, 9.

90. Hoyleman, 100.

91. Hoyleman, 10.

92. Hoyleman, 11, 95.

93. Hoyleman, 150, 152.

94. Chute reads Christopher differently: "I believe there is one Christopher (addressed or considered in many poetic ways by Merle) who Merle would like to get together with again" (personal communication with author).

95. Hoyleman, *Letters to Christopher*, 36.

96. Hoyleman, 157.

97. Mars, "8th Annual Napomo."

98. O'Donnell, "Work of Merle Hoyleman."

99. Chute, "Merle Hoyleman," 11.

100. Hoyleman, *Letters to Christopher*, 128.
101. Williams, "Parson Weems," 379.
102. O'Donnell to Hoyleman, October 6, 1960.

Chapter Three

1. Dana, *Against the Grain*, 222.
2. Thomas Meyer notes, "Finding William Blake via Patchen provided [Williams] with what would become his lifelong enthusiasm for the book as image and text intertwined." Patrick Morrissey, "An Interview with Thomas Meyer," *Chicago Review* 59, no. 3 (Summer/Autumn 2015): 122.
3. Dana, *Against the Grain*, 200.
4. As Kyle Schlesinger writes, "Williams confided in his photography professor Harry Callahan, who put him in touch with his friend, Abstract Expressionist photographer Aaron Siskind with whom he planned to co-facilitate a workshop at Black Mountain in the summer session of 1951. . . . Williams enrolled in their summer course, the climate agreed with him, and he signed on for the autumn semester when he would begin studying under Olson." "The Jargon Society," *Jacket* 38 (2009), http://jacketmagazine.com/38/jwd02-schlesinger.shtml. Williams was a notable photographer in his own right, and he published several collections, mostly consisting of (but not limited to) candid portraits of his friends and mentors, a specialty of his photography practice.
5. Dana, *Against the Grain*, 192.
6. Williams didn't know who Olson was until he went to Black Mountain in 1951. While Olson's influence on Jargon is indisputable, Patchen had more of an influence on Jargon's overall aesthetics than Olson.
7. As Vic Brand writes, "*Chants* was one of only a few publications, other than exhibition catalogs, to feature Sinsabaugh's work in his life-time." "Burr, Salvage, Yoke," *Jacket* 38 (2009), http://jacket1.writing.upenn.edu/38/jwc03-brand.shtml. A full-length collection, "The Photographs of Art Sinsabaugh," was slated as Jargon 104 but never published. Sinsabaugh's *American Horizons: The Photographs of Art Sinsabaugh* was published by Hudson Hills in 2004.
8. The New York Correspondence School was Ray Johnson's loose network of artists who sent work and collaborated via the postal service. Richard C. was one of its few foundational members.
9. Huston Paschal, *A Richard C. Chrestomathy: Fine, Medium, and Coarse Art, Or, Decorative Doodads of Cosmic Significance* (Asheville: North Carolina Museum of Art, 1987), 15. Ray Johnson committed suicide on January 13, 1995, in what many consider to be a final performance piece.
10. Julie J. Thomson, *That Was the Answer: Interviews with Ray Johnson* (Chicago: Soberscove Press, 2018), 127.
11. Thomson, 129.
12. Thomson, 26.
13. Paschal, *Richard C. Chrestomathy*, 3.
14. Michael Crane points out that mail art is more nuanced in relation to the postal service, while correspondence art is broader in scope (i.e., it can involve other forms of

correspondence). With this in mind, the terms are used interchangeably throughout the chapter. More Than Ponies, "Mail / Correspondence Art in a Time of Social Distancing," October 22, 2020, 1:29:52, https://www.youtube.com/watch?v=iyFSwm3cW1k.

15. *Richard C.* Cullowhee, NC: Department of Art, Western Carolina University, 1987. Exhibition catalog.

16. Tom Patterson, "A Polaroid Snapshot of the Artist as a Subversive, Populist Comedian," in *Richard C.*

17. Janye B. Lyons, "From: Richard Canard (Carbondale, IL)," *Mailart by Jayne*, September 11, 2020, https://mailartbyjayne.weebly.com/blog/from-richard-canard-carbondale-il9906075.

18. *Richard C.*

19. Huston Paschal, personal communication with author, 2021–23.

20. Michael Crane and Mary Stofflet, eds. *Correspondence Art: Source Book for the Network of International Postal Art Activity* (San Francisco: Contemporary Arts Press, 1984), 133.

21. Paschal, personal communication with author.

22. Paschal, *Richard C. Chrestomathy*, 8.

23. In Eric Mottram's introduction to Williams's *Niches Inches*, he quotes Williams: "I agree with one of Charles Olson's primary preachments: the poet's only obligation is to make fresh lines."

24. Crane and Stofflet, *Correspondence Art*, 84.

25. Craig J. Saper, *Networked Art* (Minneapolis: University of Minnesota Press, 2001), 31. Saper's point about the evolution of on-sending networks is bolstered by the shocking revelation—which he discusses in *Networked Art*—that the police chief investigating Johnson's suicide was inspired by "Johnson's spoofs, ruses, aliases, and other hoaxes" to "gig the *Times*," playing up certain numerical patterns, which were being used as evidence that the artist planned his death as an art project (Saper, 33).

26. Saper, 44.

27. Richard Craven, "The New York Correspondence School: Alternatives in the Making," in Crane and Stofflet, *Correspondence Art*, 118. Craven doesn't use pseudonyms for his essays or curatorial work.

28. *Richard C.*

29. Crane and Stofflet, *Correspondence Art*, 87.

30. Lucy Lippard, *Pop Art* (New York, Washington: Frederick A. Praeger Publishers, 1966), 86.

31. *Richard C.*

32. *Richard C.*

33. Richard Craven was born June 5, 1941. Southeastern Center for Contemporary Art (SECCA), *The Southeast Seven, II* (Winston-Salem, NC: Author, 1978), 100.

34. Craven received a BA from Western Carolina University in 1966 and an MA in painting from East Tennessee State University in 1973 (SECCA, 100).

35. Paschal, personal communication with author.

36. A series Richard C. started in the '60s, typically involving the rubber stamp "FAKE COLLAGE BY RAY JOHNSON."

37. Paschal, personal communication with author.

38. Craig J. Saper, "15 Minutes of Existence during a Pandemic: Pseudonyms in Mail-Art and Social Media," *Rhizomes: Cultural Studies in Emerging Knowledge* 36 (2020), http://rhizomes.net/issue36/saper/index.html.

39. As Michael Crane writes in *Correspondence Art*: "The NYCS lived until 1973. In a letter to John Willenbecher dated April 5 of that year, Johnson announced 'The New York Correspondence School died.' Johnson had killed it with a 'dead letter' to the obituary column of the *New York Times*. But it didn't really end. As Johnson points out, it had an 'instant rebirth and metamorphosis as 'Buddha University'" (87).

40. Thomas Albright, "New Art School: Correspondence and Correspondence Art," in Crane and Stofflet, *Correspondence Art*, 205. These names are associated with Dana Atchley, aside from Northwest Mounted Valise, which was Stu Horn's project.

41. Thomson, *That Was the Answer*, 108–9.

42. Bill Thelen, *Collage by Ray Johnson* (Drawing Room 1) (Raleigh, NC: Drawing Room, 2023), 1.

43. Paschal, personal communication with author.

44. Craven taught art in public schools from 1969 to 1972 (Paschal, *Richard C. Chrestomathy*, 15).

45. George Moldovan, *First Annual Alumnus Exhibition: Richard C.* (Johnson City: Department of Art, East Tennessee University, 1981).

46. Paschal, *Richard C. Chrestomathy*, 15.

47. American Institute of Graphic Arts (AIGA), *AIGA 1976 Book Show: The Catalog* (New York: Author, 1976), 188.

48. Paschal notes that Moussa M. Domit, director of the NCMA, was open to collaboration. Craven brought in Paschal to help with the organization of the show, and Elaine Sarao Beemer, art director of the NCMA, to design it (personal communication with author).

49. AIGA, *AIGA 1976 Book Show*, 188. Five dollars was less than the per-copy production cost. Today, it's quite rare and coveted by collectors. During the writing of this book, Julie J. Thomson was working on a reissue.

50. Richard Craven, ed., *Correspondence: An Exhibition of the Letters of Ray Johnson* (Raleigh, NC: North Carolina Museum of Art, 1976), https://www.rayjohnsonestate.com/publications/correspondence-an-exhibition-of-the-letters-of-ray-johnson.

51. Paschal, personal communication with author.

52. Johnson's first show was *Ray Johnson: New York Correspondence School* at the Whitney in 1970. Johnson notes: "I had no work in the exhibition at all. I was merely the vehicle" (Thomson, *That Was the Answer*, 154). Letters from Richard C. were included in the show.

53. MikeDickau "A Conversation with Ray Johnson and John Held, Jr. (December 2, 1977)," YouTube, September 16, 2010, 14:57, https://www.youtube.com/watch?v=qWUxY-NoRIM.

54. Michael Crane, "The New York Correspondence School," in Crane and Stofflet, *Correspondence Art*, 118.

55. Much can be said about this. There were artists using the mails prior to Ray Johnson, including Marcel Duchamp and Bern Porter. Johnson's particular aesthetic

and the time and effort he put into the medium are usually mentioned in connection with his crediting as its founder.

56. Thomson, *That Was the Answer*, 85.

57. The only checklist related to Jargon postcards appears in *Jargon at Forty*, which includes twenty-three postcards published between 1976 and 1991; the list isn't comprehensive.

58. A reminder of the Jargon catalog's non-ordinal ordinality.

59. Williams was at the Aspen Institute in the summer of 1962 as a writer in residence and in 1967 as a scholar residence, and was a guest instructor at Maryland Institute College of Art in Baltimore during 1968–69. Williams's time at Penland School of Crafts in Penland, North Carolina, during the '60s and '70s figures prominently in Jargon's history. He viewed the school as a kind of heir to Black Mountain College — "I would say [Penland School of Crafts'] vital community begins to replace much that Black Mountain College stood for in its last phase" (Williams, *Magpie's Bagpipe*, 177) — and was attempting to associate the Nantahala Foundation, his first attempt at forming a non-profit which eventually became the Jargon Society, with the Penland School. He published nine Jargon books at Penland: Lorine Niedecker's *Tenderness & Gristle: The Collected Poems (1936-1966)* (Jargon 48); Alfred Starr Hamilton's *Poems* (Jargon 49); *The Appalachian Photographs of Doris Ulmann* (Jargon 50); Peyton Houston's *Occasions in a World* (Jargon 52); Paul Metcalf's *Patagoni* (Jargon 58); Guy Davenport's *Do You Have a Poem Book on E. E. Cummings?* (Jargon 67); Richard Emil Braun's *Bad Land* (Jargon 70); Ronald Johnson's *The Spirit Walks, the Rocks Will Talk* (Jargon 72); and *Epitaphs for Lorine* (Jargon 74).

60. Paschal, personal communication with author.

61. Richard C., personal communication with author.

62. Richard C. to Jonathan Williams, January 26, 1971, The Jargon Society Collection, 1950–2008.

63. Williams, *Blackbird Dust*, 131.

64. Dana, *Against the Grain*, 223.

65. "Notches" wasn't the only project related to religious spoofing that Williams was pursuing at the time. William Anthony's *Bible Stories* (Jargon 85), a selection of Anthony's purposely crude drawings of stories from the Old Testament, was published in 1978. Williams also published *Bill Anthony's Greatest Hits* (Jargon 90) in 1988. Tragically, Anthony passed away on December 24, 2022, after succumbing to injuries sustained during a fire at Westbeth Artist Housing. The artist was eighty-eight.

66. Jonathan Williams, "An Attempt at a Complete List of Jargon Society Publications, including Titles in Press & Projected, as of January, 1974" (The Jargon Society, 1974) (newsletter on file with author). Jargon published all but the last two.

67. As Richard C. explains about the alternate title: "I would, upon occasion, use the term 'Bible Belch' to describe items from the collection of oddities, cliches, toys, etc. that I had found or purchased in Nawf Karolinah Religious Book Stores" (personal communication with author).

68. Jonathan Williams, "The Jargon Society: Custodian of Snowflakes" (The Jargon Society, early 1980s).

69. Paschal, personal communication with author.

70. Jonathan Williams, "The Jargon Society, Inc.: Notes for the Annual Meeting" (The Jargon Society, April 20, 1977).

71. Jonathan Williams, "The Jargon Society, Inc.: ANYTHING NOT WORTH DOING IS NOT WORTH DOING WELL" (The Jargon Society, May 2, 1977).

72. Paschal, *Richard C. Chrestomathy*, 15. Richard C. was a recipient during the program's second year. Also among the "Seven" that year was the North Carolinian photographer Elizabeth Matheson, whose *Blithe Air: Photographs of England, Wales, and Ireland* Williams published as Jargon 112 in 1995.

73. SECCA, *Southeast Seven, II*, 100. Richard C.'s "cross series" seems to be one of his more straightforward pop art projects, for example, as reflected in sculptures by Robert Rauschenberg (e.g., *Coca-Cola Plan*) and H. C. Westermann (e.g., *White for Purity*) (Lippard, *Pop Art*, 22–23).

74. Paschal, personal communication with author.

75. Tom Patterson, personal communication with author.

76. Patterson, personal communication with author.

77. Paschal, personal communication with author. Tom Patterson confirms this: "Richard is a prolific artist but one of the most humble, self-effacing people I've ever encountered, and I don't think he believed his work merited a book, so he never produced one" (personal communication with author).

78. Correspondence shows that he actually did ask Thorns Craven, Jargon's lawyer, about this issue.

79. Paschal, personal communication with author.

80. Patterson, personal communication with author.

81. *St. EOM in the Land of Pasaquan (The Life and Times of Eddie Owens Martin)* (Jargon 64) is discussed in the next chapter.

82. Jargon didn't publish either of these books. Williams's "folk art book"—*Walks to the Paradise Garden: A Lowdown Southern Odyssey*—is discussed in the next chapter.

83. Thomas Meyer, "Jargon Society Executive Committee Meeting January 1988—The Minutes as Submitted by Thomas Meyer," F. Whitney Jones Papers, courtesy of Special Collections, Appalachian State University.

84. Thomas Meyer, "Jargon Society Executive Committee Meeting Autumn 1988" (unpublished document from the personal archives of Donald B. Anderson, courtesy of Anne Midgette).

85. Williams, *Uncle Gus Flaubert*, 30.

86. Roger Manley is a photographer, folklorist, and the former director of the Gregg Museum of Art & Design at North Carolina State University. As seen in chapter 4, he frequently collaborated with Williams and for a time worked with Jargon as a consultant. Jargon also launched plans for a book called "Root & Flower: The Photographs of Roger Manley," but it never made it far enough in development to receive a Jargon number.

87. Ted Potter to F. Whitney Jones, June 16, 1988, Jones Papers.

88. Richard C. to F. Whitney Jones, July 31, 1988, Jones Papers.

89. Lynne Billings, "Eating by Scriptures Cited as Cancer Cure," *Asheville Times*, October 27, 1987.

90. Richard C. also mentions that Williams "may have written one or two (poems?) in reference to certain prospective pages of 'bible belt' notions chosen for the

so-called 'book'" (personal communication with author). Unfortunately, the poems appear to be lost.

91. Of which I'm honored to be the recipient.

92. Jonathan Williams, "The Latest Lamentations of Jeremiah Baby, Jargon's Most Sage and Most Senior Mascot, as We Prepare to Take the Show on the Campaign Trail" (The Jargon Society, 1992).

93. In the early 1990s, Williams launched plans for *The Photographs of Caroline Vaughan*, but it never received a Jargon number. The book was published by Duke University Press in 1996.

94. Thomas Meyer, who is from Seattle, is the only one mentioned here who isn't from North Carolina. Of course, he and Williams lived together at Skywinding Farm in Scaly Mountain, North Carolina, for much of their relationship.

95. Leverett T. Smith, "Twenty-Seven Batting-Practice Pitches for the John Kruk of American Letters: An Interview with Jonathan Williams," *North Carolina Literary Review*, 1995, 98–111.

Chapter Four

1. Although there were some that come very close, such as Whitney Jones and Thorns Craven.

2. There are more than a few projects that encountered a similar fate, as explored in the next chapter.

3. The Late Bronze Age was Hampton's band from 1980 to 1987, and consisted (for the most part) of Hampton with multi-instrumentalists Billy McPherson (a.k.a. Ben "Pops" Thornton), Ricky Keller (a.k.a. Lincoln Metcalf), and Jerry Fields (a.k.a. Bubba Phreon).

4. Andy Martrich, "Navigating Distance in Locality: An Interview with Tom Patterson, featuring photographs by Jonathan Williams," *Jacket2*, June 17, 2020, https://jacket2.org/interviews/navigating-distance-locality.

5. In collaboration with Whitney Jones, who was one of Patterson's professors at the time. Jones mentions that organizing the Black Mountain College Festival and later a Jargon festival at St. Andrews was "a dry run for [Patterson's] and my later roles at Jargon." Andy Martrich, "In Jargon's Penumbra: An Interview with F. Whitney Jones, President of the Jargon Society," *Chicago Review* 66, nos. 3–4 and 67, no. 1 (2023): 137.

6. While *Le Palais Idéal* and *Watts Towers* have been preserved, *In-Curiosity House*, by Stephen Sykes (1894–1964), was destroyed after his passing. Sadly, the details are unclear. Vance Lauderdale writes, "The house remained a picturesque ruin for some years. . . . It blew down one day in a storm, somebody said. Others told me it burned. Since Highway 45 is now a wide double-lane highway linking Aberdeen to points north and south, it's almost certain that In-Curiosity would have been demolished to make way for the new road." Vance Lauderdale, "Very Curious," *Memphis Magazine*, March 4, 2011, https://memphismagazine.com/ask-vance/very-curious/.

7. Mitchell Feldman, "Bruce Hampton," *Art Papers*, May/June 1983, 18.

8. Jerry Grillo, *The Music and Mythocracy of Col. Bruce Hampton: A Basically True Biography* (Athens: University of Georgia Press, 2021), 81.

9. Patterson, *Tom Patterson Years*, 21. Patterson was a staff writer for *Brown's Guide to Georgia* from 1978 to 1982.

10. Tom Patterson, "Way Out There: Inside the Jargon Society" (unpublished manuscript), 10.

11. John Russell, "Jean Dubuffet, Painter and Sculptor, Is Dead," *New York Times*, May 15, 1985, https://www.nytimes.com/1985/05/15/arts/jean-dubuffet-painter-and-sculptor-is-dead.html.

12. Julian Stern, "The Vernacular of Tom Patterson," *Brut Force*, April 23, 2015.

13. Tom Patterson, *Reclamation and Transformation: Three Self Taught Chicago Artists* (Chicago: Terra Museum of American Art, 1994), 12.

14. Nowherefast2009, "Journeys into the Outside with Jarvis Cocker (ep#3)," YouTube, September 30, 2016, 51:05, https://www.youtube.com/watch?v=oooL9vfCM6U.

15. Jonathan Williams, "The Proposal: A Wild Book of Southern (Folk) Art," January 11, 1984, Jones Papers.

16. Williams and Thomas Meyer shared an annual salary of $20,000. Patterson's salary was initially $10,000 and then was increased to $15,000 at the annual Jargon board meeting in 1986 (Patterson, personal communication with author).

17. Patterson, *Tom Patterson Years*, 105.

18. St. EOM proposed the book collaboration to Patterson three days after EOM's guest appearance with Hampton and The Late Bronze Age (Patterson, personal communication with author).

19. Patterson, *Tom Patterson Years*, 131. The title *The Tom Patterson Years* was coined by Bruce Hampton.

20. Patterson, 135.

21. The show was filmed by cinematographer William Brown.

22. The interview was also published in volume 2 of Pynyon Press's *Red Hand Book* series.

23. Patterson, *Tom Patterson Years*, 66

24. Patterson mentions in personal communication that taking on the position at Jargon in 1984 is what halted his efforts to publish Hampton's lyrics through Pynyon Press.

25. Patterson only had two visual pieces by Hampton, which were of the same drawing that appears in the interior jacket of the Hampton Grease Band's *Music to Eat*. Patterson mentions that Williams probably wanted to use Jennings's drawings instead of Hampton's because "they were more interesting" (personal communication with author).

26. *Art World* was destroyed, and the site cleared, after Jennings's death in 1999.

27. That said, Jennings was commissioned by the Jargon Society to create the sign for its offices in Winston-Salem, as seen in the photo by Roger Manley.

28. Patterson, *Tom Patterson Years*, 168.

29. Patterson, 161.

30. Williams, *Blackbird Dust*, viii.

31. Interestingly, Richard Craven (a.k.a. Richard C.) was in the process of curating a similar exhibition, *Contemporary Southeastern Folk Art*, for SECCA, which appeared in

1986. As Patterson writes in his memoir quartet, "Even though we'd inadvertently stolen [Craven's] curatorial thunder, he seemed to possess boundless, selfless enthusiasm for our project. He spent hours with us . . . helping us to position and light art of all shapes and sizes" ("Way Out There," 54).

32. Jonathan Williams, "Jargon Society, at It Again, and Still Crazy after All These Years . . ." (The Jargon Society, June 21, 1984).

33. Patterson, "Way Out There," 22.

34. Roger Manley and Tom Patterson, *Southern Visionary Folk Artists* (Winston-Salem, NC: Jargon Society, 1984).

35. Much can be said about this. Both Williams and Patterson were aware of the negative effects of attention, including price gouging, vandalism, theft, and exploitation. Of course, this was an ongoing problem well before the Southern Visionary Folk Art Preservation Project.

36. The publication never received a Jargon number and therefore doesn't appear in Jargon's book series. While it was published in 1984, the exhibition took place in 1985.

37. Manley retired from the post in 2023.

38. Photography books that Jargon published after 1987: David M. Spear's *The Neugents: "Close to Home"* (Jargon 111) in 1993; Elizabeth Matheson's *Blithe Air: Photographs from England, Wales, and Ireland* (Jargon 112) in 1995; Mark Steinmetz's *Tuscan Trees: Photographs* (Jargon 104) in 2001; Reuben Cox's *The World of Joe Webb: Appalachian Master of Rustic Architecture* (Jargon 105) in 2009; Phillip March Jones's *Points of Departure: Roadside Memorial Polaroids* (Jargon 114) in 2011; and Reuben Cox's *Corn Close: A Cottage in Dentdale* (Jargon 116) in 2015.

39. For further information on the complicated story surrounding Patterson's work on *Howard Finster, Stranger from Another World: Man of Visions*, I recommend the final two books of his memoir quartet, *The Tom Patterson Years* and "Way Out There." At the time of this writing, the latter is scheduled to be published by Spuyten Duyvil.

40. Williams's frustration was either short-lived or not serious enough to prevent him from contributing to *Howard Finster, Stranger from Another World*, and profiling Finster in several of his books, including *Walks to the Paradise Garden: A Lowdown Southern Odyssey*, whose title references a section from the Frederick Delius opera *A Village Romeo and Juliet*, but also nods to Finster's visionary vernacular environment also called *Paradise Garden*.

41. With Michael Stipe, Finster also co-designed the cover for R.E.M.'s *Reckoning* in 1983.

42. It should be noted that while Patterson was no longer employed by Jargon, he continued to collaborate with Williams and remained close with both him and Meyer.

43. Meyer, "Jargon Society Executive Committee Meeting January 1988," Jones Papers.

44. Jargon 102 would eventually be reassigned to Meyer's *At Dusk Iridescent*, published in 1999. Curiously, 102 was also assigned to the broadside *Acrostical Birthday Poem for Large Chorale, Sorghum &Grits*, which was published in 1989. It seems that Williams forgot about it, as it doesn't appear in *Jargon at Forty*, published just two years later.

45. Thomas Meyer, "Minutes of the Jargon Society board meeting, March 5, 1987" (unpublished document from the personal archives of Donald B. Anderson, courtesy of Anne Midgette).

46. "Bubba Fieldhand," one of Williams's nicknames for Patterson, is a pun on "Bubba Phreon," Hampton's name for Jerry Fields, drummer for the Hampton Grease Band and The Late Bronze Age.

47. Patterson clarifies this reference: "One of Dilmus Hall's pieces in the 'Southern Visionary Folk Artists' exhibition was a slapdash miniature model of an outhouse painted black with 'TIOLET' crudely painted on the door in bright red. The door was ajar and standing alongside it was a small figure made of modeling clay with fake-pearl eyes, also painted black and red (the University of Georgia Bulldogs' official colors). Jonathan was amused to imagine a (non-existent) small press named with Hall's misspelling of 'Toilet'" (personal communication with author).

48. Jonathan Williams to Tom Patterson, July 15, 1987, J.M. Edelstein Collection.

49. Williams also published *Joys & Perplexities: Selected Poems of Lou Harrison* (Jargon 110) in 1992.

50. Smith, "Twenty-Seven Batting-Practice Pitches."

51. Patterson, "Way Out There," 58.

52. Feldman, "Bruce Hampton," 19.

53. In his commonplace book *Quote, Unquote* (Berkeley, CA: Ten Speed Press, 1989), Williams includes a line from Hampton: "I hated music and I still do. What I love is sound" (60).

54. Grillo, *Music and Mythocracy*, 25.

55. Aquarium Rescue Unit was Hampton's band from 1988 until he left in 1993.

56. Dean Budnick, "The Space between the Notes: Oteil Burbridge on 'Comes a Time,' Dead & Company and Col. Bruce's Clairvoyance," *Relix*, September 3, 2021. https://relix.com/articles/detail/the-space-between-the-notes-oteil-burbridge-on-comes-a-time-dead-company-and-col-bruces-clairvoyance/.

57. That's not to deride the music, which was almost always technically impressive. One of Hampton's principal talents was his ability to gather very talented musicians into his bands.

58. It's important to note that Zambi was based on Hampton's friend Joe Zambie. Jerry Grillo writes about Zambi at length in *The Music and Mythocracy of Col. Bruce Hampton*.

59. *Basically Frightened: The Musical Madness of Colonel Bruce Hampton*, directed by Michael Koepenick and Tom Lawson, 2012.

60. Grillo, *Music and Mythocracy*, 99.

61. Feldman, "Bruce Hampton," 19.

62. Joseph Neff, "Graded on a Curve: Hampton Grease Band, *Music to Eat*," *Vinyl District*, February 16, 2014, https://www.thevinyldistrict.com/storefront/2014/02/graded-curve-hampton-grease-band-music-eat/.

63. Kenneth Rexroth, *American Poetry in the Twentieth Century* (New York: Herder and Herder, 1971), 59.

64. *One Ruined Life of a Bronze Tourist* was released by Terminus Records in 1978.

65. Grillo, *Music and Mythocracy*, 78.

66. Grillo, 95.

67. This comment isn't meant to be misleading regarding Robert Palmer's support for Bruce Hampton's work. He was a big fan and advocate of The Late Bronze Age, writing positive reviews of both their albums for the *New York Times*. He also praised Hampton's lyrics, in his review of *Isles of Langerhan*, for instance. That said, his concluding statement in his review of *Outside Looking Out* affirms the established division between rock/pop lyrics and poetry, and echoes Williams's reasoning when he decided not to publish "Lyrix."

68. Feldman, "Bruce Hampton," 18.

69. Tragically, Hampton suffered a heart attack on stage during Hampton 70.

70. All of the lyrics presented here follow the same formatting as in *Red Hand Book III* and are reproduced with permission of the publisher.

71. Feldman, "Bruce Hampton," 19.

72. Grillo, *Music and Mythocracy*, 84.

73. Grillo, 84.

74. Tan Lin, *Seven Controlled Vocabularies and Obituary 2004. The Joy of Cooking* (Middletown, CT: Wesleyan University Press, 2010), 40.

75. Katherine Elaine Sanders, "Tan Lin," *BOMB Magazine*, May 29, 2010, https://bombmagazine.org/articles/tan-lin/. Emphasis in original.

76. Sanders, "Tan Lin."

77. *Basically Frightened*.

78. *Basically Frightened*. In Hamptonian fashion, he follows up the line by saying, "or do something completely familiar."

79. Jerry Grillo, personal communication with author, April 2022.

80. Grillo, *Music and Mythocracy*, 54.

81. "Is one writing or reading? It's kind of hard to tell"—Tan Lin, *Purple/Pink Appendix* (Philadelphia: Edit Publications, 2010).

82. Williams and Hampton were huge sports fans. They met when Tom Patterson invited them to watch Superbowl XV at his house.

83. Billy Bob Thornton, *Sling Blade* (script), *Daily Script*, https://www.dailyscript.com/scripts/sling_blade.html.

84. Grillo, *Music and Mythocracy*, 91.

85. Martrich, "In Jargon's Penumbra," 142.

Chapter Five

1. "The bibliographic checklist . . . is built from the following publications: J. M. Edelstein's *A Jargon Society Checklist* (Books & Company 1979); Additions by Michael Basinski in *Jargon at Forty: 1951–1991* (The Poetry / Rare Books Collection, SUNY at Buffalo 1991); Additions by Richard Owens and Jeffery Beam in *Jonathan Williams: The Lord of Orchards* (Westport: Prospecta Press, 2017); Later additions and edits by Carissa Pfeiffer, Black Mountain College Museum + Arts Center." "The Jargon Society," Black Mountain Museum + Art Center, accessed February 20, 2020, https://www.blackmountaincollege.org/the-jargon-society/.

2. *Four Stoppages / A Configuration*.

3. Charles Olson's *The Maximus Poems* / 1–10.

4. Jonathan Williams to Fielding Dawson, April 5, 1953, Fielding Dawson Papers, Archives & Special Collections, University of Connecticut.

5. Jonathan Williams, "JARGON (in conjunction with)."

6. Williams, "JARGON (in conjunction with)."

7. Jonathan Williams, "Issue #2 of An Occasional Jargon Newsletter" (The Jargon Society, February 25, 1960).

8. Williams, "JARGON (in conjunction with)."

9. BMCM+AC, "Jonathan Williams Oral History," Vimeo, April 12, 2021, https://vimeo.com/539322342.

10. The recording is available at PennSound.

11. "Charles Olson," PennSound, accessed September 10, 2021, https://writing.upenn.edu/pennsound/x/Olson.php.

12. "Charles Olson—Charles Olson Reads from *Maximus*, Poems IV, V, VI," Discogs, 1975, https://www.discogs.com/master/2032663-Charles-Olson-Charles-Olson-Reads-from-Maximus-Poems-IV-V-VI.

13. As Ross Hair writes in *Avant-Folk*: "It seems fitting that Migrant's first book, Robert Creeley's *The Whip* (1957), was co-published by three small presses: Migrant, in the United Kingdom, Jargon in the United States, and Contact Press in Canada" (17). Migrant Press was founded by Gael Turnbull in 1957. Contact Press was established by Louis Dudek, Raymond Souster, and Irving Layton as a "poets' co-operative" in 1952 ("Contact Press," The Canadian Encyclopedia, accessed August 14, 2023, https://www.thecanadianencyclopedia.ca/en/article/contact-press).

14. Jonathan Williams, *A Palpable Elysium: Portraits of Genius and Solitude* (Boston: David R. Godine, 2002), 62.

15. Thomas Meyer, personal communication with author.

16. Williams, "Issue #2."

17. Bern Porter had been working on Bob Brown's selected poems since "roughly 1949." Bern Porter to Jonathan Williams, March 19, 1960, Jargon Society Collection. Porter's manuscript also featured introductions from Kay Boyle, Gertrude Stein, Walter Lowenfels, and Carl Sandburg. Bern Porter to Jonathan Williams (postcard), March 22, 1960. Jargon Society Collection. Bern Porter Books was one of the many imprints Williams was selling out of his car in the '50s and '60s (Williams, *Magpie's Bagpipe*, 26).

18. Jonathan Williams to Bob Brown, April 7, 1958, Jargon Society Collection. It is a bit surprising that Williams wrote this in 1958, as Porter had made the proposal in 1955. Bern Porter to Jonathan Williams, September 28, 1955, Jargon Society Collection.

19. Bob Brown to Jonathan Williams, April 26, 1958, Jargon Society Collection.

20. Bob Brown to Jonathan Williams, April 27, 1958, Jargon Society Collection.

21. Williams to Brown, May 6, 1958.

22. The manuscript can be found in the Poetry Collection at SUNY Buffalo.

23. Initially, the book was to feature "monoprint decorations" by Enid Foster.

24. I suspect that Williams used Moore's "botanical pressings" that were to be featured in *Letters to Christopher*; I couldn't confirm this.

25. Williams, "Parson Weems."

26. Jonathan Williams to Jess Collins, November 16, 1966, Jargon Society Collection.

27. James Maynard, "Some Notes on Jonathan Williams and Robert Duncan," *Jacket* 38 (2009), http://jacketmagazine.com/38/jwb04b-maynard-jim-jw-rd.shtml.

28. Later on, Creeley was tapped to write the introduction.

29. Hutcheson, "Inclemented That Way," 402.

30. Other pseudonyms include Willard Emory Betis, Trumbull Drachler, Cerise Farallon, and Tobi Macadams, among others.

31. Williams, *Uncle Gus Flaubert*, 19.

32. Judson Crews taught at the University of Zambia from 1974 to 1978. "Judson Crews," Verdant Press, accessed March 22, 2024, https://verdantpress.com/checklist/judson-crews/.

33. Dana, *Against the Grain*, 212.

34. Stuart Mills and Martin Parnell founded the Trent Bookshop in 1964, which functioned as a hub for Mills' Tarasque Press and for the avant-garde poetry scene in the United Kingdom outside of London. Trent Bookshop closed in 1972.

35. Williams, *Blackbird Dust*, 81.

36. Williams, 83.

37. Tom Patterson, "If You Can Kill a Snake with It, It Ain't Art: The History of a Maverick Poet-Publisher," *Jacket* 38 (2009), http://jacketmagazine.com/38/jwd03-patterson.shtml.

38. I also have a copy in my personal collection.

39. Dean taught photography at Penland on and off from 1969 to 1979 and was a visiting scholar in 1973. Cindy Gibson to Huston Paschal (email), February 15, 2023.

40. A paperback edition sans Dean's photographs was designed by Jonathan Greene and published by Duke University Press in 1985.

41. Nicholas Dean, Letters to Jonathan Williams, November 1 and 24, 1967, Jargon Society Collection.

42. Williams, *Magpie's Bagpipe*, 37.

43. Jeffery Beam, "Blue Darter," in Beam and Owens, *Lord of Orchards*, 436.

44. Williams, "American Society."

45. Willams, *Magpie's Bagpipe*, 94.

46. John Kingsley Shannon, "FESTSCHRIFT FOR GUY DAVENPORT'S 50TH BIRTHDAY: TENTATIVE OUTLINE," J. M. Edelstein Collection.

47. Alex Harris, "Decatur County," *SF Camerawork Quarterly* 14, no. 2 (Summer 1987): 9–11.

48. Jonathan Williams to Charles H. Kirbo, May 15, 1978, Jargon Society Collection.

49. Williams, "ANYTHING NOT WORTH DOING."

50. Meyer, personal communication with author.

51. Jonathan Williams, "A Jolly Gardyloo from the Locologodaedalist's Desk on November 8, 1980 in Buffalony" (The Jargon Society, November 8, 1980).

52. Mills founded Tarasque Press in 1962 and Simon Cutts joined in 1965. They were later joined by Ian Gardner. Mills also founded the Aggie Weston's imprint in 1973, which published work by both Williams and Meyer.

53. Although Williams had planned on publishing Mills via Jargon, a specific title was never slated.

54. Simon Cutts, personal communication with author, 2023.

55. Williams detested Moore's cover design so much that it essentially destroyed their friendship.

56. It was at the Institute of Design that he became interested in photography via Harry Callahan and learned about Black Mountain College from M. C. Richards (BMCM+AC, "Jonathan Williams Oral History").

57. Williams, *Blackbird Dust*, 199–200.

58. Brand also mentions that Charles Olson was a fan of *Six Mid-American Chants*: "My God, it's like a train, like getting a train for Christmas, even including the tracks." Vic Brand, "Burr, Salvage, Yoke," *Jacket* 38 (2009), http://jacket1.writing.upenn.edu/38/jwc03-brand.shtml.

59. Jaffe, "Jonathan Williams, Jargonaut."

60. Meyer, "Jargon Society Executive Committee Meeting January 1988." Curiously, in the same document, Williams suggests Hallmark Greeting Cards as a potential co-publisher.

61. Art Sinsabaugh died in 1983.

62. Jonathan Williams, "The Jargon Society, Inc.—Newsletter March 15, 1977" (The Jargon Society).

63. Williams, "Custodian of Snowflakes."

64. Mike Spear, "*The Sherwood Anderson Review*," https://facultystaff.richmond.edu/~mspear/00summer.html.

65. Dale Smith, "Devotion to 'The Strange': Jonathan Williams and the Small Press," *Jacket* 38 (2009), http://jacketmagazine.com/38/jwd05-smith-dale.shtml.

66. Meyer, personal communication with author.

67. F. Whitney Jones, "Memorandum" (unpublished, 1981).

68. Jaffe, *Jonathan Williams / The Jargon Society*, x.

69. Jonathan Williams, "The Jargon Society," Wayback Machine at Internet Archive, accessed April 1, 2022, https://web.archive.org/web/20040604145953/http://www.jargonbooks.com/works.html.

70. Jonathan Williams to Larry Walldrich, July 7, 1955, Jargon Society Collection.

71. Jonathan Williams, "SLEEPERS, AWAKE" (The Jargon Society, 1959).

72. *Black Mountain Review* #7 was the final issue, as #8 was never published.

73. Dana, *Against the Grain*, 212.

74. Jonathan Williams to Jim Roman, January 31, 1963, James S. Jaffe Collection of Jonathan Williams and the Jargon Society, Yale Collection of American Literature, Beinecke Rare Book and Manuscript Library.

75. Williams, *Blackbird Dust*, 202.

76. Jargon books that Dawson contributed to include "Jammin' the Greek Scene" (Jargon 13c); *The Suicide Room* (Jargon 17); *The Empire Finals at Verona* (Jargon 30); *14 Poets, 1 Artist* (Jargon 31) (Dawson is the "1 Artist"); and *The Darkness Surrounds Us* (Jargon 40). In 1959, Jargon also issued *Ajax* by Dawson as the second installment of its very brief broadside series.

Notes to Chapter Five 169

77. Biltmore Press was "Asheville's leading commercial job printer" and was frequently used by Black Mountain College's faculty and students. Philip Blocklyn, "It's Right the Way It Is": Printing at Black Mountain College," *Black Mountain Studies Journal* 12 (May 2021), https://www.blackmountainstudiesjournal.org/blocklyn-printing/.

78. Jonathan Williams to Fielding Dawson, November 22, 1954, Fielding Dawson Papers.

79. Williams, "The Jargon Society," Wayback Machine at Internet Archive.

80. Hair, *Avant-Folk*, 156.

81. "John Furnival: Somewhere between Poetry and Painting: A Survey of Prints, Drawings and Collaborations from the 1960s to Today," England & Co. Gallery, accessed May 3, 2023, https://www.englandgallery.com/john-furnival-somewhere-between-poetry-and-painting/.

82. Williams, *Blackbird Dust*, 101–2, 109.

83. Anne Midgette, personal communication with author, 2022.

84. Williams, "The Jargon Society," Wayback Machine at Internet Archive.

85. Roger Manley, personal communication with author, 2023.

86. Meyer, personal communication with author.

87. It was first printed in an edition of 17,500. At the time, Jargon's largest production was Patchen's *Hurrah for Anything* (Jargon 21) at "2500 copies and 100 copies prepared and painted by Kenneth Patchen." "The Jargon Society," Black Mountain College Museum + Arts Center, https://www.blackmountaincollege.org/the-jargon-society/.

88. Robert Shelton, "Jazz Man Is Changing His Beat," *New York Times*, August 27, 1962, https://www.nytimes.com/1962/08/27/archives/jazz-man-is-changing-his-beat-charlie-mingus-at-work-on-story-of.html.

89. Jaffe, personal communication with author, 2021.

90. Williams, "The Jargon Society," Wayback Machine at Internet Archive.

91. Jonathan Williams, *Jargon (A Checklist, 1959)* (The Jargon Society, 1959).

92. Williams, "Parson Weems."

93. Williams wanted to publish other works by Stevie Smith, but I only spotted the one title; I'm sure there are more (Williams to Roman, January 31, 1963).

94. Williams, "EPISTLE DE PROFUNDIS."

95. Smith, "Twenty-Seven Batting-Practice Pitches."

96. Jonathan Williams, "Jammin' the Greek Scene" (unpublished proof, 1959).

97. Jonathan Williams to Vincent Ferrini, September 29, 1954, Vincent Ferrini Papers, Archives & Special Collections, University of Connecticut.

98. Jonathan Williams, "(PERHAPS) A LAST LETTER" (The Jargon Society, 1963).

99. Caroline Vaughan, personal communication with author, 2022.

Epilogue

1. Jonathan Williams, *Eight Days in Eire: Or, Nothing so Urgent as Mañana* (Rocky Mountain, NC: North Carolina Wesleyan College Press).

Index

Abeles, Sigmund: missing Jargon book of, 124
Abrams, Sam: missing Jargon book of, 124
Adams, Dobree, 4, 123
ambient reading. *See* Lin, Tan
Ammons, A. R.: missing Jargon book of, 124
Anderson, Donald B., xi, 4, 91, 103, 135–36, 143n11, 145n11
Anderson, Sherwood, 127; missing Jargon book of, 124–25; *Six Mid-American Chants*, 63, 111, 123
The Anthology of Black Mountain College Poetry, 124
Anthony, William: *Bible Stories*, 118, 160n65; *Bill Anthony's Greatest Hits*, 119, 125; missing Jargon book of, 125
Appalachian State University (Belk Library), xiii, 143n9
archives, 2–3, 44, 60, 82, 113, 116, 138, 141, 143n9
Argus Book Shop, 16
Art brut, 81, 84–85. *See also* Outsider (art)
Asphodel Book Shop, 38, 47, 111, 147
Atchley, Dana, 69, 159n40
attention, 1–3, 7, 19, 67, 93–94, 99, 140

Baraka, Amiri, 19, 31. *See also* Jones, LeRoi
Basinski, Michael, 11, 166n1. *See also* The Poetry Collection at SUNY Buffalo
Baum, L. Frank. *See* childhood books
Baxter, Glen: missing Jargon book of, 125
Beam, Jeffery, xi, 1, 81; as bibliographer, 11, 116–17, 147n43, 166n1;

A Hornet's Nest, 15, 123, 147n53; on *Jammin' the Greek Scene*, 24, 28–29; *Visions of Dame Kind*, 124
Beamish, Rae, 12, 46–47
Beats, The, 7, 34, 146n29, 152n82
begging bowl letters, 4–5, 135
Bell, Millicent, 3, 10
Belli, Giuseppe Gioachino. *See* Norse, Harold
Benton, Williams: missing Jargon book of, 125
Bertholf, Robert J., 39, 121, 152n7. *See also* The Poetry Collection at SUNY Buffalo
Beye, Holly, 5–7, 63
bibliographical: checklists, 10–11, 14, 91–92, 105, 115, 147n42, 147n43, 160n57, 166n1; description, ix, 2–3; hauntology, ix–xi, 2, 3, 14–15
Bishop, Elizabeth, 51, 155n64
Bishop, Robert, 89
Black Mountain College, 1, 33, 35, 44, 70, 83, 108, 131, 160n59, 170n77; Black Mountain College Museum + Arts Center, xiii, 11, 15, 104, 105, 143, 166n1; Black Mountain poets, 11, 22, 124, 144n9, 146n29; *Black Mountain Review*, 126, 169n72; Closure, 32–33, 35–36, 141. *See also* Olson, Charles; Williams, Jonathan
Black Sparrow Press, 13, 112, 117, 127
Blake, William, 62, 157n2
Blizzard, Georgia, 1, 84, 89
Bongé, Lyle, 11, 131; missing Jargon book of, 115; *The Sleep of Reason*, 117; *The Photographs of*, 118
Boyle, Kay, 109, 110, 167n17

171

"Boys" (Baron Corvo, Baron Von Gloeden, Baron von Plüschow), 118
Braun, Richard Emil: *Last Man In*, 123
Broughton, James, 1; *High Kukus*, 114; *A Long Undressing*, 114; *75 Life Lines*, 115
Brown, Bob, 1, 44; *The Selected Poems of*, 14, 91, 109–10, 167n17, 167n18
Brown, Pete: missing Jargon book of, 125
Bunnen, Lucinda. See *Scoring in Heaven*
Bunting, Basil, 135; *Madeira & Toasts for Basil Bunting's 75th Birthday*, 116; missing Jargon book of, 125–26
Burbridge, Oteil, 93, 94
Burroughs, William S.: *Naked Lunch*, 7, 126, 146n29

CAConrad, 51, 153n28; missing Jargon book of, 126
Cage, John, 70, 108, 132; missing Jargon books of, 126, 132
Callahan, Harry: Black Mountain College, 11, 62, 148n1, 157n4; Institute of Design, 169n56; Lorine Niedecker's missing Jargon book, 109; *On My Eyes* (Eigner), 63, 110; *A Red Carpet for the Sun* (Layton), 110
Cantz, Dr. Walter, 9, 10
Caplan, Ronald, 47, 147n46
Catullus: "Catullus: Carmen XVI," 31, 36; influence on Williams, 17–18, 23–24; missing Jargon book of, 14, 126
Cendrars, Blaise: missing Jargon book of, 126
Chand, Nek, 85
channeling, 12, 19, 22, 57, 138–40
Cheval, Ferdinand: *Le Palais Idéal*, 83, 162n6
childhood books, 7, 20–21
Christianity, 33–34, 59, 72, 73, 76, 78, 79, 80
Christmas, 68, 70, 71, 91, 111, 112, 169n58

Chute, Ken, 39, 41–42, 53, 147n47, 152n9, 153n11, 155n50, 156n77, 156n94
Clare, John, 9, 94
Clark, Mark, 75
Clark, Thomas A., 72; *Some Particulars*, 117; *A Still Life*, 118; *Ways through Bracken*, 120
Collins, Jess: missing Jargon book of, 13, 112, 127–28
concrete poetry, 77, 112, 116, 128
Coracle Press, 120, 128. See also Cutts, Simon
Corinth Books, 3, 107, 108, 109, 154n41
Corn Close, 9, 15, 124, 129, 135–37, 143n11
correspondence art, 63–64, 67–71, 157n8, 157n14, 159n39, 159n40, 159n52, 159n55
Cory, Jim, 126; missing Jargon book of, 126
Cox, Reuben: *At Dusk Iridescent* (Meyer), 122; *Corn Close*, 15, 124, 135–37, 164n38; *The World of Joe Webb*, 123, 164n38
Craven, Richard. See Richard C.
Craven, Thorns, xii, 74, 87, 103, 143n9, 147n51, 161n78, 162n1
Creeley, Robert, 1, 19, 23, 50–51, 132; *All That Is Lovely In Men*, 106; connection to Mason Jordan Mason, 113, 168n28; *A Form of Women*, 30–31, 109; *The Immoral Proposition*, 10, 23, 106; issuing of a record by Olson, 108; missing Jargon books of, 105–6, 126; *The Whip*, 108, 167n13
Crews, Judson, 168n32. See also Mason, Mason Jordan
Crosby, Caresse, 51, 52, 109–10
cummings, e. e., 51, 65; *Do You Have a Poem Book on E.E. Cummings?* (Davenport), 116, 160n59; influence on Williams, 16
Cutts, Simon, xii, xiii, 135, 168n52; missing Jargon book of, 120; *Piano-*

172   Index

stool Footnotes, 120; *Quelques Pianos*, 118; *See pages*, 115. See also Coracle Press

Dahlberg, Edward, 20; *14 Poets, 1 Artist*, 109; missing Jargon books of, 14, 127; *Six Mid-American Chants* (Anderson), 111, 127
Davenport, Guy, x, 12, 22, 44, 72; *Do You Have a Poem Book on E.E. Cummings?*, 116, 160n59; *Flowers and Leaves*, 111; missing Jargon book on, 118–19; *The Spirit Walks, the Rocks Will Talk* (Johnson), 117
Dawson, Fielding, 105–6; as artist for "Jammin' the Greek Scene," 23, 24, 107, 150n41; as artist for Jargon books, 107, 109, 111, 169n76; at Black Mountain College, 11; *The Empire Finals at Verona*, 109; missing Jargon projects of, 108, 127, 132
Dean, Nicholas, 168n39; *Blues and Roots / Rue and Bluets*, 168n40; missing Jargon book of, 116
Dodd, Baby: missing Jargon book of, 14, 127
Domit, Moussa M., 70, 159n48
Donahoe, Edward, 46, 53
Dove, Arthur, 14, 129
Duberman, Martin, 16, 20, 32
Dubuffet, Jean, 85
Duchamp, Marcel, 73, 110, 159n55
Duke University: Archives, 44; Press, 133, 134, 162n93, 168n40
Duncan, Robert, 1, 28, 108, 146n29, 151n81; at Black Mountain College, 20; contention with Williams, 112, 127–28; *Elegies and Celebrations* (Williams), 24, 107; *Letters*, 107, 112; missing Jargon book of, 14, 127–28; poetics, 22, 27, 32; *Three Choruses from Opera Libretti* (Harrison), 111
Du Plessix Gray, Francine, 11, 17
DuVernet, Kay: missing Jargon book of, 14, 128

Edelstein, J. M., 10–11, 147n42, 166n1
Eden, Glen: missing Jargon book of, 128
Eigner, Larry, 1, 95; correspondence with Williams, 4–5; *On My Eyes*, 63, 110
epigrams, ix–x, 17–19, 32

Feld, Ross: *Plum Poems*, 117
Ferren, John: missing Jargon book of, 128
Fields, Jerry (Bubba Phreon), 162n3, 165n46
Finlay, Ian Hamilton, 114; *The Blue and the Brown Poems*, 116; *Epitaphs for Lorine*, 117; missing Jargon books of, 14, 112–13, 128
Finster, Reverend Howard, 86, 88, 89, 90, 92, 102; album cover art by, 90, 164n41; *Howard Finster, Stranger from Another World*, 90, 132, 164n39; *Paradise Garden*, 86, 164n40; Williams's contention with, 90, 164n40. See also Patterson, Tom
Fisher, Sandra, 135; missing Jargon book of, 128
Fletcher, John Gould, 51
Fluxus, 63, 67
Folk art. See visionary folk art
food, 5–6, 58, 76, 78, 84. See also *White Trash Cooking*
Ford, Ford Betty (Ellen Patterson), 84
Foster, Enid: *Letters to Christopher*, 45, 167n23
found material: ephemera, 65, 121, 160n67; lyrics, 94–95; poetry, 9, 13, 19, 22, 65–66, 71–72, 77–78, 85, 94, 95, 99, 135; sculpture, 65; speech, 17, 22, 56, 94
Fuller, Buckminster, 4, 12; *Untitled Epic Poem on the History of Industrialization*, 36, 111
Furnival, Astrid, 129n29, 135, 137
Furnival, John, 117–18, 129n29, 135, 137

Index 173

Gardner, Ian, 168; *Pairidaeza*, 117; *Quelques Piano*, 118; *Six Variations on a Chrysanthemum of William Morris*, 118
gay literature, 1, 12, 16, 28–30
George, LaVerne: missing Jargon book of, 14, 129
Georgia: Albany, 128; Atlanta, 82, 84, 120, 121; *Brown's Guide to Georgia*, 84, 85, 163n9; Buena Vista, 85; Decatur County, 120; Dublin, 83, 84; Summerville, 86
Gerhardt, Rainer Maria: missing Jargon book of, 105–6
Ginsberg, Allen, 95; *14 Poets, 1 Artist*, 109; *Howl*, 7, 146n29
Goodman, Paul: missing Jargon book of, 129
Gould, Wallace, 44; missing Jargon book of, 129
Gowin, Emmet: missing Jargon book of, 72, 129
Graves, Robert, 23, 30–31
Greek mythology: Minoan myth, 26–27, 50; Prince Ganymedes, 29–31; Williams's use of, 25–27, 29–32
Greene, Jonathan, 9, 119, 146, 154, 168; work on Jargon books, 117, 118, 122, 124, 132
Gregg Museum of Art & Design, 89, 161. *See also* Manley, Roger

Hair, Ross, 4, 10, 20, 28, 29, 128, 167n13
Hall, Dilmus, 1, 89, 165n47
Hamilton, Alfred Starr, 1, 7, 12, 44, 85; *Poems*, 45, 112, 160n59
Hampton, Bruce (a.k.a., Col. Hampton B. Coles (Ret.), 165n57, 166n69, 166n78; Aquarium Rescue Unit, 93, 95, 103, 165n55; friendship with Patterson, 82, 84, 163n19; friendship with Williams, 92, 165n53, 166n82; Hampton Grease Band, 84, 94, 100, 163n25, 165n46; influences of, 92–93; *Isles of Langerhan*, 90, 95, 99, 166n67; *The Late Bronze Age*, 94, 95, 97, 100, 103, 121, 162n3, 165n46, 166n67; *The Lyrix of Col. Hampton B. Coles (Ret.)*, xiii, 13–14, 81–82, 86–87, 90–104, 121, 163n24, 163n25, 166n67; *Outside Looking Out*, 90, 95, 96, 97, 99, 100, 166n67; performance with St. EOM, 85–86, 94, 163n18; psychic abilities of, 93–95; *Sling Blade*, 102–3; Zambi, 93, 165n58
Hanes, DeWitt, 122
Hanes, R. Phillip, 4, 103, 136, 145n11
Hanes Foundation, 25, 29, 75
Harding, Mike, 135; *Corn Close* (Cox), 124; *Eight Days in Eire* (Williams), 137; missing Jargon book of, 129, 135–36
Harrison, Jane, 23, 30
Harrison, Lou, 11, 135, 136; *Joys and Perplexities*, 123, 165n49; missing Jargon books of, 129, 130; *Three Choruses from Opera Libretti*, 91, 111
Hawkins, Spike: missing Jargon books of, 114, 122
Hayter, Stanley William, 5, 62, 148n1
H. D., 149n26, 151n81
Hesiod, 20, 143n9
Hölderlin, Fredrich: missing Jargon book of, 129
Holmes, Flournoy, 94, 96
Homer, 20, 26, 139; missing Jargon book of, 129
Homer, William Innes: *Heart's Gate*, 121
Hooper, Annie, 1, 88–89
Horn, Stu, 159n40
Houédard, Dom Pierre-Sylvester: missing Jargon books of, 128, 130
Houston, Peyton: *Arguments of Idea*, 121; *The Changes Orders Becomings*, 123; *The Garden Prospect* (Yates), 118; *Occasions in a World*, 113; *Sonnet Variations*, 109
Howe, Susan, 20
Hoyleman, Merle, 75; *Asp of the Age*, 12, 45–51, 52, 57, 60, 154n44, 154n46, 155n52, 155n53, 155n54, 155n55, 155n56, 155n63; biographical

information of, 38–42, 59–60, 152n9, 153n12, 153n13, 153n15; death of, 38–39, 152n2, 152n5; family, 40–41, 53, 144n13, 153n14, 156n76; institutionalization of, 40–41, 153n18, 153n19; *Letters to Christopher*, xii, 12, 36, 38, 44–46, 53–61, 91, 111, 139–140, 147n48, 152n1, 152n4, 156n73, 156n77, 156n81, 156n94; *New Directions in Prose & Poetry*, 51; papers of, 39, 147n47; relationship with Williams, 42–45, 61; research projects, 51, 55, 153n25; the Scum, 41–42, 153n28; on television, 52–53

Institute of Design (Chicago), 17, 62, 122, 145n22, 148n1, 148n8, 169n56
Ives, Charles: missing Jargon book of, 130

Jackson, Mahalia: *Movin' On Up*, 14, 130
Jaffe, James S., xi–xiii, 2, 11, 15, 23, 115, 143n8, 147n43
The Jargon Society: benefactors, 135–36, 143n11, 145n11; bibliographers of, xi, 10–11, 143n8, 147n43; board members, 25, 75, 103, 130; contracts, 45–46, 154n41; later years, 81, 103–4, 113; name of, 7, 35, 145n22, 152n86; networks, xi, 9–10; as non-profit, 4, 25, 41, 45, 130, 160n59; origins of, 1, 6–7, 9–10, 11–12, 16, 25, 62–63, 108, 144n9, 145n18, 157n6; postcard series, 71, 160n57; volunteers, 4, 74, 85, 145n16. *See also* Southern Visionary Folk Art Preservation Project; Williams, Jonathan
jazz (music), 14, 25–26, 92, 108, 114
Jennings, James Harold, 13, 82, 89, 102, 121, 163n25, 163n27; *Art World*, 87, 163n26; death of, 88, 163n26
Johnson, Ray, 13, 63–64, 67–69, 159n52; death of, 157n9, 158n25; as founder of correspondence art, 70, 159n55; friendship with Jonathan Williams, 70–71; *The Roman Sonnets* (Belli), 110–11; *What a Man Can See* (Edson), 110. *See also* New York Correspondence School; Richard C.
Johnson, Ronald, 1, 32, 72; *Eyes & Objects*, 72, 118; "Eyes in Leaves" (Shannon), 118–19; *The Family Album of Lucybelle Crater* (Meatyard), 117; *A Line of Poetry, a Row of Trees*, 111; relationship with Jonathan Williams, 9, 12, 147n45; *The Spirit Walks, the Rocks Will Talk*, 117, 160n59; on Jonathan Williams's practice, 25, 26–27, 148n1
Jones, F. Whitney, 5, 74, 75, 87, 103, 143n9, 145n16, 147n51, 162n1, 162n5
Jones, Harold L. (Count M'Butu), 95
Jones, LeRoi, 32. *See also* Baraka, Amiri
Jones, Phillip March, 90, 133; *Points of Departure*, 124, 164n38

Kalos, Victor: *The Double-Backed Beast*, 105
Keller, Ricky (Lincoln Metcalf), 97, 162n3
Kelly, Robert, 147n49; "Eyes in Leaves" (Shannon), 118–19; *The Umbrella of Aesculapius*, 118
Kenner, Hugh, 7, 9; "Eyes in Leaves" (Shannon), 118–19
Kirstein, Lincoln, 45, 46, 52
Kitaj, R. B., 135; *Lullabies Twisters Gibbers Drags* (Williams), 115; *Madeira & Toasts for Basil Bunting's 75th Birthday* (Williams), 116; missing Jargon book of, 14, 130
Knaths, Karl, 148n1; "Poems" (Eigner), 110
Kwilecki, Paul, 128; missing Jargon book of, 120

Landslide Records, 90. *See also* Hampton, Bruce
Larsson, R. E. F., 44; missing Jargon book of, 130

Laubiès, René: *The Immoral Proposition* (Creeley), 106; "An Olson Miscellanea" (Williams), 133; *Poems: 1953-1956* (Williams), 23; *The Whip* (Creeley), 108
Laughlin, Clarence John, 118
Laughlin, James, 12, 38, 45, 51, 152n1
Layton, Irving: *The Improved Binoculars*, 107; *A Laughter in the Mind*, 109; *A Red Carpet for the Sun*, 110; Contact Press, 167n13
letters (correspondence), 4, 9, 44, 69-70, 116, 131, 135, 138, 159
Levertov, Denise, 1, 108, 112; *14 Poets, 1 Artist*, 109; *Lunar Baedeker and Time-Tables* (Loy), 108; *On My Eyes* (Eigner), 110; *Overland to the Islands*, 108
libraries, ix-x, 2
Lilith, 34-35, 151n81
Lin, Tan, 99, 101, 166n81
Lovecraft, H. P., 7, 85
Lowenfels, Walter, 132; association with Bob Brown, 110, 167n17; *14 Poets, 1 Artist*, 109; *Some Deaths*, 109
Loy, Mina, 1, 4, 7, 12, 44; *Lunar Baedeker and Time-Tables*, 108; *The Last Lunar Baedeker*, 113; missing Jargon book of, 132

MacDonald, George. See *Lilith*
Mail art. See correspondence art
Manley, Roger, xiv, 81, 87, 161n86, 163n27, 164n37; missing Jargon book of, 130, 161n86; "Notches Along the Bible Belt," 75; Southern Visionary Folk Art Preservation Project, 88-90; *St. EOM in the Land of Pasaquan* (Patterson), 115; *Walks to the Paradise Garden*, 86, 133, 136
Marshall, Edward: *14 Poets, 1 Artist*, 109; missing Jargon book of, 130
Martial, ix-x, 11, 13, 23, 27-28, 31, 33
Martin, Eddie Owens (a.k.a. St. EOM), 1, 89, 92, 94, 102; death of, 88;

Pasaquan, 85; *St. EOM in the Land of Pasaquan* (Patterson), 74, 85-86, 89-90, 115, 132, 163n18. *See also* Hampton, Bruce; Patterson, Tom
Mason, Mason Jordan: *The Selected Poems of*, 14, 113-14
Matheson, Elizabeth, xiv, 81, 161n72; *Blithe Air*, 124, 164n38
McClure, Michael, 1; *Passage*, 108
McGarrell, Ann: missing Jargon book of, 14, 130
McPherson, Billy (Ben "Pops" Thornton), 96, 100, 162n3
Meatyard, Ralph Eugene, 12, 44, 85; "Eyes in Leaves" (Shannon), 119; *The Family Album of Lucybelle Crater*, 63, 117; *Flowers and Leaves* (Davenport), 111; *Spring of the Lamb* (Woolf), 117
Menapace, John: *Letter in a Klein Bottle*, 121
Mendes, Guy: *Elite/Elate Poems* (Williams), 119; *The Family Album of Lucybelle Crater* (Meatyard), 117; *St. EOM in the Land of Pasaquan* (Patterson), 115; *Walks to the Paradise Garden*, 86, 89, 133, 136; *Who is Little Enis?* (Williams), 118
Metcalf, Paul C., 1; *Araminta and the Coyotes*, 123; *BOTH*, 92; "Eyes in Leaves" (Shannon), 119; *Genoa*, 111; *The Middle Passage*, 72, 117; *Patagoni*, 114, 160n59; *Spring of the Lamb* (Woolf), 117; *Will West*, 108
Meyer, Thomas, x, 28, 81, 82, 85, 87, 95, 143n8, 143n9, 162n94, 163n16, 164n42, 168n52; accepting *White Trash Cooking*, 10; "Acrostical Birthday Poem for Large Chorale, Sorghum & Grits," 122, 164n44; *The Bang Book*, 117, 129; *Blithe Air* (Matheson), 124; Corn Close, 135-37, 143n11; *Corn Close* (Cox), 124; on "Decatur County," 120; *At Dusk Iridescent*, 122, 147n52; *EPitaph*, 117; on "Eyes in

176   Index

Leaves," 119; *Feuilles Albigenses* (Cutts), 120; on "Frank," 126; on *Jammin' the Greek Scene*, 24, 29; *Names & Local Habitations* (Oppenheimer), 115; on "Olson / By Ear," 108; on "The Photographs of Art Sinsabaugh," 122; *Pianostool Footnotes*, 120; *Points of Departure* (Jones), 124; relationship with Williams, 1, 13, 147n49; *Sappho's Raft*, 121; *Staves Calends Legends*, 118; *The Umbrella of Aesculapius*, 72; *A Valentine for L. Z.*, 113; *Visions of Dame Kind* (Beam), 124; on Williams's practice, 157n2; works with Sandra Fisher, 128–29

Mickler, Ernest Matthew. See *White Trash Cooking*

Midgette, Anne, 9, 91, 120; *Corn Close* (Cox), 124, 135–37

Miles, Lisa A., 39, 40, 41, 147n47

Miller, Henry, 6, 113; *The Red Notebook*, 108

Mills, Stuart: missing Jargon book of, 14, 130, 169n53; Tarasque Press, 120, 168n34, 168n52

Mingus, Charles, 25, 150n47; *Beneath the Underdog*, 14, 130

minimal poetry, 56, 66–67

missing books, x–xi, 2–3, 14–15, 138, 140–41

Monk, Thelonious: missing Jargon book on, 132

Moore, A. Doyle: *Do You Have a Poem Book on E. E. Cummings?* (Davenport), 116; *Epitaphs for Lorine* (Williams), 117; *Heart's Gate*, 121, 169n55; *Letters to Christopher* (Hoyleman), 45, 111, 167n24; *Madeira & Toasts for Basil Bunting on his 75th Birthday* (Williams), 116; *The Siesta of the Hungarian Snake* (Morgan), 115; *Tenderness & Gristle* (Niedecker), 111; *The Umbrella of Aesculapius*, 72

Moore, Raymond: missing Jargon book of, 130

Morgan, Edwin: *The Siesta of the Hungarian Snake*, 115–16

Morgenstern, Christian. See Collins, Jess

Morley, Hilda: missing Jargon book of, 14, 131

Mosier, Jeff, 95, 96

Mottram, Eric, 19, 32, 158n23

MTV, 92, 103

Music Pocket-Book Series, 126, 127, 129, 130, 132, 134

Nantahala Foundation, 25, 130, 160n59

National Endowment for the Arts, 4, 45, 72, 73

Nelson, Martha, 84, 87

New Directions, 13, 39, 47, 51, 112, 155n52, 155n53, 155n63. See also Laughlin, James

New York Correspondence School, 13, 63–64, 67–70, 79, 140, 157n8, 159n39, 159n52

Niedecker, Lorine, 1, 7, 51, 72; *From This Condensery*, 121; missing Jargon projects of, 109, 132; *Tenderness & Gristle*, 111

Norse, Harold: *The Roman Sonnets*, 71, 110

North Carolina, 18, 69, 70–73, 81, 83, 92, 115, 116, 132, 136; Asheville, 127, 143n9, 148n12; Boone, 143n9; Buncombe County, 131; Cape Hatteras, 88; Cullowhee, 64; Graham, 71; Highlands, 8, 36, 133; Pinnacle, 87; Scaly Mountain, 17, 148n12, 162n94; Thomasville, 68; Toxaway, 71; Winston-Salem, 14, 71, 82, 87, 88, 163n27

North Carolina Museum of Art (NCMA), 65, 67, 69–70, 159n48

O'Donnell, George Marion, 44–47, 50, 53, 61

Oklahoma, 12, 39, 59, 153n15

Index 177

Olson, Charles, 50, 70, 149n26, 169n58; connection to "Jammin' the Greek Scene" (Williams), 11, 23–24, 25, 27, 28–36, 107; *The Maximus Poems*, 1, 9–10, 16, 105, 106, 108, 154n41; missing Jargon projects of, 14, 108, 131, 133; poetics of, 17, 19–20, 28, 29–30, 32, 158n23; relationship with Williams, 4, 11–12, 16–17, 20, 28–36, 62–63, 126, 146n29, 148n1, 152n86, 157n4, 157n6
on-sending, 67, 158n25
Oppenheimer, Joel, 1, 11; *The Dancer*, 9, 105; *The Darkness Surrounds Us* (Sorrentino), 111; *The Dutiful Son*, 107; *14 Poets, 1 Artist*, 109; *Just Friends / Friends and Lovers*, 4, 114; missing Jargon projects of, 14, 131, 132; *Names & Local Habitations*, 115
Orpheus, 25, 29–30, 36, 152n88
outsider (art), 52, 81; criticism of, 84–85
Ovid, 23, 25, 30, 139
Owens, Richard, xi, 11, 166n1

pacifism, 16, 17, 35
Palmer, Robert, 95, 97, 99, 166n67
Parker, Bart: missing Jargon book of, 131; *Some Particulars* (Clark), 117
Paschal, Huston, 64, 65, 68, 69, 70, 71, 73, 74, 159n48
Patchen, Kenneth, 4, 6, 126, 145n21, 147n44; *Fables and Other Little Tales*, 6–7, 9, 23, 105, 106; *Hurrah for Anything*, 108, 170n87; influence on Williams, 7, 16, 28, 62–63, 108, 157n2, 157n6; missing Jargon books of, 13, 112, 131; *Poemscapes*, 106
Patterson, Tom, x, 7, 163n9, 166n82; *Howard Finster, Stranger from Another World*, 86, 90, 132, 143n5, 164n39; Pynyon Press, 13, 84, 87, 95, 121, 163n24; relationship with Williams, 83–84; on Richard C., 64–65, 73–74, 79, 161n77, 163n31; *St. EOM in the Land of Pasaquan*, 85–86, 89–90, 115, 163n18; *The Tom Patterson Years*, 10, 124, 163n19; work with the Jargon Society, 13–14, 82–83, 85, 88, 92, 103, 121, 162n5, 164n42, 163n16, 165n46. *See also* Hampton, Bruce; Martin, Eddie Owens; Southern Visionary Folk Art Preservation Project; visionary folk art
Penland School of Crafts, 71, 116, 160n59, 168n39
Pfeiffer, Carissa, 105, 166n1
Phillips, Esther, 39–40, 147n47. *See also* Hoyleman, Merle
photography, 11, 13, 14, 61, 62–63, 89–90, 120, 127, 157n4, 164n38, 169n56
The Poetry Collection at SUNY Buffalo, 11, 23, 24, 60, 116, 143n9, 152n7, 167n22
Pop art, 63, 64, 161n73
Porter, Bern, 159n55. *See also* Brown, Bob
Potter, Ted, 75
Pound, Ezra, 17, 19, 105, 117, 149n26, 151n76
preservation, 44, 64, 140. *See also* Southern Visionary Folk Art Preservation Project
Princeton University, 17, 33, 148n1, 148n8

Rexroth, Kenneth, 20, 23, 28, 44; *Lunar Baedeker and Time-Tables* (Loy), 108; missing Jargon books of, 3, 13, 106–7, 132, 144n9
Richard C., 67–70, 72, 81, 121, 139, 158n33, 158n34, 159n52; anonymity & identity, 68–69, 130; casual art, 67, 158n36; collecting/hunting ephemera, 72, 79; *Correspondence: An Exhibition of the Letters of Ray Johnson*, 69–70; as curator, 69–70, 158n27, 159n48, 163n31; as essayist, 67, 70, 158n27; "Notches Along the Bible Belt," 12–13, 62–63, 72–81, 121, 160n67, 161n90; *Poems by Richard C.*,

178 Index

And/Or Another Notepad for All Those Endless Lists, 65–67; prank, 64–65, 68, 79; pseudonyms, 68–69; relationship with Williams, 70–72; sculpture, 65, 73, 161n73; Southeast Seven, 73, 161n72; as teacher, 69, 159n44. *See also* New York Correspondence School
Richards, M. C., 3, 148n1, 169n56
Rodia, Simon: *Watts Towers*, 83, 162n6
Roselli, David, 75
Ruff, David, 5–6, 127, 145n18, 146n35; *Garbage Litters the Iron Face of the Sun's Child*, 9, 105
Ruggles, Carl: missing Jargon books on, 116, 129
Rumaker, Michael, 17, 35, 151n61
Russell, Bill: missing Jargon book of, 132

Saper, Craig J., 67, 68, 110, 158n25
Sappho, 109, 139, 148n18
Satie, Erik: missing Jargon books of, 132
Schlesinger, Kyle, 10, 116, 157n4
Scoring in Heaven, 125
sex, 25–28
Shannon, John Kingsley: "Eyes in Leaves," 118–19
Sinsabaugh, Art, 169n61; missing Jargon book of, 14, 74, 122–23, 157n7; *Six Mid-American Chants*, 63, 111, 112, 124, 157n7
Siskind, Aaron, 11, 62, 128, 148n1, 157n4; *Elegies and Celebrations* (Williams), 107
Sitwell, Dame Edith, 20–22
Skywinding Farm, 17–18, 36, 125, 148n12, 162n94
Smith, Gordon Royce, 45, 46, 154n42
Smith, Henry Holmes: missing Jargon book of, 132; *Sonnet Variations*, 109
Smith, Keith: missing Jargon book of, 132
Smith, Mary T., 1; *Araminta and the Coyotes* (Metcalf), 123
Smith, Stevie: missing Jargon projects of, 132, 170n93

Smith, Virginia Warren. See *Scoring in Heaven*
song lyrics, 13–14, 33, 91–92, 94–95, 103, 166n67. *See also*, Hampton, Bruce
Sorrentino, Gilbert: *The Darkness Surrounds Us*, 111
Southeastern Center for Contemporary Art (SECCA), 71, 73, 75, 163n31
Southern Visionary Folk Art Preservation Project. See Finster, Reverend Howard; Hooper, Annie; Manley, Roger; Martin, Eddie Owens; Mendes, Guy; Patterson, Tom
SPACES (Saving and Preserving Arts and Cultural Environments), 88
Spear, David M.: *The Neugents*, 123
St. Andrews College (St. Andrews University), 83, 162n5
Stein, Gertrude, 51, 167n17
Steinmetz, Mark: *Tuscan Trees*, 123
Stipe, Michael, 192, 164n41
subscription, 3
Sykes, Stephen: *In-Curiosity House*, 83, 162n6

Tarasque Press. See Mills, Stuart
time, 19, 56, 64, 97, 98–99, 138–41
Tolkien, J. R. R., 85. *See also* childhood books
travel, 6, 7, 9, 83, 86, 115
Turnbull, Gael, 51; Migrant Press, 113, 167n13
Twombly, Cy, 69, 129
Tworkov, Jack: missing Jargon book of, 132

Ulmann, Doris, 85; *The Appalachian Photographs of Doris Ulmann*, 63, 89, 112, 160n59

Vargo, Mike, 39, 42, 52, 147n47, 152n9, 153n11
Vaughan, Caroline: missing Jargon book of, 14, 81, 134, 162n93

Index 179

visionary folk art, 1, 83–85, 88–89. *See also* Southern Visionary Folk Art Preservation Project

Vogrin, Hak: *High Kukus* (Broughton), 114; missing Jargon projects of, 126, 134

Walldrich, Larry. *See* Music Pocket-Book Series

Warhol, Andy, 64–65, 70

White Trash Cooking, x, 10, 13, 74, 90, 103, 121, 147n51

Williams, Jonathan: at Black Mountain College, 1, 9, 11, 16–20, 22, 29–30, 32–33, 35–36, 62–63, 126, 127, 146n29, 148n1, 157n4, 157n6, 169n56; *Blues and Roots / Rue and Bluets*, 72, 85, 116, 132; *An Ear in Bartram's Tree*, 23, 25, 32, 37, 150n44, 150n53; fundraising efforts of, 3–5, 24, 44, 123, 126, 131; *Garbage Litters the Iron Face of the Sun's Child*, 9, 10, 62, 105, 145n18; "Jammin' the Greek Scene," 11–12, 16, 22–37, 107, 140, 150n41, 150n53; Jargon books authored by, 105, 107, 109, 111, 115, 116–17, 118, 119, 122; living in New York, 5–6; on mavericks and eccentrics, 12, 44, 89–90, 113; military service, 9–10, 35, 105–6; missing Jargon books of, 115, 116, 129, 132–33, 135–37; on music, 5–6, 9, 14, 91–92; poetics of, 1, 17–22, 65, 148n18, 158n23; pre-Jargon, 5–7, 16, 148n1, 148n12; residencies and teaching, 71, 160n59; sexuality, 28–30; *Walks to the Paradise Garden*, 86, 90. *See also* The Jargon Society; Meyer, Thomas

Williams, William Carlos, 17, 51, 105, 127, 129; *The Improved Binoculars* (Layton), 107; *Lunar Baedeker and Time-Tables* (Loy), 108; *The Roman Sonnets* (Belli), 110

Wolpe, Stefan, 11; missing Jargon book of, 134

Woolf, Douglas: missing Jargon projects of/on, 132, 133; *Spring of the Lamb*, 117

Yates, Peter: *The Garden Prospect*, 118; missing Jargon book of, 134

Zukofsky, Celia, 14, 107, 126

Zukofsky, Louis, 1, 20, 24, 109; missing Jargon books of, 14, 126, 134; *Some Time*, 10, 16, 107, 132; *A Test of Poetry*, 3, 107, 125

Printed in the USA
CPSIA information can be obtained
at www.ICGtesting.com
CBHW021904171024
15937CB00017B/332